Anonymous

Easy Lessons

In natural Philosophy, natural History, Mechanics, Chemistry, Electricity, Optics,

and Acoustics

Anonymous

Easy Lessons
In natural Philosophy, natural History, Mechanics, Chemistry, Electricity, Optics, and Acoustics

ISBN/EAN: 9783337072483

Printed in Europe, USA, Canada, Australia, Japan

Cover: Foto ©ninafisch / pixelio.de

More available books at **www.hansebooks.com**

IN

NATURAL PHILOSOPHY
NATURAL HISTORY
MECHANICS, CHEMISTRY
ELECTRICITY, OPTICS, AND ACOUSTICS

WITH NUMEROUS ILLUSTRATIONS.

LONDON
HOULSTON AND WRIGHT
65, PATERNOSTER ROW.
MDCCCLXIV.

GRANDFATHER WHITEHEAD'S CATECHISMS.

I.—NATURAL PHILOSOPHY.

TO TEACHERS AND PUPILS.

The object of every tutor should be to convey the knowledge the pupil requires in as simple, clear, accurate, and concise a manner as possible. The object of every pupil should be to acquire the knowledge imparted by the tutor, not in *words only*, but in *ideas*; so that the information gained should not be of a superficial character—a mere catalogue of scientific names—but an acquaintance with the phenomena of Nature, and a distinct and comprehensive idea of the laws which regulate them.

Montaigne aptly remarked that "a tutor should not be continually thundering instruction into the ears of his pupil as if he were pouring it through a funnel; but, after having put the lad, like a young horse, on a trot before him, to observe his paces, and see what he is able to perform, should, according to the extent of his capacity, induce him to taste, to distinguish, and to find out things for himself; sometimes opening the way, at other times leaving it for him to open; and by abating or increasing his own pace, accommodate his precepts to the capacity of his pupil."

Once excite curiosity, then inquiry will follow, and the consequence will be a desire to gratify that curiosity by acquiring knowledge. The ignorant or uneducated mind requires cultivation quite as much as the unproductive land on the road-side. In the following Catechisms the pupil is led step by step, by a familiar and easy method, to acquire the requisite knowledge of the subject studied, which is still further elucidated by numerous diagrams and experiments.

The experiments are so contrived, that the apparatus required is of the most simple and inexpensive **kind in most** instances, **and** due regard has been paid throughout to simplicity and usefulness, rather than magnificence ; the object being to render everything as plain and intelligible as possible, commensurate **with the subject.**

The introductory narratives are all founded upon facts, or are **the actual** biographies of eminent scientific men. The lessons have been constructed for weekly tuition, it being desirable that the first *five* days should be devoted to catechising, and the *sixth* to recapitulation, examination *viva voce*, or essay writing upon the subjects contained in the week's course of study.

Teachers are recommended to give additional illustrations of the subjects under consideration, to perform the experiments given in the lessons before the pupil, and to adduce other familiar and simple experiments to elucidate them.

Pupils should perform the experiments themselves *before studying* the lessons, and repeat them again when master of the lesson. If possible, they should also perform other experiments bearing upon the question, and explain their analogy to those previously exhibited.

Each lesson has a few important questions appended, to assist the teacher in the examination of the pupils.

GRANDFATHER WHITEHEAD'S CATECHISMS.

INTRODUCTORY NARRATIVE.

LESSON I.

NEARLY a century and a half ago, great distress prevailed in a certain district in England, where there were but a few houses, peopled by labourers in the humblest condition of life; and, as the land was unproductive, and marshes hemmed in by mountains were to be seen far and wide, the earth did not bring forth sufficient to supply the wants of the people, so that many of them were obliged to leave the home of their childhood, and settle elsewhere. A poor lad, who had only received sufficient education to enable him to read, was removed from school to assist his father in his employment of stuff-weaving. The love of knowledge—the ardent desire of becoming a scholar—had taken possession of the youth, who devoted all his leisure moments, and even a portion of the time which his father required of him, to reading and writing. The father, instead of encouraging his son's fondness for study, forbade him to open a book, behaved with great harshness, and at length drove him from the house, telling him to go and seek his fortune where and how he chose. Weary, and uncertain where to go, he threw himself upon the heath to reflect upon the course he must take; and, having refreshed himself at an adjoining brook, walked to the neighbouring village, and took up his abode in the house of a tailor's widow, with whose son he had been previously acquainted. He contrived to support himself by industry and frugality, and to add to his stock of knowledge by careful observation and reading. Soon after his arrival, a pedlar, who combined fortune-teller and astrologer with his own trade, came to lodge in the same house; and becoming intimate with Hallam—for such was the boy's name—instructed him in the various branches of knowledge that he was acquainted with, while pursuing his own trade of pedlar and itinerant merchant. From the astrologer-pedlar he obtained the knowledge of the first principles of Natural Philosophy; and his naturally active and intelligent mind, improved by reading, extracted new and important facts from the incidents of every-day life with which he was surrounded.

The time for the departure of the pedlar arrived, and previous to setting off on his journey, he lent Hallam *Cocker's Arithmetic*, which had bound up with it a treatise on Algebra, and a work upon *Physics and Somatology*. These he studied so thoroughly that when the pedlar returned he was astonished to find his quondam pupil had almost eclipsed his tutor, and forthwith proceeded to draw his horoscope, as he termed it, in order to discover the probable career of this wonderful lad.

Having concluded his observations, the pedlar predicted that in two years Hallam would surpass his tutor, and ultimately rise to be a great man; and the youth promised that if such came to pass, he would not forget in his prosperity the instruction of the pedlar, and his kindness towards him.

* * * * * * *

Eighteen years have elapsed, and the prediction has been fulfilled: the lad abandoned his trade of weaver, turned schoolmaster, and married his landlady—the tailor's widow. He has passed through many phases in his journey through life, and, notwithstanding the privations and hardships he encountered, has risen to considerable eminence as a scholar, has been appointed Professor of Mathematics, and elected a Fellow of the Royal Society.

The few houses that were scattered upon the borders of the wild and desolate district where Hallam's father formerly lived, have increased in number and size; the marshes have been drained, the land tilled, the mountains quarried, and the whole aspect changed from desolation to the busy hum of commercial activity. Jacquard-looms have been erected, mills and factories built, and long lines of streets; so that from being a village at first, it has grown into a city. He seeks out the aged pedlar, who still instructs the young and labours for his bread; the old man has almost forgotten his pupil, but tears of joy suffuse his eyes, as the remembrance of other days is recalled. At eve, the two stroll towards the brow of the hill, Hallam supporting his aged tutor, and as they approach a mill on the road-side, they halt, for the pedlar is wearied and wishes to rest himself.

"This spot," said Hallam, "is where I reclined when my father drove me from his house; but how changed the prospect! The mountain's side is now peopled; and where the heath and furze grew amid marshy land, the golden-eared corn bends to the breeze. Observe yon waggon as it moves along the road; 'tis mine—aye, and all the factories beyond! So you must now leave off toiling, and share them with me; for to your instruction I owe all."

"To mine?" replied the pedlar.

"Yes! 'twas through the knowledge obtained from you, that I have risen to my present position. Your prediction ever before me, and with the desire of reaching the highest pinnacle of fame and honour, I worked incessantly; success crowned my efforts; and now, surrounded with wealth and honours, I must not forget the pedlar-astrologer, and his gift-book of—NATURAL PHILOSOPHY."

NATURAL PHILOSOPHY.
QUESTIONS AND EXPLANATIONS.

1. *Teacher.*—WHAT is Natural Philosophy?

Pupil.—It is that branch of the natural sciences which treats of phenomena that do not depend upon a change of the construction of bodies; and makes us acquainted with the nature, causes, properties, and effects of the various objects and events which surround us. It will enable **us to** discover why a room smokes when there are two fires in it. Why the handles of cooking vessels are often made of wood. Why persons interpose a piece of woollen material between their hand and the handle of an iron kettle. Why plunging the hands into water produces a sensation of cold. Why water is fluid; or why a cracked bell makes a discordant sound.

[The pupil should be required to give satisfactory answers to all these queries.]

2. *T.*—What is the term Philosophy derived from?

P.—**From the Greek** *philosophia*—(φιλοσοφία), **which literally** signifies **" love** of wisdom or **knowledge."**

3. *T.*—Then **it** appears from what you **have** stated, that Philosophy affords a wide **field** for observation, embracing as it does so many objects of opposite character. Is this the case?

P.—Yes. The vast realm of Nature, however, presents such an infinity of subjects for our consideration, that it has been found desirable to divide the natural sciences into two great branches—Natural History, and Natural Philosophy.

4. *T.*—What does Natural History **treat** of?

P.—It instructs us in the nature of individual objects, and arranges them in systems according to their different characters.

5. *T.*—If such be the case, of what does Natural Philosophy treat?

P.—It endeavours to teach us the manner in which inorganic substances act upon each other; laying open, in fact, the laws of the material world.

6. *T.*—What do you mean by inorganic substances?

P.—Inorganic substances are bodies that are not endowed with life, such as minerals, being the reverse of organic, or living bodies.

7. *T.*—What do you mean by the term *bodies?*

P.—All objects recognisable by the senses, whether fluid or solid, **are** generally described as *bodies;* thus **water** is a fluid body, ice a solid body, and steam a gaseous body. All these substances excite certain sensations in our minds, and the powers which excite them are called their *qualities* or *properties.*

8. *T.*—Give me some examples of the qualities or properties of bodies.

P.—Each body has some peculiar property or quality by which it is distinguished from another. It is the property of glass to be transparent and brittle; of fire to burn; of charcoal to be inodorous and insipid; of amber to be brittle, light, hard, and transparent; and of the loadstone to attract iron.

[**The** pupil should be requested to give other examples of the properties of bodies.]

9. *T.*—You said that certain sensations were excited in our minds by bodies: give me some examples.

P.—One body excites the sensation of green, another of blue, and a third is devoid of all colour, or may be said to be **white,** such as lime.

10. *T.*—Why is lime white?

P.—Because the particles of matter of which it is composed are piled so densely one upon another, that they are able to reflect all the coloured rays of light.

11. *T.*—What do you mean by the term *matter?*

P.—The substance entering into the composition of all bodies has received the general name of matter, which possesses certain essential characteristic qualities.

12. *T.*—What do you mean by the expression *general name?*

P.—A general name is one that is used to express a large *genus* or class of things **of** similar character; thus, *hats* may include straw hats, gutta-percha hats, cork **hats,** silk, beaver, **or** felt hats, and many other kinds; and **when we** say *apples,* we use an indefinite term, **if we** allude to any particular kind, such as crab-apples, **or** golden russet, and only employ the *general name* to express the class. Generalisation of facts can only be accomplished by persons **of** experience, well acquainted with **science.** The vast and heterogeneous mass of phenomena which puzzle ignorant people, are compared, classified, and generalised by the philosopher, and rendered familiar and useful to mankind.

13. *T.*—What do you mean by *phenomena?*

P.—They are all extraordinary appearances in the works of Nature; the word phenomenon being derived from the Greek word *phaino* (to appear), and signifying, literally, an appearance.

14. *T.*—Give me **some** illustrations of natural phenomena.

P.—Heat applied to ice drives the particles entering into its composition further asunder, and changes it from a *solid* **to a** *liquid form;* and if the temperature is increased, and the process prolonged, **the** water or liquid is converted into a *gaseous* fluid or steam, because the component particles are driven still further apart. Heat rarefies air and causes it to expand; for example, [Experiment 1,] let a bladder, half full of air, be tied tightly at the neck and then laid before a fire, or held over the flame of a spirit-lamp sufficiently high to prevent the flame injuring the bladder, and the air will expand and fill the bladder.

[The pupil should give some further illustrations of natural phenomena.]

GENERAL QUESTIONS UPON LESSON I.

1. What is the derivation and meaning of the term Philosophy?
2. How is Philosophy divided?
3. Name the senses by which the existence of bodies are made known to us.
4. What is the quality of a body?
5. What constitutes the composition of bodies?
6. What **is** matter?
7. What is a natural phenomenon?
8. Prove that the same cause may **produce** various effects.

LESSON II.*

We have an excellent example for the youth of the present age **to** follow, in the case **of the** poor boy Hallam, who, by untiring zeal in study, and perseverance, raised himself from obscurity to affluence, and an honourable position in the scientific world. The chief points in the story are true, but some little incidents have been introduced for

---

* Grandfather Whitehead requests that the Pupil will commit to memory the *ideas* of each lesson, and endeavour by experiments of a different character from those given here, to *demonstrate* to the Teacher that he has thoroughly mastered the subject.

especial reasons. It is founded upon the career of Thomas Simpson, the celebrated mathematician, who was born in the town of Market-Bosworth, in Leicestershire, in the year 1710. By studying the books given to him by the pedlar-astrologer, the boy was enabled to comprehend many of the laws of nature; and the knowledge he thus acquired was applied to the daily purposes of life, for Natural Philosophy explains the principles of the various arts which are practised, elevates **and** improves the mind, **and** extends man's power over nature. It unfolds to us the magnificence, order, and beauty of construction in the material world, and adduces the most powerful evidence of the wisdom and beneficence of the Creator. It was the knowledge of its laws that enabled Hallam to change the desolate tract of land into a populous and productive district. We can understand the manner in which bodies act upon each other, and the reason they do so, by means of its laws; for example:—[Experiment 2,] take a sheet of glass and place some water upon it; the glass will be wetted. You know this already from daily experience; but you require to know Natural Philosophy to explain the reason. If we wipe the glass dry, and place some mercury upon it, [Experiment 3,] the same effect is not produced, the glass remains dry; and Natural Philosophy explains why the glass is differently affected. Suppose we substitute a thin sheet of lead or tin, [Experiment 4,] and use the mercury as we did with the glass, the effect will be different; the metal plates will be wetted with the mercury, and if there is sufficient mercury, the plates will be dissolved in a short time. Again, take a lump of sugar, [Experiment 5,] and place it upon the glass plate we used a short time ago; examine it carefully, and you will observe how compact it looks; place a teaspoonful of water upon the glass and allow it to flow towards the sugar, you see it falls to pieces, and has now disappeared; and when you know more of Natural Philosophy the reason will be obvious.

QUESTIONS.

15. *T.*—From what you have shown respecting the manner in which some bodies act upon each other, it would appear that the phenomena we have witnessed *always* happen under similar circumstances, and therefore, that there must be a natural law to govern the action of bodies. Do you think that this is the case?

P.—Yes, undoubtedly. It is a natural law that bodies always act in the same manner under the same circumstances, and each body **has** its own law. Pure water will always dissolve sugar, but does not affect gold in the same manner, because it is not its nature to do **so**.

16. *T.*—Do you understand **what is** meant by a natural law?

P.—It is the external connexion of the phenomena of nature. If we apply heat to water it converts the water into steam, cold will not; therefore we say it is a natural law that governs its action. It is a natural law that all bodies at the earth's surface, if left to themselves, descend in straight lines towards **the** surface.

17. *T.*—Do you think that I can dissolve sand in water?

P.—No; I know you cannot, because it is contrary to its natural law.

18. *T.*—How have these laws been discovered?

P.—By experiments and observations.

19. *T.*—What is the use of experiments?

P.—Experiments verify observations and truths, elicit facts, establish theories, impress the principles more strongly upon our minds, and exemplify the application of general principles to the demonstration of individual facts.

20. *T.*—Having observed that sand, gold, and other bodies are insoluble, or oil incapable of mixing with water, you say that it is a natural law that governs this; but as it would be impossible for one person to observe and experiment upon all the bodies by which he is surrounded, how can we obtain the knowledge we require?

P.—From the experience of philosophers, who have observed and experimented upon the many and various bodies around them, and left their knowledge to us. Galileo was the first to test theories by practical experiments, and Lord Bacon showed that this was the only method of acquiring a knowledge of the laws of nature.

21. *T.*—Where can the recorded experience of philosophers be found?

P.—In works upon Natural Philosophy, **in** which the nature and properties of bodies, the laws which govern them, and the phenomena of nature are explained.

22. *T.*—As bodies differ materially one from another, the comprehension of the nature of their individual properties appears to be almost impossible.

P.—So it would be, if there were not general properties which we observe to exist in all bodies, whatever other differences they exhibit. Thus, it is essential to the existence of a body that it possess the power of extension, occupy a limited space, and be impenetrable; but in addition to these properties, without **which** we cannot form any idea of matter, **there** are other properties which we observe, as divisibility, extensibility, compressibility, porosity, inertia, and gravity.

23. *T.*—Can you always recognise these properties in bodies?

P.—Yes; some are essential to the existence of a body, others are not, as I stated before.

24. *T.*—How do you expect to understand all the phenomena that occur when experimenting upon bodies?

P.—By studying Natural Philosophy.

GENERAL QUESTIONS ON LESSON II.

1. What is the object of Natural Philosophy, and to what purposes is it applied?
2. What is meant by a natural law?
3. What is the use of experiments?
4. What is essential to the existence of a body?
5. Do all bodies possess peculiar characteristic properties?

[The pupil should be required to state the properties of various bodies in a concise manner—Example: *Lead* is solid, heavy, soft, malleable, deficient in tenacity, and readily fusible. *Water* is fluid, inodorous, clear, and tasteless. **Carbonic** *acid* is gaseous, colourless, pungent, **insoluble in** water, and acidulous, &c.]

LESSON III.

HALLAM learned **from the** book on Natural Philosophy that the pedlar-astrologer lent him, many of the laws of nature and their application, and by reading, reflection, and observation, he was enabled to add much to his store of knowledge, and apply his experience in such a manner, that he not only enriched himself, but benefitted his neighbours. The only source from whence we can derive our knowledge of nature is the perception of the senses, practical experience and observation; the facts observed and collected are arranged, and inferences drawn either from analogy or induction; but we derive all the certain and accurate knowledge of the laws of nature from the latter. Having mastered certain points, his next object was to apply his experience, and this he did so effectually that he drained the marshy lands, **and** made the mountain streams move machinery. We trust our pupils will all endeavour to be Hallams.

QUESTIONS.

25. *T.*—You have said that one of the properties of matter was divisibility. Now, do you think that there is any limit to this; that is to say, can it be infinitely divided?

P.—As far as we know, all bodies **are** divisible, being capable of division into smaller and still smaller portions; and, provided the instruments of division are fine enough, there is no limit as far as our senses are concerned. Yet, as all particles of matter must be possessed of a finite magnitude, we should rather say that it is limited, though too small to be seen even when magnified by the most powerful microscope.

26. *T.*—Give me some examples of the DIVISIBILITY of matter?

P.—One of the best examples of extreme divisibility of matter is musk, which will continue to diffuse its odour year after year without any perceptible loss of weight. It is stated* that "a clean cork, which stopped a phial in which there was musk, which it seemed never to have touched, in 1712, smelled of musk more than twenty years after;" and Fée says that one part of musk will communicate its odour to 3,000 parts of inodorous powder. It is very evident that some particles of the musk must have been diffused, otherwise the odour would not have been discovered by the sense of smelling; touch and vision could not assist in the perception of its existence. Again: the silk, spun by the silk-worm, is about the 500th part of an inch thick; but a spider's line is, perhaps, six times finer, or only the 3,000th part of an inch in diameter; insomuch that a single pound of this attenuated substance might be sufficient to encompass our globe. Another remarkable instance of the divisibility of matter is seen in the dyeing of silk with cochineal, where a pound of silk, containing eight score threads to the ounce, each thread seventy-two yards long, and the whole reaching about 104 miles, when dyed with scarlet does not receive above a drachm additional weight; so that a drachm of the colouring matter of the cochineal is actually extended through more than 100 miles in length, and yet this minute quantity is sufficient to give an intense colour to the silk with which it is combined. The animal kingdom also affords us an excellent example of the divisibility of matter in the animalcules of the iron-ochre, which are found in certain marshes. Each animalcule is only about $\frac{1}{1000}$th of an inch in diameter; and therefore a cubic line would contain 1000 *millions* of them, or nearly *two million millions* in a cubic inch!

[The pupil should be required to give other illustrations of the divisibility of matter, such as *gold* in gilding, or when beaten out; *plati-*

---
* Alston's *Letters on Materia Medica*, vol. ii. p. 542.

num, when formed into wire; *soap bubbles, wings of insects, puff-ball fungus, &c.*]

27. *T.*—What you have stated seems almost incredible without some further explanation; will you therefore demonstrate to me how matter is capable of division?

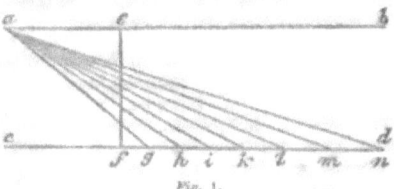

Fig. 1.

P.—Draw a line, A, B, and parallel to that another, C, D; then draw E F perpendicular to C, D, and between the two. Let E F represent the particle of matter to be divided; then draw lines from A to *g, h, i, k, l, m, n,* D, and the line E F will be divided into eight parts. If the line, C, D, be lengthened or extended, and the lines drawn from A increased in number, then the line E F, which represents the particle of matter, will be divided into a greater number of parts of less magnitude.

28. *T.*—Although you have explained to me in a very satisfactory manner the division of matter by means of a diagram, I wish to have a familiar instance. Can you furnish one?

P.—Yes; when large rocks are divided from the mass, for the purposes of building, the smaller portions are again divided to mend the roads, and then subdivided by the wheels of waggons, &c., till they form dust, the particles of which are frequently so exceedingly fine, that we cannot readily distinguish them without the aid of a magnifying glass.

29. *T.*—Give **me an** example **to prove** that the divisibility of matter **passes the** limits of sensual perception.

P.—Cinnabar, which is composed of sulphur and mercury, may be separated into these constituents; but we cannot distinguish the particles of sulphur from those of mercury, even under the microscope.

30. *T.*—Do you consider that the divisibility of matter **is** wholly unlimited?

P.—No; to adopt such an assumption would be to admit that the size of the ultimate undivisible particle is null; while it is evident, **that if** the ultimate particle have *no* extension, it cannot enter into **the** composition of a body occupying space.

31. *T.*—What do you gather from all the facts and observations you have stated?

P.—That all bodies are composed of minute particles, which cannot be further disintegrated, but are undivisible.

32. *T.*—What name have these particles received from natural philosophers?

P.—Atoms. If, however, we speak **of** the particles **of** a mass, without wishing actually to describe them as the ultimate portions, **we** employ the term molecules.

33. *T.*—Then it appears that a molecule is not the same as an atom; will **you** explain the difference?

P.—A molecule **is** supposed to be formed of several atoms, arranged according to some determinate figure, and generally signifies the component parts of a body too small for sensual perception.

34. *T.*—Has the knowledge of the constitution of bodies thus formed been applied?

P.—Yes. Natural philosophers and chemists have universally embraced the view, which has received the name of the **atomic** theory, **or** theory of atoms.

GENERAL QUESTIONS ON LESSON III.

1. Are all bodies divisible?
2. Give some examples of the divisibility of matter from the organized world.
3. Can you give a familiar example of the divisibility of matter?
4. Can we always prove the divisibility of matter by our senses?
5. Is there any limit to the divisibility of matter?
6. What is the difference between an atom, a molecule, and a particle?
7. What name has the fundamental view of the constitution of bodies received?

LESSON IV.

RECAPITULATION, &c.—THE study **of the** laws **of Natural** Philosophy enabled Hallam to discover that matter was capable of division, and he applied his knowledge **to** many useful purposes. The mountain **on the borders** of the marsh where he had **taken up** his abode, was barren, and he therefore rented a portion **of it for** a small sum: **on this he** built a hut, and formed lime. The lime he sold to the farmers; and by frugality and industry, was enabled to purchase a plot of ground on which to build his house. The house he now built was formed of stone, procured from the mountain's side, united with mortar made from lime he manufactured himself. To procure this stone, he was obliged to have recourse to Natural Philosophy as his assistant, and by means of judiciously conducted experiments and observations, he was enabled to accomplish ten **times the** amount of work he otherwise could have done, if unacquainted with Natural Philosophy.

QUESTIONS.

35. *T.*—I **remember** that you said one of the essential properties of a body was EXTENSIBILITY. Pray what do you mean by the term?

P.—Every body must occupy a certain amount of space, which space will, of course, **be** in proportion to its magnitude. Extensibility is the property observed in bodies to have their volume enlarged without increasing their mass.

36. *T.*—What do you mean by the volume **of a body?**

P.—It is the bulk or size of **a** body, being the quantity of space included within its external surfaces.

37. *T.*—How do you estimate **the bulk** or volume of bodies?

P.—By the quantity of their dimensions; **or** in other words, by their length, breadth, and depth.

38. *T.*—You have just said that a body may have its volume enlarged without increasing its mass; how is this possible?

P.—I will prove it to you by an experiment. [Experiment 6.] Take a glass tube (*a*, *b*,) with a bulb at the **end** (*b*); let the bulb (*b*), and part of the tube be filled with some infusion **of** logwood, solution of indigo, or other coloured fluid, as far **as** *c*. Plunge the bulb into hot water, and **if you** observe, you will see the decoction of logwood, which is **in this** tube, rapidly rising towards **A**, because the fluid has dilated **or** extended under **the influence** of the increased temperature, **and is occupying a greater space than before, therefore its volume is increased. We will now allow the fluid to cool, and you will** observe that it will return to the level at *c*, therefore we prove that the mass **is the same** as before. If you repeat the experiment with the bladder, [Experiment 1], you will have another illustration of extensibility. In both these experiments **the** elevation of the temperature produces **an** increase of volume, which will be easily comprehended by examining these two diagrams.

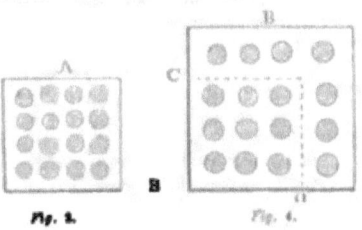

Fig. 3.

Fig. 3 represents **a cubic** inch of **cold** air, **which we will suppose** contains **sixteen atoms of air, but when** expanded, **the** same space only **contains** nine atoms, (as indicated by the **dotted** lines B, C,) because the volume has **increased** to the **size of** *Fig.* 4, but when the air again becomes **cold,** it will return to the original **size.** Yet the warm cubic inch of air **contains the same** number of atoms, and **weighs the same as** before.

39. *T.*—You have only given **me two** illustrations, the one relating to **a fluid, the other** to a gaseous body. **Can you illustrate the** subject by a solid body?

P.—**Yes.** When the stopper of **a decanter has become** firmly fixed, **so that it** cannot easily be withdrawn without the probability of breaking the decanter, if a flannel is dipped into hot water, and applied to the neck of the bottle, it will cause the glass to expand [Experiment **7**], and when the neck is enlarged the stopper can be easily extracted.

40. *T.*—Has the volume **of a body any** relation to its figure?

P.—No. Bodies having **very different** *volumes* may have the same *figure ;* **and** bodies **with** different *figures* may have the same *volume*. Thus, a box may be ten times as large as a die, or another box, but yet have the same *figure ;* and a square and a sphere may, though of different figures, yet have **equal** *volumes*.

41. *T.*—**Do you think that bodies can be diminished in bulk, without diminishing** their mass?

P.—Yes ; all bodies possess the property of compressibility as well as extensibility.

42. *T.*—What do you mean **by compressibility?**

P.—It is **that quality which all bodies** possess of having **their volume diminished** without decreasing **their mass.**

43. *T.*—Can you furnish **me** with some familiar examples of the compressibility of bodies?

P.—The most elastic, and therefore the most compressible bodies, are aëriform fluids, and the most familiar of these is the atmospheric air, which varies in bulk, according as it is near or remote from the earth's surface. It may appear very extraordinary that the **bulk** of the atmosphere should vary, but nevertheless it is the **case,** and I will explain this by a simple **experiment.** [Experiment 8]. Take four bags of seed or flour, and place them one above the other, and you will easily understand how those **at** the bottom **of** the pile are **not** so thick **as** those at the top. [The experiment is better illustrated by increasing the number of the bags, **and** employing horsehair.] It is on account of the weight of the bags above

Fig. 5.

pressing upon the lower ones. So it is with the particles of air at the surface of the earth: they are pressed upon by those above them, at a pressure of about 15 lbs. to every square inch. If you examine the bags, you will perceive that *a* is very much compressed, *b* not quite **so** much, **c** less, and *d* almost uncompressed; so that **as we ascend you** observe the pressure is less, the same as it is with atmospheric pressure.

44. *T.*—Can you compress gases the same as you do atmospheric air?

P.—Yes; all gases can be compressed; and one of the most familiar illustrations of the truth of this, is the compression of carbonic acid gas in the manufacture of **soda-water**.

45. *T.*—Are fluids or liquids **compressible**?

P.—Yes; but **in so slight** a degree that, in a hydrostatic **sense, they are** considered incompressible; yet **they are** not absolutely incompressible, but only yield slightly to very intense pressure.

46. *T.*—Are you certain that liquids have been compressed?

P.—Yes. Canton proved this by experiment in the year 1761. He placed **a** tube with a bulb, similar to the one we employed [Experiment 6], in a condenser, and submitted the surface of the liquid to a very intense pressure of condensed air. The result was, that the level of the liquid fell perceptibly, and rose again to its original height upon removing the pressure.

47. *T.*—Can solids be compressed?

P.—Yes. You observe this piece **of** lead is round, in fact, it is what is called a bullet; now immediately that it receives **a** stroke of this hammer it will be partially compressed. [Experiment 9.] You see that it is somewhat flattened, and now that it has received six strokes, the size of it is diminished, but its weight is the same. In the same manner, iron, steel, gold, and other solids may be compressed.

48. *T.*—How can you account for this?

P.—All bodies have interstices between the different particles of matter, and it is therefore very evident that the atoms are not in immediate contiguity with each other. The spaces between the atoms are capable of being compressed or extended, and therefore the volume of the body may be diminished or increased.

49. *T.*—What do you call the spaces between the particles of bodies?

P.—They **are called pores.**

50. *T.*—Have *all* bodies spaces or pores between their particles?

P.—Yes; every body is porous.

51. *T.*—Then the property of being porous is a general one?

P.—It is; and the quality of being so is called Porosity.

GENERAL QUESTIONS ON LESSON IV.

1. When bodies have their volume enlarged without increasing their mass, by what term do you express this property?
2. What is the volume of a body?
3. How is the volume of a body estimated?
4. **Prove by experiments that the volume of a body may be enlarged without increasing the mass.**
5. Are all bodies capable of being extended?
6. What relation has the volume **of a** body to its figure?
7. Can bodies be diminished in bulk without decreasing their mass?
8. What term has been applied to this property of diminishing the bulk of bodies?
9. Are all bodies capable of being compressed?
10. Give some familiar examples of the compressibility of bodies, and illustrate the fact by experiments.
11. How do you account for the compressibility and extensibility of bodies?
12. What term has been applied to the spaces between the particles of bodies?
13. What is the name of the general law, "that all bodies have spaces between their particles?"

LESSON V.

RECAPITULATION, &c.—We have learned how bodies may be extended, and how compressed, and have also ascertained that all bodies are porous. Now these facts are all very important, especially when they are associated with other matters which we shall consider hereafter. They are intimately connected with the affairs of every-day life, and are therefore of great consequence. Hallam had become conversant with the laws which regulate them, and was led on step by step until he applied the knowledge he thus acquired to useful purposes. He learned that even solid bodies may be made to expand or contract without diminishing their mass, and he also learned that solid bodies have pores or interstices between their particles. Hallam had yet to learn more of the principles of Natural Philosophy; so have we.

QUESTIONS.

52. *T.*—You said that *all bodies* have pores or interstices between their particles; how do you know this?

P.—It has been discovered by experiment, and I know it by reading. More than two centuries ago it was proved by experiment, at the Academy *Del Cimento*, in Florence, that gold was porous; the experience was the result of accident, but it established the fact that water may be made to pass *through* gold.

53. *T.*—Then you would imply, that because all bodies are compressible, there are interstices between their particles.

P.—Certainly, but the size of the pores varies in different substances. Thus, one substance may contain 10,000 pores in a square inch, and another 100,000 pores in the same space. In the former case, the pores are considerably larger than in the latter.

54. *T.*—What is the effect of the pores of a body being closer together?

P.—The substance itself is rendered more dense.

55. *T.*—What do you mean by being dense?

P.—The density of bodies depends upon the proximity of their particles; and therefore, the greater the density of any substance, the less will be the porosity. The density of a body is the relation of its weight to its volume, and therefore indicates its specific gravity, a property we shall consider on another occasion.

56. *T.*—How can you prove **that bodies** have pores?

P.—By a very simple experiment. [Experiment 10.] I have here a piece of wood, with a wire fastened to it, and a tumbler of water. I will plunge the wood into the water, and keep it at the bottom of the tumbler by means of the wire [performing the experiment]. You see that several bubbles of air are rising to the surface, they have escaped from the pores of the wood, which are being filled with water instead. If there were not any interstices it would be impossible for the air to be in the substance of the wood, because it is contrary to one of the established general laws of Natural Philosophy.

57. *T.*—Is the knowledge of the porosity of bodies applied to any useful or scientific purposes?

P.—Yes; filtration is based upon, and electrotyping is under obligations to it.

58. *T.*—Can you adduce any further proofs of the universal porosity of bodies?

P.—Yes; many bodies are capable of compression merely by mechanical force, and this I will explain by a simple experiment. [Experiment 11.] I have here a basin of water, and a piece of cork floating upon the surface; I will take an empty tumbler (as it is commonly termed, but actually filled with air) and invert it over the cork, so that **the** edge shall just be below the water; **the air is** now confined within the tumbler **and** occupies a given space, but if I plunge the tumbler below the surface, and keep it there, it will be found that the water rises to a certain height above the level of the brim, and the deeper that it is plunged the more the cork rises in the tumbler; but as the pressure is removed and the goblet rises, it will be found that the water descends and the cork with it, because the air expands. Thus you will see that air is capable of being compressed—a sufficient proof of its porosity.

59. *T*—Why did not the water fill the tumbler when you plunged it below the surface?

P.—Because, as the air was in the tumbler, the water could not occupy the same space at the same time, and, therefore, the experiment also proves the IMPENETRABILITY of the air.

60. *T.*—What do you mean by impenetrability?

P.—By the impenetrability of bodies is meant, that no two particles of matter can occupy the same identical portion of space at the same moment.

61. *T.*—How can you prove this?

P.—By experiment. [Experiment 12.] I have here a piece of clay, and a bullet, which I will enclose within the clay. Now it is quite impossible to make another bullet occupy the cavity that contains the first bullet as long as it is there. This you will readily understand, because it is like trying to pour a pint of water into a pint measure already full of water. Again, if I drive a nail into a piece of wood, the effect is only to compress the wood, because it is impossible that the wood and nail can be in the same identical space at the same precise time.

Fig. 6.

62. *T.*—Has this knowledge of the impenetrability of bodies been usefully employed?

P.—Yes; the principle of the wedge is founded upon it. In the above diagram you will see the explanation of the law; the point of the wedge has been inserted into a block of wood by a blow from a hammer, and has displaced the wood by compression. The substance of the wood is dividing, because it cannot be compressed any more.

63. *T.*—If you remove the wedge, does the wood resume its former shape, and occupy the space it did before the wedge was driven in?

P.—No; because, unlike the air in the tumbler, it is not elastic, otherwise it would resume its former dimensions.

64. *T.*—Are not all bodies elastic?

P.—No; lead or iron may be compressed or diminished in size, but they cannot resume their former volume; and therefore we learn, that elasticity does not always accompany compressibility.

65. *T.*—Then am I to understand that elasticity is the power by which a body resumes its figure or volume, after that figure or volume has been altered by the action of any force?

P.—Yes, undoubtedly, after the force that caused the alteration of the figure has ceased to act; not otherwise, and that power is found in solid and fluid bodies.

GENERAL QUESTIONS ON LESSON V.

1. How do you know that all bodies have pores between their particles?
2. What is the result of the greater proximity of the pores of bodies?
3. What is meant by the density of bodies?
4. Can you prove the porosity of bodies?
5. Is it possible for two bodies to occupy the same space at the same time?
6. What do you call this natural law of bodies?
7. How can you prove the impenetrability of bodies?
8. Has the knowledge of the impenetrability of bodies been practically applied?
9. Do all bodies possess the property of resuming their former volume after being compressed?
10. What is this property of matter named?

LESSON VI

RECAPITULATION, &c.—When Hallam commenced the study of Natural Philosophy, he learned that there were certain laws relating to bodies, called Natural Laws, which have been in force since the creation; and having stored his mind with the information contained in the gift-book of the pedlar-astrologer, having reflected upon the various applications of the principles he had learned, and experimentally proved the practical use of his knowledge, he was enabled to overcome the many difficulties with which he was surrounded. He discovered that the stones in the vicinity of his hut were fit for building, and by means of the application of the wedge, he was enabled to separate large masses from the parent rock. Thus, he applied the knowledge of the impenetrability of bodies to a useful purpose. He read, that all bodies near the earth's surface, if left to themselves, descend in straight lines towards that surface, and that the directions in which they fall in different places of the earth, tend nearly to the centre of it. This is a general natural law, and is seen daily. He also learned that philosophers had discovered by observation, that matter is incapable of spontaneous change,—a fact of great importance.

QUESTIONS.

66. *T.*—Do bodies possess **the** power of spontaneous action?

P.—No; all bodies, when at rest, *must remain* passive or inactive, unless influenced by some external force.

67. *T.*—What does this prove?

P.—That mere matter is void of life; for spontaneous action is the only test of the presence of the living principle.

68. *T.*—Then it is impossible for any body of itself to commence to move from a state of rest.

P.—It is. A body cannot be in a state of motion and rest at the same instant; and, as I have explained before, all bodies must remain passive unless put in motion by force.

69. *T.*—Can you tell me the name of this quality of matter?

P.—It is called INERTIA, or *inactivity*.

70. *T.*—Can you give **me an** example of inertia?

P.—A stone, if left to itself, cannot possibly move; but if I kick the stone, it will continue to move with unchanging **velocity** in the same direction until its **course** is arrested by some external force.

71. *T.*—Am I to understand, that when a body is put in motion it has not the power to arrest its progress, and become quiescent?

P.—Certainly. It **cannot be reduced** from a state of **motion without the agency** of some force. **Thus, the wheel** of **an engine** continues to **move after** the force which impelled it has been arrested, and would continue to run on for ever if the motion were not constantly impeded by friction.

72. *T.*—Do you think that mechanical causes, or friction, are the only impediments to which moving bodies on the same surface of the earth are liable?

P.—No. The air offers considerable resistance; and no doubt you remember, that when you have been running fast with a cloak on, that you have found, as your speed increased, that the resistance of the air also increased.

73. *T.*—Can you give me a good example to prove that bodies will continue **to** move when not impeded?

P.—The vast bodies of the universe, which received motion from the Creator, have continued to move with unchanging velocity since the time they were launched into space.

74. *T.*—Are organised bodies an exception to the law of inertia?

P.—No; for example, when horses are racing, they always pass far beyond the winning-post before their speed can be arrested; and **a man** standing upright in a boat or carriage will fall backwards **when the boat is** suddenly pushed from the shore, or the carriage starts; and when either of them stops suddenly, the man will be thrown forwards.

75. *T.*—Why **would the man be** thrown backwards when **the boat or** carriage started?

P.—**Because his body, by** obeying the **law of inertia, remains where** it was; but **his feet being pulled** forwards, his body **falls backwards.**

76. *T.*—If such be the case, how does it happen that the man falls forward **when** the carriage or boat stops?

P.—Because his body has acquired the same velocity as the boat or carriage, and is impelled forward with that speed, while his feet remain **passive.**

77. *T.*—Do you think that bodies can increase or diminish their velocity?

P.—Certainly not; they must move with an **unchanging** speed, because **of** themselves **they cannot** change the rate of motion. **An increase** of its rate could only be the result of some applied force, and a diminution **of it** must be caused by some impediment.

GENERAL QUESTIONS ON LESSON VI.

1. Can bodies move of themselves?
2. What is the only test of the living principle?
3. What name has been applied **to** passiveness of bodies?
4. What is inertia?
5. Give me some examples of inertia.
6. Have bodies the power to arrest their speed?
7. How are organised bodies affected by inertia?
8. Can **bodies increase or** diminish their velocity?

LESSON VII.

RECAPITULATION, &c.—THE fact of matter being inert, and unable to pass from a state of rest into one of motion, is important, and therefore when we see that a body commences to move the instant we deprive it of its support, we know that it is in consequence of the force of gravity. But there are other phenomena in connexion with **gravity** that require our attention:—the air-balloon, the falling rain, the rising smoke, are all **familiar** illustrations of the attraction of gravitation; but there is also another attraction **to** which bodies are subject—a mutual attraction. For example, [Experiment 13,] place two **balls of** cork or wood in a basin of water, and they will be attracted and come into **contact with each** other. If, however, two balls of wood or lead be **suspended by** strings, they cannot approach each other, without moving out of the vertical **line of** the earth's attraction; and as their mutual attraction cannot overcome this, they remain at rest. Hallam learned all this by studying Natural Philosophy. It was the knowledge that bodies are possessed of inertia, and the law of the attraction of gravitation, that enabled him to apply the mountain-streams as a motive power for his machinery; but this he could not have done, if he had not also learned other important laws in Natural Philosophy, which we shall consider hereafter.

QUESTIONS.

78. *T.*—What is GRAVITY?

P.—It is the force which compels bodies to fall. Thus, a stone or any other body thrown by a person, when left to itself, will fall until it reaches the earth, or any other object that impedes its progress.

79. *T.*—Is this power limited to this action, or not?

P.—No; the actions produced by its influence are various; for example—the rising of a piece of cork from the bottom **of a** tumbler **of** water to the surface; the falling of an apple; and the direction of rivers to find their lowest level, are all the effects of the force of gravitation.

80. *T.*—How can you ascertain the direction of the force of gravity?

P.—Fasten a string at one extremity (*a*), and attach a small heavy weight (*w*) to the other end of the string. The direction of the string, when it is tightened and at rest, will give the direction of gravity with accuracy. The weight (*w*) is called a plummet; and the line which the string (*v*) forms in a state of equilibrium, the vertical line.

81. *T.*—Can you always determine the direction of gravitation?

Fig. 7.

P.—Yes; by means of the plummet, it may easily be ascertained at all times and in all places.

82. *T.*—Where is the force of gravity always directed?

P.—Towards the centre of the earth.

83. *T.*—If this is the case, the direction of the plummet must be different in various parts of the earth.

P.—So it is; the directions of the plummet, at two different parts of the earth, are not parallel, because they make a certain angle with each other, the point of which coincides with the central point of the earth.

84. *T.*—Can you explain to me how it is that bodies do not descend in parallel lines, as they appear to do?

P.—I have a diagram here that will explain it very easily. Let A B C represent a part of the circumference of the earth, and *a* & *b* two balls of lead. When these balls are left to themselves, they will descend in the direction of the lines *a* A and *b* B. Now, if it was possible for the balls to descend to the centre of the earth they would meet at o, the same as

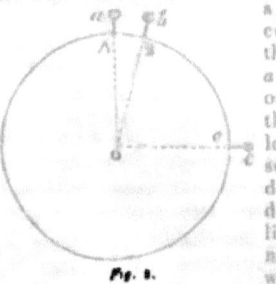

Fig. 8.

the lines do. If the ball *c* was let fall at that part of the globe, it would descend in a straight line (*c c*) so as to form a right angle with the line *a* A.

85. *T.*—Is gravity a general **property of all bodies**?

P.—Yes; fluids, solids, and gaseous bodies are alike subject to its laws.

86. *T.*—Suppose that the body is interrupted in its descent by some other **supporting body**, what is the result?

P.—The action of the force of gravity does not cease; but expends itself by pressure upon the object intervening.

87. *T.*—What is the weight of a body?

P.—It is the amount of pressure exercised by one body upon another body on which it rests; the pressure increasing with the number of the material particles **of** the body.

88. *T.*—What is the mass of a body?

P.—It is the quantity of matter of which it is composed; and therefore the larger the quantity of matter, the greater the resistance it will offer.

89. *T.*—You have stated that gravity **is** the force which compels bodies to fall. Explain to me how it is that smoke, clouds **of** vapour, and air-balloons *ascend*, if the theory of the attraction of gravitation is correct.

P.—These are only additional proofs of the effect of gravitative attraction; because the smoke, vapour, and balloon are driven upwards solely by the force of the atmospheric air through which they pass; as they are lighter than the air, they ascend, and displace or thrust down portions of air equal to their volume.

90. *T.*—This does not prove to me that they are influenced by the attraction of gravitation: explain the fact more fully?

P.—All substances that are lighter than the atmospheric air of the surface of the earth, will ascend until they reach that part of the air that is not so dense; and **as two** bodies cannot occupy the same space at the same time, the smoke, vapour, or balloon will displace a portion of air equal to their bulk. The smoke, however, only remains suspended till its particles unite and form flakes of soot, which being heavier than the air, descend; and the vapour becomes condensed into drops of water, which descends, because it is heavier than the air, and its weight draws it down.

91. *T.*—Suppose that I could remove the atmosphere from the surface of the globe, while the smoke, vapour, and balloons were suspended, what would be the result?

P.—They would fall to the ground, because their support would be withdrawn.

92. *T.*—How can you prove this?

P.—By an experiment. [Experiment 14.] I have here a tall bell-glass (*a*), open at the bottom, which shall be placed on the plate of an air-pump (*f*), and the air it contains exhausted. You observe that the top is closed by a brass cap (*b*), which has two small stages (*c c*) attached to its sides, and a wire (*a*) passing through the centre, but fitted so that it will turn without admitting the air. The ends of the stages being made to rest upon the lower part of the wire, a piece of lead (*d*) is placed upon one, and a feather (*e*) upon the other, or any two bodies differing in density. I will now exhaust the air, [performs the experiment,] and as soon as the handle of the wire (*a*) is turned, the stages will fall, and the lead and feather also. Observe, you see the lead and feather have both reached the stage of the air-pump at the same instant. I will now replace them and admit the air, and you will see that the lead reaches the stage long before the feather. So it is with the air; being heavier than the smoke, it descends, and pushes the smoke, vapour, or balloon upwards, which may be easily proved by means of the air-pump [Experiment 15.] You observe that I place a small piece of candle with a long ignited wick, upon the stage of the air-pump, and cover it with the bell-glass we used in our last experiment. The smoke from the wick ascends because the air in the glass descends and pushes it up, but when the air is exhausted the effect will be very different; and, to illustrate it better, I will place the candle upon an inverted wine-glass. [Performs the experiment.] Now you see that the smoke falls to the bottom of the glass.

93. *T.*—Are there other kinds of attraction?

P.—Yes; there is the attraction of cohesion, capillary attraction, chemical attraction, magnetic attraction, and electrical attraction.

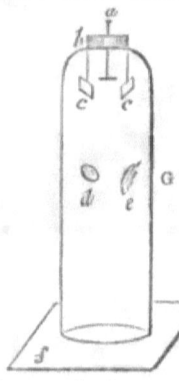

Fig. 9.

GENERAL QUESTIONS ON LESSON VII.

1. WHAT is meant by gravity?
2. Can you discover the direction of the force of gravity by any means?
3. What is the direction of the force of gravitation, and how can you determine it?
4. Does the direction of the force of gravity differ?
5. How is it that falling bodies do not descend in parallel lines?
6. Are all bodies subject to the laws of gravity?
7. What do you mean by the weight and the mass of a body?
8. How can you account for smoke rising?
9. What would be the result if the globe was not surrounded by the atmosphere?
10. How many kinds of attraction are there?

LESSON VIII.

RECAPITULATION, &c.—The attraction of the earth's mass binds the atmosphere around its surface, producing what is termed atmospheric pressure, a force equivalent to about fifteen pounds on the square inch at the level of the sea, but less as we ascend; a fact we have considered before. If this pressure, or force, were not exercised, we should not be able to remain upon the surface of the earth, but would be thrown off the same as the dirt from the wheel of a carriage, or the water from a mop, when the servant causes it to revolve rapidly. We have now to consider other forms of attraction, of equal importance in their way with the attraction of gravitation.

QUESTIONS.

94. *T.*—What is meant by the **ATTRACTION OF COHESION**?
P.—It is that power which causes particles of matter to stick together, or cohere?

95. *T.*—Are all bodies kept together by this power?
P.—Yes; but it is much stronger in some bodies than in others. It is stronger, or more **powerful**, in solid bodies, than in fluids, and weakest in gaseous bodies.

96. *T.*—What is the effect of the influence of this power?
P.—That some bodies are hard, **others** tough, soft, brittle, elastic, and so on.

97. *T.*—Is the attraction of cohesion limited to the particles of the bodies?
P.—No. It may exist between the molecules of bodies, and between bodies themselves; and in the former case is termed *molecular*, or *atomic* attraction.

98. *T.*—Give me an example of molecular attraction?
P.—A piece of lump-sugar is kept together by molecular attraction, because the atoms mutually attract each other; and other bodies are operated upon in the same manner, in a greater or less degree.

99. *T.*—Suppose that this force was not exercised, what would be the result?
P.—The bodies would be without **form** or figure, and the molecules would be a confused mass.

100. *T.*—Is actual contact necessary for the exercise of this property?
P.—No; it acts at insensible distances, when the particles appear to us to touch one another; but we learn, by means of the microscope, that they do not.

101. *T.*—Suppose that I break a stone by a blow from a hammer, will the various molecules unite again?
P.—No. The attraction of **cohesion has been** overcome by the force **of the blow;** and the particles have not **sufficient mutual attraction** to unite again, **independent of other causes.**

102. *T.*—Can you explain to me how it is that **a** drop **of** rain or dew, or a globule of mercury, unites **and forms** a sphere when it comes into contact with another **body of a similar nature**?
P.—Yes; it is **a law of nature, that** the particles **of** matter are attracted towards a common centre, and therefore they arrange themselves thus.

103. *T.*—Can you give me a familiar illustration of the attraction of cohesion?
P.—You **see** that I have two pieces of lead with **flat and smooth** surfaces. [Experiment 16.] **Press** the surfaces firmly together with **a twist, and you** will find that it will require a considerable **force to** separate them.

104. *T.*—If **a** sponge is placed in **a plate** of water, what is the effect?
P.—The greater part of the **water is drawn** into the pores of the sponge **by capillary** attraction.

105. *T.*—What do **you mean by capillary** attraction?
P.—It is the force **by which fluids are** raised above their levels, the attraction **that** causes hair-like tubes **to raise liquids.**

106. *T.*—How **can you** illustrate this?
P.—I have **here a glass** vessel which contains some **infusion of** logwood, and there **is a piece of wood** fitting to the upper

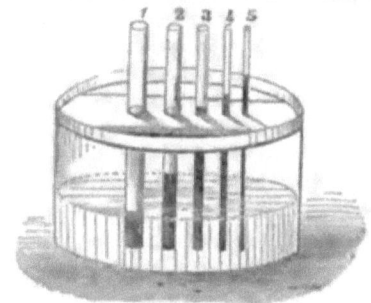

Fig. 16.

part, which has **five tubes of glass** in it. [Experiment 17.] **Immediately** the tubes are immersed in the **liquid, it** will rise in each tube, but will **vary** in **the** height to which the liquid is raised; thus, No. 1 will not have any great height of fluid, because the centre of the tube is more distant from the circumference than it is in

No. 2, and so on until No. 5, in which the fluid is raised to a considerable height; it being an established rule, that the smaller the tube, the greater will be the height of the surface of the fluid.

107. *T.*—Give me a familiar example of capillary attraction?

P.—[Experiment 18.] I have a basin of water here, and a skein of cotton. You observe that one end of the cotton is immersed in the water, and if this basin is left sufficiently long in its place, the whole of the water will be extracted from the basin by the force of capillary attraction, and fall into the tumbler I now place beneath.

GENERAL QUESTIONS ON LESSON VIII.

1. What is the attraction of cohesion?
2. What are its effects?
3. How can you prove the property?
4. What is capillary attraction?
5. How does it act?
6. Prove that it exists.

LESSON IX.

RECAPITULATION, &c.—When a plate falls it breaks into several pieces; the attraction of cohesion being overcome by the force of the fall; and when a piece of wood is split with a chisel, the power of cohesion is overcome by the force employed. These are examples we may witness every day. We have also learned that the force of gravitation may be overcome by the force of capillary attraction, (from *capilla*, the Latin for a hair), and that fluids may be raised above their levels by its power; this we proved by tubes of different diameters being immersed in a coloured fluid, but we can demonstrate it also by another simple experiment, [Experiment 19.] Take two sheets of glass of the same size, and place them in the contact at *a, b,* but separate them by means of a piece of cork (*c*) at *d, e*. Immerse them in a solution of logwood, or ink and water, contained in the trough *f*. It will then be found that the fluid will ascend higher between the glasses at *a, b,* than at *e*, where it is scarcely above the level, because the attraction is greater at *a, b*, than at *e*. You observe that the fluid is curved from *a* to *e*; this curve has received the name of the *hyperbola*. When we consider the other branches of science, we will enter into the phenomena attending chemical, magnetic, and electrical attraction, which do not *essentially* pertain to Natural Philosophy.

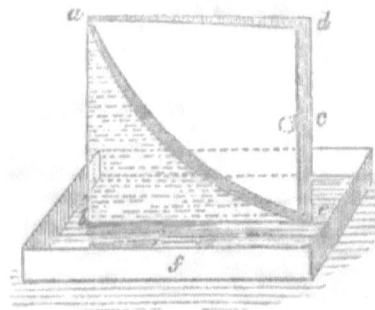

Fig. 11.

QUESTIONS.

108. *T.*—What is meant by REPULSION.
P.—It is that power by which the particles of bodies, or the bodies themselves, are made to recede from one another.

109. *T.*—Does the power of repulsion exist in all bodies?
P.—Yes; all the particles of material substances possess the power of attraction and repulsion.

110. *T.*—What is the great agent of repulsion?
P.—Caloric or heat, which pervades all things.

111. *T.*—What is caloric?
P.—It has been called an *imponderable body*, because it does not cause any perceptible difference in the weight of any body.

112. *T.*—Can you give me a more definite idea of it?

P. It is a very subtile, elastic fluid, which we know only by its effects, and the sensations it produces. It penetrates all bodies, more or less, and exists in all bodies, but cannot be wholly separated from them. It exists in a *free*, and in a *latent* or concealed state. Its particles are supposed mutually to repel each other, and its rays are capable of reflexion and polarization, and are refrangible.

113. *T.*—How do you know that heat exists?

P.—Because I can detect its presence in various ways; for example, if I rub a button upon my coat, it will soon become so hot that it will ignite a lucifer-match; and if I hammer the end of a piece of iron wire it will become hot enough to ignite phosphorus or gunpowder.

114. *T.*—What is the reason that heat is developed by friction, and hammering the iron?

P.—Because the atoms of which the materials are composed are compressed, and the heat which was latent or concealed is forced out, and made sensible, or set free.

115. *T.*—What effect does heat produce upon bodies?

P.—It modifies attraction, and regulates their solidity or density.

116. *T.*—How is heat communicated?
P.—By conduction and radiation.

117. *T.*—What do you mean by conduction?

P.—When the heat passes from atom to atom slowly along a body, it is conducted; thus, if I place one end of a small piece of iron or copper wire in the flame of a candle, the heat will soon be conducted or conveyed to my fingers; but the effect is different when we employ wood, because **it** is a bad conductor—but still the heat is conducted. The reason of this is, that metals are the best conductors; then fluids, and last of all, gases.

118. *T.*—What do you mean by the radiation of heat?

P.—It simply means, that the heat is given off in rays or lines.

119. *T.*—Can you give me **some other** peculiarities and properties **relating to** heat?

P.—Yes; **but** they will be more suited to the subjects of Chemistry and Pneumatics.

120. *T.*—Although you have explained to me that heat is the great agent of repulsion, yet you have not given me a single example to prove that.

P.—This is easily done: [Experiment 20]—Take two feathers, rub a glass tube about 1½ inch in diameter pretty briskly with a silk handkerchief, and then touch both feathers, one after the other; the first effect produced will be attraction. Now place them near to each other, and the result will be repulsion: they will separate themselves.

GENERAL QUESTIONS ON LESSON IX.

1. What name has been **given** to the property which causes the atoms of bodies to separate, or recede from each other?
2. Does this property exist in all bodies?
3. What is the chief cause of its acting?
4. What is caloric?
5. Prove that it exists.
6. What are the sources of heat?
7. What effect does it produce upon bodies?
8. How is heat communicated?
9. What do you mean by conduction and radiation of heat?
10. Give examples of the repulsion of bodies.

[The pupil should give other examples than those furnished in the Lesson; such as the friction of two similar bodies, like wood, to prove that heat is latent, &c. &c.]

LESSON X.

RECAPITULATION, &c.—We have learned that heat possesses remarkable properties; and although it is unequally distributed over the surface of the globe, yet it has a constant tendency to preserve an equilibrium in all situations. When we know more respecting heat, we shall be able to understand how the heat-measurer or *thermometer* is constructed, and in what manner it acts, and many other phenomena connected with it. Hallam *observed*, that when all the forces acting upon a body counteracted each other, it remained in a state of equilibrium, or was balanced; and having gained a knowledge of the properties of matter, he applied it to the study of the *laws of motion* and forces.

QUESTIONS.

121. *T.*—What is **motion**?

P.—It is **the** very **reverse** of rest, and means the change of place, which may be uniform **or** variable, according **to** its rate **or relative** velocity.

122. *T.*—What do **you mean by rest; because it** appears a **direct contradiction to the** laws of nature?

P.—There is no such thing as absolute rest, because the earth upon which we stand is always in a state of motion, therefore the term is only *relative*, and not positive.

123. *T.*—What do you mean, by saying that rest is only relative?

P.—If I let a stone fall from my hand, it will remain in the same place and in **the same** position where it fell, until removed by some applied force; and, therefore, we say it is now at rest, but we mean to say that it is at rest only as regards the earth, because we know that there is no such thing as *absolute* rest in creation. The earth, the planets, and the sun move; **in fact,** all creation moves.

124. *T.*—**Which is more** natural, for a body **to be in a state of rest** or motion?

P.—Rest, of course; **because** bodies must be arrested **in their progress by** atmospheric pressure, **friction, the attraction** of the earth, or their **own gravity.**

125. *T.*—What causes motion?

P.—Its causes are various, but **it is** certain that all bodies must continue at rest unless acted upon by some force **or** forces impressed upon them. In the animal economy it is produced by a principle of life, which we do **not** quite understand; inanimate bodies **are** put in motion or arrested by certain **forces** or powers.

126. *T.*—Is motion variable or constant?

P.—It is variable, and must ever be so, although its degree of velocity is in accordance with the force applied. Thus, if I push a cart with one hand, it will move slowly; with two hands faster, but if six or seven men all push at once, and with considerable force, **its** velocity will **be augmented.**

127. *T.*—What do you mean by velocity?

P.—It is the degree of speed that bodies possess, which is increased by the space **or** distance passed over.

128. *T.*—But does not this speed vary?

P. Unless any impediment is presented to moving bodies their velocity is uniform, **and** their speed is calculated by the time they take to pass over a given distance or space. Thus, **any** body that takes thirty seconds to pass over sixty feet, is said to possess a velocity of two feet per second.

129. *T.*—Is motion always uniform?

P.—No; it may be retarded or accelerated.

130. *T.*—Explain these terms.

P.—If it decreases gradually, it **is** said to be retarded; if it increases, it is accelerated, and the force that governs or regulates this, is called the retarding or accelerating force.

131. *T.*—How are forces distinguished?

P.—They are called *instantaneous* or *continued* forces.

132. *T.*—What is the difference?

P.—An instantaneous force is an impulse; it is sudden, like a blow, but a continued force has always the same degree **of** power, and is called a constant force when it has no intermission.

133. *T.*—Can forces vary

T.—Yes; of course they vary when the power is not constant, or when there is intermission.

134. *T.*—What **is meant by** absolute motion?

P.—When **any** body moves towards another body at rest, or passes it, or moves from one point **of** space to another, it is influenced by absolute motion.

135. *T.*—What do you mean by relative motion?

P.—It is the motion of one body considered in relation to that of another body; thus: suppose I roll two balls, one of wood and the other of lead, along a table, and they both move in the same direction, the difference between their motions is the relative motion.

136. *T.*—If I let a bullet fall at the same moment as cork, but of the same **size, will** there be any great difference in **the descent** of them?

P.—Yes; because it **will** depend upon the momentum.

137. *T.*—What do **you** mean **by** the momentum?

P.—It is the motal force of a body. All bodies, whether light or heavy, *may* move with the same speed, but the momentum of a body being proportionate to its mass and velocity, it is very evident that the difference will be relative.

138. *T.*—How can you estimate the momentum of a body?

P.—If you multiply the weight of a body by the number of feet it passes through or over in a second, the produce will be the momentum. If the velocity of a cannon ball, weighing 30 lbs., **be** 1,800 feet a second, its momentum **will be** 54,000.

139. *T.*—Suppose that I let a bullet, weighing an ounce, fall at the same moment with a thin sheet of lead, weighing an ounce, which will reach the ground sooner?

P.—The bullet; because the resistance of the atmosphere impedes the descent **of** the sheet.

GENERAL QUESTIONS ON LESSON X.

1. What is meant by motion and rest?
2. Is rest in accordance with the established laws of Nature?
3. What is meant by the terms absolute and relative rest?
4. Is it more natural for bodies to be in a state of rest or motion?
5. What are the causes of motion?
6. Is motion constant or not?
7. What is the difference between **the** velocity and momentum of a body?
8. How can you estimate the momentum of a body?

LESSON XI.

RECAPITULATION, &c.—HALLAM found that the velocity of every falling body is uniformly increased as it approaches the **earth,** no matter from what height it falls; that is, without taking into account atmospheric resistance. Experiment determined his observations, for he found that the motion of falling bodies is increased in regular arithmetical progression, and, by computation, he was enabled to ascertain the space fallen through in a given time. Thus he found that a dense or compact body passed through a space of 16 feet 1 inch during the first second of time that it was descending towards the earth; and, in order to ascertain the time a body occupied in falling, he multiplied the square of that number by 16, and the result was, the number of feet the body had fallen. For example, he observed that a stone occupied 6 seconds in falling from a certain height, and he took the square (the number multiplied by itself) of 6, which is 36; **then,** by multiplying 36 by 16, the result was 576, or the number of feet fallen. In making **these** calculations, he omitted the odd inch, because it is near enough for all *practical* purposes; and he knew that even the best calculation would only be an approximation of the actual distance, in consequence of the gravity **of** bodies,—a fact he had learned by experi**ment** [See Experiment 14].

QUESTIONS, &c.

140. *T.*—What do you mean by the CENTRE OF GRAVITY?

P.—It is that point in all bodies at which the influence of gravitation is, as it were, concentrated, and upon which a body *will* rest if it be freely suspended; it is consequently the central point of parallel and equal forces.

141. *T.*—If a body is not suspended with due regard to the centre of gravity, what will be the result?

P.—It will move until it settles in a position in which the centre of gravity cannot fall lower.

142. *T.*—What is the **use** of finding out the centre **of gravity?**

P.—**When we** know the weight of bodies and their centre of gravity, we can substitute the weight for all the forces acting upon the body, and a single point (the centre of gravity), for the collective points forming the body.

143. *T.*—Have all solid bodies a centre of gravity?

P.—Yes; the centre of gravity is sure to be in the centre of all round, square, and regular bodies of the same density; and no matter what form a body has, it is sure to have a centre of gravity. In irregular bodies it is situated at that point which will place the body in a state of equilibrium when fixed or suspended from it.

144. *T.*—Can I stand an egg, or place it in a state of equilibrium, upon its narrow end?

P.—Not without following the example of Columbus. Because, if there is not anything to support the egg, it will assume such a position, that a line drawn from the centre of gravity to the point below, where the body comes in contact with the surface, will be the shortest that can be drawn from the centre to any other part of its superficies. If you observe this diagram carefully, you will see that the egg could not remain in the position it is in the figure; it would roll over, and instead of the line *a c* being perpendicular to the line *d e*, it would be the line *c b*.

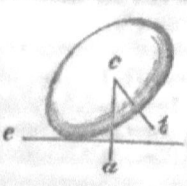
Fig. 12.

145. *T.*—If the centre of gravity of a body be a fixed point, the body itself will always be in a state of equilibrium, no matter how we turn or place it. Is this so?

P.—Yes; the only thing that is actually necessary to the equilibrium of any body is, that the centre of gravity should be supported.

146. *T.*—How will you find the centre of gravity of an irregular figure?

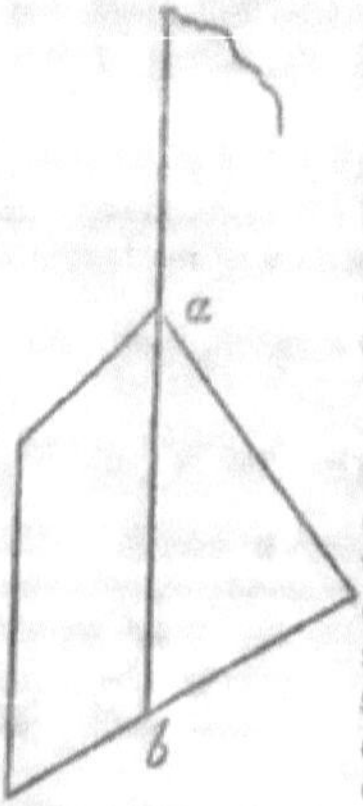

P.—Very easily; or that of any body. If you suspend the body at a point *a*, (*Fig.* 13,) the direction of the string supporting it will pass through the lower part of the body at *b*, and therefore it is very evident the centre of gravity is in the direction of the line *a b*. Again, suppose we suspend the same body at the point *d* (*Fig.* 14), the centre of gravity is still in the direction of the suspending string *d e*, and therefore the centre of gravity lies where the two lines *a b* and *d e* cross one another at *c*. Although it is easy to determine the centre of gravity of some bodies of regular form and uniform density by geometric principles, yet there

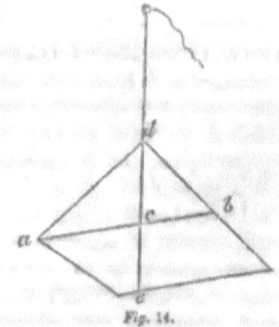
Fig. 13.

Fig. 14.

are certain bodies in which it is difficult to ascertain the line of direction exactly.

147. *T.*—What do you mean by the line of direction?

P.—It is the imaginary line drawn from the centre of gravity of a body toward the centre of the earth; therefore it is evident that, if the line of direction fall within the base of any body, it will stand; if not, the body will fall over, or, what is generally termed, over-balance itself.

148. *T.*—Where is the centre of gravity in a straight line?

P.—In the centre of the line, so that it will be maintained in a state of equilibrium?

149. *T.*—How would you find the centre of gravity of a homogeneous triangle?

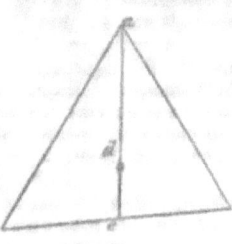
Fig. 13.

P.—By drawing straight lines from two of its angles to bisect the opposite sides, and the point of intersection, *d*, of these two lines, is the centre of gravity. Thus, the point *e* is the centre of gravity of the line *b, c*, and any line drawn parallel to *b c* in the triangle must be bisected or divided by the line *a e*, which proves that the centre of gravity lies upon the line *a, e*, as regards all lines parallel to *b c*, and, by the same reasoning it would lie in the line *a b*.

150. *T.*—Is the centre of gravity of a body always in its substance?

P.—No; because in a circle or ring it is in the centre of the circle, and in a drum it is in the axis of the drum.

[The pupil should give some other illustrations of the situation of the centre of gravity, such as coaches heavily laden upsetting; attitudes of men and women dancing upon the tight-rope, tendency of trees to grow in a direction perpendicular to their base, &c.]

151. *T.*—If I attempt to stand upon one leg and fall down, is it because I cannot keep the centre of gravity?

P.—Yes; the equilibrium is not **preserved**, and therefore you fall over.

GENERAL QUESTIONS ON LESSON XI.
1. What is the centre of gravity?
2. Why do bodies fall down when inclined to one side?
3. Have all bodies a centre of gravity?
4. How can you find the centre **of** gravity of a body?
5. Give some examples of the direction of the centre of gravity?
6. Are the animal and vegetable kingdoms subject to its laws?
7. Give some examples of **other bodies** being affected by it.

LESSON XII.

RECAPITULATION, &c.—If Hallam had not known anything about the centre of gravity, it **is** possible that he might have built his house in such a position that it would have fallen down, or he might have overloaded his waggons, and then there would have been a probability of their upsetting when they ran over any uneven ground. The only requirement for the equilibrium of any solid body is, that its centre of gravity should be supported, which may be done in various ways. A body attached to an axis may either be in a state of stable, unstable, or indifferent equilibrium, according **to** whether the centre of gravity is below, above, or within the axis.

QUESTIONS.

152. *T.*—What do you mean by the term, stable equilibrium?

P.—When any body is displaced from its position by a very slight force, and recovers its former state, the equilibrium is said to be *stable*.

153. *T.*—What is unstable equilibrium?

P.—When a body is in such a position that it may easily be disturbed, and not able to recover its former state, because the line of direction falls outside **its** base, it is said to be in a state of *unstable equilibrium*, because it must fall. When a man carries a weight he must change his position according to the weight and the manner of carrying it, otherwise the direction of the common centre of gravity of his body and the load would be beyond the base, and he would fall. For instance, if **he** carries **a** bale of cloth, or any load upon his back (*Fig.* 16) he must bend forward; and if he carries a load in his left hand

Fig. 16.   *Fig.* 17.

(*Fig.* 17), **he must** bend the upper part of his body to the right.

154. *T.*—What **do you mean by** indifferent equilibrium?

P.—When any body is balanced in all positions it is in a state of *indifferent equilibrium*. For example, when the wheel of a carriage is raised from the ground to wash it, we have a body in a state of indifferent equilibrium, upon a fixed axis. **The** common balance is an excellent example of this state, when both scale-pans **are of equal** weight.

155. *T.*—We will try an experiment [Experiment 21]. I have here a bullet with a hole in it, through which a string passes, and you will see that when the bullet **is** drawn out of the perpendicular and let go, that it will swing backwards and forwards. [Performs the experiment.] You observe that it swings or oscillates, as it is termed, **and** in doing so describes a segment **of** a circle, which is called its arc. Can you tell me what **is** the cause of this?

P.—Gravity, which **causes bodies to fall.**

156. *T.*—What is the name applied to a rod of iron with a weight at the lower part, like my bullet and string?

P.—A pendulum; which hangs perpendicularly when at rest. The uppermost part is called the axis or point of suspension, and the part where the ball is placed is called **the** point of rest.

157. *T.*—You have not explained to me how it is that the pendulum swings to and fro.

P.—When the ball of the pendulum is raised to a height upon one side and set at liberty, it has a tendency to fall to the ground by the force **of** gravity, but being confined by the **rod it** makes **a** sweep to the point **of rest, and** having acquired a certain degree **of** velocity it **sweeps on** until it ascends **on** the other side to nearly the same height as that from which it was set free. Its weight **again** draws it down, and its velocity raises **it** to nearly the same height as the point from which it originally fell, and thus it continues **to** swing to and fro until the force of gravity overcomes the propelling force, and it ultimately settles in a state of rest in its original position.

158. *T.*—Then it appears that each sweep of the pendulum decreases the length of the arc. What is the reason?

P.—The resistance of the atmosphere, and the friction at its axis or point of suspension.

159. *T.*—What is the length of the arc traversed by the fall of a pendulum?

P.—It is impossible to fix any certain length, because it will depend upon **the** force exercised in setting the pendulum free; it may be made to traverse any number of degrees under 180, which is half a circle; but generally the extent of the arc is from ten to twenty degrees.

160. *T.*—Does the length of the rod by which the weight is suspended make any difference in the oscillations of the pendulum?

P.—Yes; the one with a long rod vibrates or oscillates slower than the one with **a** short rod, and here we have a motion **analogous to** that of falling bodies?

161. *T.*—Why is the vibration analogous to the falling of bodies?

P.—Because we have learned (see Lesson XI.) that the motion of falling bodies is increased in regular arithmetical progression; and, in the case of the pendulum, their lengths are as the squares of the times of vibration. Thus, if the times occupied by one vibration of two pendulums be 2 and 3 respectively, their lengths will be as 4 and 9.

162. *T.*—What is the use of a pendulum to a clock?
P.—On account of its uniform vibration it regulates its motion, for without it the wheels would go very irregularly.

163. *T.*—As pendulums are required to vibrate only sixty times in a minute, that is, neither slower or quicker; how **is** this managed?
P.—By adjustment of the length.

GENERAL QUESTIONS ON LESSON XII.

1. How many kinds of equilibrium are there, and how are they distinguished?
2. What is a pendulum?
3. What causes its oscillation?
4. Why does the sweep of a pendulum, left to itself, decrease in length each time?
5. Why does the length of the rod affect the vibrations of the pendulum?

LESSON XIII.

RECAPITULATION, &c.—It is quite as natural for a body to be in a state of motion as rest, according to the laws of Natural Philosophy, because it has been shown that matter is passive, and must therefore be influenced by some external force to make it change its condition from a state of rest to that of motion, or *vice versa*. Sir Isaac Newton laid down three propositions, which have been called the "laws of motion." They are as follow:—

1st. "Every body must persevere in its state of rest, or of uniform motion in a straight line, unless it be compelled to change that state by forces impressed upon **it.**"

2nd. "Every change of motion must be proportional to the impressed force, and must be in the direction of that straight line in which the force is impressed."

3rd. "Action must always be equal to and contrary to reaction; or the actions of two bodies upon each other must be equal, and directed towards contrary sides."

It will be our duty to consider these laws, and examine the phenomena they present. We have already found that bodies cannot possibly continue in a state of motion for any length of time upon or near the earth; for the attraction of gravitation, atmospheric resistance, and friction, would operate so powerfully, that the bodies would be arrested in their course. It is therefore evident, that permanency or uniformity of motion can only be fully demonstrated by the heavenly bodies, which have continued to move, with uniform force, since the time the Creator launched **them** into space.

QUESTIONS.

164. *T.*—Suppose that there are two equal forces acting upon one point from opposite directions, what is the result?
P.—The body acted upon will remain in a state of equilibrium.

165. *T.*—If the two forces act in the same direction, what is the result?
P.—The effect produced will be equal to that of a double load, and so on for every additional force. Whatever be the number **of** forces acting upon one point, and the direction of them, they can only produce one **motion** in **one** definite direction; consequently we imply that a single force would produce the same effect.

166. *T.*—What is this single force called?
P.—The *resultant* or *equivalent*. For example, when a ship is impelled by the combined action of the stream, rudder, and wind, it will move in a definite direction; but if the actions of these forces were to cease, the ship would be impelled in the same direction by employing a single force, such as a rope, which would act in the same line of direction as the ship was impelled by the three forces; consequently

the single force (the rope) would be the resultant of the three forces.

167. *T.*—How can you explain the action of forces?

P.—By means of diagrams. Thus, the various lines are made to represent the quantity or intensity of the forces, the effects produced, and the directions in which they act.

168. *T.*—When several forces act in concert upon a given point, what are they termed?

P.—The system of forces. If, however, we speak of them in reference to the equivalent or resultant force, they are then termed latent or component forces.

169. *T.*—How can you determine the resultant of forces?

P.—When two or more forces act in the same direction, their resultant is the sum of the separate forces; but if they act in opposite directions upon one point, their resultant is equal to the difference of the two, and the line of action is in the direction of the greater force.

170. *T.*—Suppose that two forces act upon one point, and make an angle with each other, how will you find the resultant of them?

P.—By means of the law called the parallelogram of forces, which is explained by this diagram. Suppose that a ball is placed at the point *a*, and two forces are

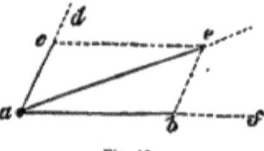

Fig. 18.

acting upon it at the same moment, the one in the direction *a f*, the other in the direction *a d*. Now let us take it for granted that the one force will move the ball of itself in a second from the point *a* to *b*, while the other force will only move it from *a* to *c* in the same space of time. It is, therefore, very evident that the same result would ensue, as if one force acted upon the ball in the direction of the line *a e*, because if in one second the ball would be impelled as far as *a b*, and then the action of the force cease, and the ball only subjected to the action of the second force, it would reach *e* in another second. Therefore it is certain, that if the two forces acted at the same instant, that the ball would reach the point *e*, and the single force that would produce the same result, if applied in the direction of the line *a e*, is the resultant.

171. *T.*—What is meant by the composition of forces?

P.—It is the process of finding a single force that is equivalent to two or more forces.

172. *T.*—What is the resolution of forces?

P.—It is the process by which we can find forces that will produce a motion equal to that of a single force.

173. *T.*—Give me an example of this.

P.—Let *e f* represent a boat, *f i* the rope by which it is drawn along, and also the

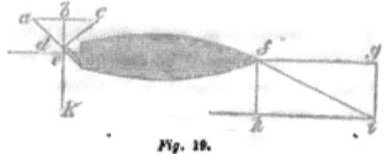

Fig. 19.

force of draught. It may then be assumed that there are two forces acting, *f g*, which draws the boat forward, and *f h*, which would draw the head in the direction *f h* were it not counteracted by the helm *e d*, which is parallel to the line *f i*. When the boat is moving the resistance of the water acts upon the helm, which may be explained thus. If *c a* represents the resistance, it may be resolved into *a d* and *e c*. Now, as *a d* produces no effect upon the helm, it is evident that the pressure is in the line *e c*, which tends to turn the stern of the boat in the direction *b e k*, and thus counteracts the force *f h*.

174. *T.*—How can you prove the correctness of the law of the parallelogram of forces?

P.—By experiment. For example, suppose that we have three forces, each equal, and opposed to the resultant of the other two, a state of equilibrium will be the result. You observe that I have two vertical pieces of wood attached to the table, and that each of them has a moveable slide, to which a pulley, that turns easily upon its axis in a vertical plane, is attached. Let the vertical planes of both pulleys coincide, then **pass a** line having a weight (*a*) at one **end,** and another weight (*c*) at the **other;** **now** suspend a weight (*b*) at **any point**

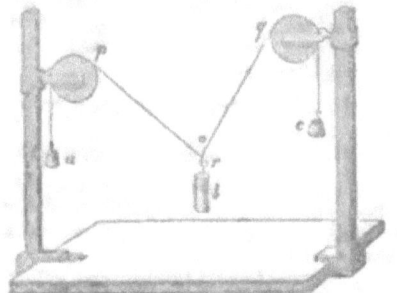

Fig. 20.

(*o*) between the pulleys, the whole will be in a state of equilibrium in **any** definite position of the lines. There **are** three forces acting upon the point **o, in the** directions *o p*, *o q*, and *o r*, **and we** may ascertain the resultant **by construction.**

175. *T.*—Will you explain this **more** fully ?

P.—Suppose that the weight *a* was equal to 2, and *c* to 3 ounces, **the** force or the weight at *b* requisite to produce an angle of 75° must be four ounces. Let

the angle *a b c* measure 75°, and *a b* = 2, and *b c* = 3 (the length being given), then the diagonal *b d* = 4. **To prove this, if we attach a four ounce weight to the line, we shall find** that the angle *p o q* measures 75°. From this it appears that the greater the weight at *o* the less will be the

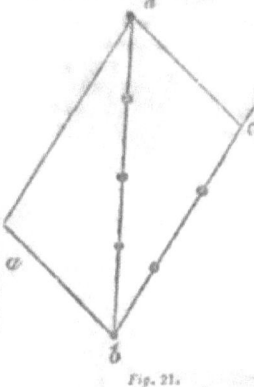

Fig. 21.

angle *p o q*, and the less the weight the greater the angle.

GENERAL QUESTIONS ON LESSON XIII.

1. How do you define force ?
2. What are the laws of **motion laid** down by Sir Isaac Newton ?
3. What is the resultant ?
4. What is meant by the diagonal of the square ?
5. What is the parallelogram of forces ?
6. Prove the correctness of the law of the parallelogram of forces.

LESSON XIV.

RECAPITULATION, &c.—THE **laws of** equilibrium in all **simple machines are derived** from **the knowledge of the** parallelogram of forces; **for example, the inclined plane,** the screw, **the wedge, the pulley,** and **the lever. We have now to consider the motions** produced by **gravity, where the directions of the force of** gravitation in **various points** are no longer **parallel. Bodies have a** tendency to proceed in a straight line when **flying** off from a centre, which we **may see every** day; and this property is termed the *centrifugal* or *centre-flying force.*

QUESTIONS.

176. *T.*—What is CENTRIFUGAL FORCE ?
P.—It **is** that force which causes all bodies **to fly** off from the centre.
  [The pupil should give examples of centrifugal force, such as the trundling of a mop, the **whirling** of a sling with a stone in it, &c.]

177. *T.*—Is the earth subject to this force ?
P.—Certainly. Whenever there is rotation round a fixed **axis,** and the separate particles are prevented from deviating from this axis in **any** way, this force must prevail.

178. *T.*—Does the centrifugal force vary with the distance from the earth's axis?

P.—Yes; all the different points of the earth are not equidistant from the axis of rotation, and this force is greatest at the equator, and diminishes as it approaches the poles, acting against gravity, and lessening its intensity. This apparatus (*Fig.* 22) will explain how it is that

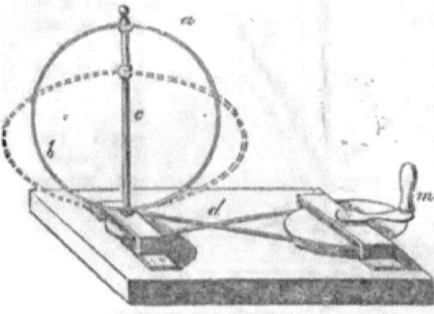

Fig 22.

the earth is flattened at the poles. You observe there are two discs, which revolve horizontally. When the handle *m* is turned it conveys the motion of the larger disc by means of the string *d* to the lesser disc, which has the vertical axis *c* fixed in its centre. A spring *a b*, is fastened by its lower end to the axis, and the upper part can be moved up and down, and when the machine is at rest it forms a spherical figure, but assumes an elliptical figure when the axis revolves rapidly, owing to the centrifugal force acting upon those points most remote from the axis.

179. *T.*—Can you give me any other examples of centrifugal force overcoming the force of gravity?

P.—A horseman at a circus, when standing upon the horse which is running round the ring, inclines his body inwards, and when the horse is going round at full speed, any one may see both rider and horse influenced by this force.

180. *T.*—Why does the horseman incline his body inwards?

P.—To counteract the centrifugal force.

181. *T.*—If this force impels bodies outwards, how do you account for bodies inclining towards the centre when going round a circle?

P.—Because there is another force acting, called the *centripetal*, or *centre-seeking* force, which draws them towards the centre, so that all bodies moving in circles are acted upon by both forces.

182. *T.*—What is the axis of a body?

P.—The real or imaginary line round which a body rotates.

183. *T.*—The other matters in connection with Natural Philosophy must be left for another occasion.

GENERAL QUESTIONS ON LESSON XIV.

1. What is centrifugal force?
2. How does it act?
3. Prove its existence.
4. What is centripetal force?
5. What does a body rotate upon?

II.—NATURAL HISTORY.

INTRODUCTORY NARRATIVE.

LESSON I.

The celebrated Carl Von Linné, or Linnæus, was born 24th May, 1707, at Râshult, in the parish of Stendrohult, in the province of Smaland, Sweden. His father, Nils Linnæus, was descended from a humble peasant; but after struggling with poverty, and overcoming many difficulties, obtained the office of curate of Stendrohult, and resided in a beautiful spot upon the borders of a lake, surrounded by woods, hills, and valleys; and being very fond of botany, employed all his leisure hours in cultivating his garden, **which** contained many rare and foreign plants. Here the young Carl followed his father as soon as he could walk, so that, **as one** of his **pupils** has remarked, "from the very time that he first left his cradle, he almost lived in his father's **garden."** There cannot be a doubt that his early acquaintance **with the beauties of nature laid** the foundation for the study of those sciences which he afterwards so greatly adorned. **His own** relation of the manner in which his **first lessons in** botany were given, are worthy **of notice.** When **about four** years old, **he went to** a feast at Mökler with his father; and, **as the** evening was fine, **the young Carl was** seated upon a flowery bank with many of the guests, listening to **the** eloquent and instructive remarks **of** the curate upon the various plants around **them.** His curiosity was awakened; **but one** so young could only ask questions, the answers to which were speedily forgotten, especially the *names* of the plants. **As he** grew older, his inaptitude to remember names was a source of constant annoyance to his father; but, by perseverance and practice, he overcame the defect. When Linnæus was seven years old, he was placed under the **private charge** of John Tiliander, and two years afterwards, was sent to school at **Wexio, being intended** for the church; and here, and **at the** gymnasium of the **same place, he remained until** nearly eighteen, **without making much progress** in **languages, literature, or the studies his father** desired, **although he eclipsed most of his schoolfellows** in physical and **mathematical science. All his leisure hours were** devoted to the study of botany; and his library, consisting **of a few books, showing a decided** taste for that science, his fellow-students dubbed him **the "little botanist."** The **father** was so disgusted with his son's distaste for clerical studies, **that he determined** to bind **him** apprentice to a shoemaker, or tailor, but was fortunately prevented by the kind offer of Dr. Rothmann, a provincial physician, who proposed to receive the young Linnæus into his own house, and instruct **him** in medical literature. This offer was not without its service, for we find that he **made** considerable progress in physiology and botany, and therefore, the following year, **was sent to the** university of Lund, with the following introductory certificate from the **head master of the** gymnasium:—" Youth at school may be compared to shrubs in a **garden, which will** sometimes, though rarely, elude all the care of the gardener, but if **transplanted into a different** soil, may become fruitful trees. With this view, therefore, **and no other, the** bearer is sent to the **university,** where it is possible he may meet with **a climate propitious to his progress."** An **old** tutor and friend suppressed this **extraordinary document, and introduced him as his** private pupil.

At Lund, he **lodged in the house of** Dr. Stobæus, physician to the king, and professor **of medicine, who soon became aware of his** acquirements, and was delighted to find he **possessed such a** knowledge of botany. This excellent man allowed Linnæus free access to his library and collection of shells, minerals, birds, and plants; instructed him how to form a *hortus siccus*, and first turned the attention of Linnæus to other branches of Natural History. Next year he repaired to the University **of** Upsala, with only eight pounds in **his** pocket, which was all the money his parents could give him; and after a short time was reduced to such a state, that he was **often** obliged to trust to chance for a meal, and mend his shoes with folded paper instead of sending them to a **cobbler.**

Linnæus, notwithstanding all these difficulties and privations, studied early and late, **and soon** attracted the attention of Professor Rudbeck and Dr. Celsius; and the latter, **requiring an** assistant, received him into his own house. It was here that he contracted **a friendship with** the celebrated ichthyologist, Artedi, and composed his *Spolia Botanica*, which was never published. Soon after this, he drew up a sketch of his system of botany, and submitted it to Dr. Celsius, who showed it to Professor Rudbeck. The latter was so pleased with it, that he appointed him tutor to his children, and eventually employed him as his assistant in lecturing.* He lectured publicly, improved the garden, gave botanical excursions in the vicinity of Upsala, and commenced several of his works.

His **fame was** now established, and the Royal Academy entrusted him with **the care of the scientific** expedition to Lapland, which started on the 13th **of** May, 1732, Linnæus being only twenty-five years of age. In this expedition he encountered many hardships and dangers, travelled over the greater part of Lapland, and, skirting the borders of Norway, returned to Upsala by the Gulf of Bothnia, having travelled more than 4,000 miles. He arranged the plants, and other natural productions collected during the journey, and lectured publicly upon the result of the expedition. In 1736 he visited England, afterwards repaired to Holland, where he remained some time, then visited Paris, and, in 1739, returned to Stockholm, where he took up his residence as a physician, having married the daughter of Dr. Moreus. In 1741, he was appointed professor of medicine at Upsala, and by a private arrangement with Dr. Rosen, professor of botany, he effected an exchange, receiving the superintendence of the Botanic Garden, and charge of the Natural History department. In 1758, he **was** created a knight of the order of the Polar Star, by King Frederic Adolphus of **Sweden**, was admitted member of most of the scientific societies of Europe; and, in 1761, **having** received letters of nobility from the king, his name was changed to Von Linné. **His** various appointments and an excellent practice placed him in affluent circumstances, and he therefore purchased the villa of Harmanby, about a league **from** Upsala, where he spent the last fifteen years of his life, and died on the 10th of January, 1778, in the seventy-first year of his age. He was buried at Upsala, near the main door of the cathedral, with his wife by his side, under a stone, without even his name upon it; but at a short distance from the grave there is a bust of the great naturalist, in *alto relievo*, on black marble, with the following inscription engraved on a tablet of Swedish porphyry:—

BOTANICORUM PRINCIPE,
AMICI ET DISCIPULI.
M.DCC.XCVIII.

His memory **was** most comprehensive, seizing upon **the** useful, and rejecting the useless; and his love of order most remarkable. "In winter," he tells us in his diary, "he slept from nine to six; in summer, from ten to three," and that, as soon as he felt tired, he ceased to study. He noted everything in its proper place immediately, never trusting to memory. As a teacher, he was kind, made himself easily understood, **and** never failed to interest his pupils in the subject under consideration. He was frugal in his living, and very temperate; thought much, read slowly, and was most devout.

GRANDFATHER WHITEHEAD has given his pupils this sketch of the life of one of the most celebrated naturalists, because it is instructive both to the young and more aged: the former should endeavour to imitate him; the latter to repair their misspent time, by studying the great kingdoms of nature around them.

---

* The system of Linnæus owes its origin to Le Vaillant's *Treatise on the Sexes of Plants*, which he read a short time before he drew up his sketch.

It was Linnæus who first practically pointed out the necessity and utility of studying natural history by some system, and to him we are indebted for the first PRINCIPLES OF CLASSIFICATION.

NATURAL HISTORY.

QUESTIONS AND EXPLANATIONS.

1. *T.*—WHAT is Natural History?
P.—It is the study of Nature in all her departments, treating of, and examining abstractedly, each of the properties of all moveable and extended bodies, animate or inanimate, and having for its object the special application of the laws recognised by the various branches of General Physics to the numerous and different beings which exist, in order to explain the phenomena they each present in their single characters and relation to each other, to the proximate objects among which they are found, and to nature generally.

2. *T.*—What is a naturalist?
P.—A person who studies nature, especially the three great kingdoms.

3. *T.*—What do you mean by the three great kingdoms?
P.—The animal, vegetable, and mineral kingdoms.

4. *T.*—Does not Natural History include all natural objects existing in space?
P.—Yes; but as the subject would be too extensive, it has been divested of such sciences as astronomy, meteorology, geology, and metallurgy, &c., that properly belong to it, and is now generally understood to signify only the three great kingdoms.

5. *T.*—How have these divisions in Natural History been accomplished?
P.—By learned men observing, comparing, and classifying the bodies that surround them.

6. *T.*—What is the use of classifying objects?
P.—To establish systems or methods.

7. *T.*—What do you mean by a *system*?
P.—A system is a great catalogue, in which all objects have their appointed place, distinguished by known names, distinctive characters, and relations.

8. *T.*—Is there more than one system?
P.—Yes; there is a *natural* and an *artificial* system, and various naturalists have established systems of their own.

9. *T.*—What is meant by a *natural* system?
P.—A classification and arrangement of the objects in nature, based on certain fundamental principles, which, so far as the laws of Nature are known, are found to be general throughout all her productions.

10. *T.*—What, then, is an *artificial* system?
P.—A method established to elucidate the resemblances which one species bears to others in all their varied and complex relations, directing us to the precise point upon which we require information.

11. *T.*—What are the uses of these systems?
P.—The natural system depends upon the artificial. Thus, we turn to the latter to arrive at a fact; but if we desire to know how that fact bears upon *other* facts, we turn to the former.

12. *T.*—You have made use of the terms nature and natural very often; will you explain their meaning?
P.—NATURE is used to denote the laws which govern the beings that surround us in the works of creation; *nature* is employed to denote the peculiarity of a body —thus it is the NATURE of some bodies to burn; others; to become converted into vapour, &c.; and *nature* may be intended to convey to the mind that such bodies are not altered by art or civilization, that they are, in fact, in a state of nature. *Natural* may be applied to express to another that such a body is not artificial or made by human agency; it may be used to particularize certain qualities in an object; thus, it is natural for a dog to bark, and walk

upon four legs, but unnatural to walk upon two, dance, and perform tricks.

12. *T.*—What is the natural division of objects that surround us?

P.—Into the *organic* and *inorganic* kingdoms.

13. *T.*—What class of objects belongs to the *organic* kingdom?

P.—Animals and vegetables of every kind.

14. *T.*—What class belongs to the *inorganic*?

P.—Every kind of body destitute of the vital principle, or life; such as earths, minerals, salts, &c.

15. *T.*—What is the study of the animal kingdom termed?

P.—ZOOLOGY: from two Greek words, signifying a *discourse* upon *life*; and the person who studies the science is called a *zoologist*, or observer of life.

16. *T.*—What is the study of vegetables termed?

P.—BOTANY; from a Greek word, which means an herb or grass; and the student of that science is termed a *botanist*, or one who studies the vegetable kingdom.

17. *T.*—What is the study of earths, salts, &c., termed?

P.—MINERALOGY; because it teaches the properties, composition, and relations of mineral bodies, and the art of describing and distinguishing them; the student of this branch of Natural History is termed a *mineralogist*.

GENERAL QUESTIONS ON LESSON I.

1. What is Natural History?
2. How is Natural History divided?
3. How do you define the three great kingdoms of Natural History?
4. What is a system, and its use?
5. How many systems are there?
6. What is the difference between the natural and artificial system?
7. Define the terms nature and natural.
8. How is the realm of Nature divided?
9. Give the definition of the terms zoology, botany, and mineralogy.
10. What do **you mean** by a zoologist, botanist, or **mineralogist**?

LESSON II.

It is absolutely necessary for us to have names and places for animals, vegetables, and minerals, the same as for the various articles in an ironmonger's shop. By this **means we** are enabled to distinguish **one** animal **from** another; and by the whole of **the** animal kingdom being divided into different groups, we can, by paying attention **to the** peculiarities of an individual, at once assign a proper place for it; and the **same** applies **to the** vegetable and mineral kingdoms. It has **been** found desirable, in studying **Natural** History, **to** commence with the highest and descend to the lowest divisions **or** groups, which are nine in number:—1. Kingdom; 2. Sub-kingdom; 3. Class; 4. Order; 5. Tribe; 6. Family; 7. Sub-family; 8. Genus, or kind; 9. Sub-genus. GRANDFATHER WHITEHEAD intends to follow the system laid down by Cuvier, because it is the most complete. The Linnæan system, although excellent and practical, is very deficient in some of the most essential parts; for we find animals grouped together, which differ materially in **their** nervous systems and general anatomy.

QUESTIONS.

18. *T.*—What do you mean by a KINGDOM?

P.—It is a grand or primary division of nature.

19. *T.*—How many divisions are there?

P.—Three grand ones: the animal, the vegetable, and the mineral kingdoms.

20. *T.*—What is meant by a SUB-KINGDOM?

P.—It is a primary division of a kingdom. Thus, the animal kingdom has four sub-kingdoms, each of which includes all animals possessing certain peculiarities, which will be noticed as we proceed.

21. *T.*—What is a CLASS?
P.—It is the first division of a sub-kingdom.

22. *T.*—What is an ORDER?
P.—A division including several families.

23. *T.*—What is a TRIBE?
P.—A group between a family and an order. Thus, the order *Incessores*, or perching birds, has several tribes, which are again divided into *families* or groups, containing many *sub-families*.

24. *T.*—What do you mean by a GENUS?
P.—It is a number of species closely resembling each other, but yet differing slightly in some point; in fact, a collection of sub-genera.

25. *T.*—What is a SUB-GENUS?
P.—Several species, all of the same type of formation.

26. *T.*—What is a SPECIES?
P.—It is an animal distinguishable from another animal on account of certain peculiarities of structure, size, or otherwise.

27. *T.*—Are all the individuals of one species alike?
P.—Yes, they all resemble the parent.

28. *T.*—Is there not another division which naturalists notice?
P.—Yes, *varieties*. These are generally the result of accident, such as food, situation, or malformation, and do not perpetuate their peculiarities.

[The pupil should be required to give some examples of the causes of varieties, such as unusual heat or cold, scarcity of food, &c.]

29. *T.*—You have now learned that there are certain points for the practical naturalist to attend to; and, as the vegetable and mineral kingdoms will be examined hereafter, we must now confine ourselves to the principles of classification in the animal kingdom alone.

GENERAL QUESTIONS ON LESSON II.

1. Why do we have fixed names for objects of Natural History?
2. What is the usual method of dividing Natural History?
3. Why is the Linnæan system not so good as the Cuvierian?
4. What do you mean by the terms kingdoms, sub-kingdoms, classes, and orders?
5. Explain the meaning of the terms tribes, families, and sub-families.
6. What is the difference between a genus, sub-genus, and species?
7. Are varieties perpetuated?
8. Why are not varieties perpetuated?

LESSON III.

IT is the aim of scientific men to classify and arrange the various objects of Natural History that surround them; and, in doing so, they have to confine themselves to certain laws. They observe the difference in structure of animals from plants—the habits, actions or functions, and peculiarities of each. Those animals or plants that closely resemble each other are grouped together, and naturalists have found that certain individuals possess the means of perpetuating their species: thus we know that pointers will not produce spaniels, or *vice versa*; and therefore we commonly call such a series of families a *race*. It is our duty to endeavour to discover whether these races have a common origin; for instance, Is it possible that all dogs, of whatever breed, are descended from two parents? Naturalists must pay attention to the anatomical structure of animals, before they can classify them correctly. The Animal Kingdom is divided into four sub-kingdoms—VERTEBRATA, MOLLUSCA, ARTICULATA, and RADIATA; and we shall now consider their principal characteristics consecutively.

QUESTIONS.

30. *T.*—You have said that the Animal Kingdom is divided into several parts; what is the name of the first sub-kingdom?

P.—VERTEBRATA, or vertebrate animals, so called because the individuals comprised in this division have a backbone or vertebral column, composed of several parts, each of which is called a *vertebra*.

31. *T.*—Why have these animals a backbone or spine composed of several parts?

P.—Because it affords them more strength and flexibility, and gives their movements **more** precision.

32. *T.*—Is **there no other use for** this vertebral column?

P.—Yes: it protects a bundle of nervous cords, confined within a sheath, which is called the spinal marrow, or *medulla spinalis*; and also supports the skull.

33. *T.*—What is the use of the skull?

P.—To protect the brain, and organs of sense connected with it.

34. *T.*—What is attached to the other end of the spine?

P.—It is prolonged, and contracted into a tail, the size and length of which usually increases in proportion as the skull decreases.

35. *T.*—What other attachments has the spine?

P.—It is connected at the sides with a series of peculiar shaped bones, called the ribs, which are again attached in front to a breast-bone.

36. *T.*—What is the use of the ribs?

P.—To enclose and afford protection to the organs of respiration, circulation, &c.

37. *T.*—What is there peculiar in the structure of vertebrated animals?

P.—They have an *internal* skeleton, **a** highly organised nervous system, are **endowed** with all the senses, have red **blood, which** is propelled through the system by **a** muscular heart, and separate sexes. Their organs **of** locomotion do not exceed two pairs **of** limbs; the mouth is furnished with only two jaws, placed one *above* or *before* the other, never opening sideways, and usually furnished with teeth. The largest animals belong to this division, and are remarkable for possessing a greater degree of intelligence than any other class of animals.

38. *T.*—Do all the animals comprised in this class present the same peculiarities?

P.—Yes, there may always be found some analogy, even in the most remote species, of an uniform plan.

39. *T.*—You named another sub-kingdom. What is it called?

P.—ARTICULATA, **or** articulate animals.

40. *T.*—Why are they called articulate?

P.—Because the skeleton **is in** pieces, jointed, or *articulated* together.

41. *T.*—In what respect do they differ from the vertebrate animals?

P.—The skeleton is *external*, covering the whole body; while, in the former, the muscular part is external. The nervous system is not so highly developed, the organs of hearing and smell being generally deficient. The legs are frequently numerous, but never less than six. The jaws always open laterally, and they usually possess more than one pair; and the blood is *white*.

42. *T.*—What is the second sub-kingdom called?

P.—MOLLUSCA, or molluscous animals.

43. *T.*—What is there peculiar in their organization?

P.—They have not any skeleton—the muscles being attached to the skin, which constitutes a soft contractile envelope, in which strong plates, called shells, are found in many species, the production and position of which are analogous to those of the mucous body. The viscera and nervous system, which are composed **of** several scattered masses connected by nervous filaments, are contained within this general envelope. The brain is placed over the *œsophagus*, or gullet, and is merely the principal connecting nervous filament. One family only possesses the organs of hearing; and taste and vision are the only senses, with this exception, which this class presents; frequently vision is wanting.

They have a complete circulatory system, and particular organs for respiration.

44. *T.*—What is the last sub-kingdom named?

P.—RADIATA, or radiate animals. They have their organs of sense and motion arranged as rays around a centre. They have no very distinct nervous system, or particular organs of sense; and in some of them it is is extremely difficult to discover any circulation. The respiratory organs are generally on the surface of the body.

45. *T.*—Have not the radiated animals been divided, so as to form another sub-kingdom?

P.—Yes, by Macleay, who formed another called ACRITA, or acrite animals; but as we have yet to learn more of the peculiarities of each, we must wait until we commence Zoology.

GENERAL **QUESTIONS** ON LESSON III.

1. What is the aim of all scientific men when studying Natural History?
2. How is the Animal Kingdom divided?
3. Describe the peculiar characteristics of the sub-kingdoms Vertebrata, Mollusca, Articulata, and Radiata.
4. Are there only four sub-kingdoms?

LESSON IV.

THE celebrated Baron Cuvier, whose method we shall adopt in this Catechism, observes, that "the habit necessarily acquired in the study of natural history, of mentally classifying a great number of ideas, is one of the advantages of this science which is seldom spoken of; but which, when generally introduced into the system of common education, will perhaps become the principal one. It exercises the student in that part of logic which is termed method, as the study of geometry does in that which is called syllogism: because natural history is the science which requires the most precise method, as geometry is that which demands the most rigorous reasoning. Now, this art of method, when once well acquired, may be applied with great advantage to studies the most foreign to natural history. Every discussion which supposes a classification of facts, every research which requires a **distribution** of subject, is performed after the same manner; and he who has cultivated this science merely for amusement is **surprised** at the facilities it affords for disentangling all sorts of affairs."

Those who desire to master natural history must adopt a system to facilitate its study, and this is only done by observing and noting the characters and attributes of the vast numbers of objects in organic and inorganic creation. It is absolutely necessary, just as much as it is to arrange the various matters in a house. If you wanted a spoon, and had to look for it amongst a heap of knives, forks, scissors, and other things, you would lose much time, and perhaps after all your labour it might not be there. So it is with natural history; if you wanted to find the description of a kangaroo you would refer to Division I. *Vertebrata*, Class I. **Mammalia**, Order IV. *Marsupiata*; and then you would procure the information required; and nothing is more easy, because every animal has some leading feature, which fixes its position in the catalogue of nature, and this is chiefly determined by its organization.

QUESTIONS.

46. *T.*—Why did Cuvier place the vertebrate animals first?

P.—Because they are more highly organised than the others.

47. *T.*—Explain how this is.

P.—In the first place, the nervous system is better developed, consisting of a brain and prolongations; whereas in the molluscous animals, it is only two long chords, running longitudinally through the abdomen, and enlarged at intervals into **small knots**, which are called *ganglions*. Secondly, the **muscles** cover the bones, which form **the framework** of the body, **and the** important organs are inclosed within a bony case **or** framework.

48. *T.*—**How can you assign the** proper **place to an animal in the Cuvierian** system**?**

P.—**Because every one** of them must be **placed in one of the four great** divisions; **and the peculiarities of the** animal determine **the naturalist whether it** belongs to **the first, or the other three.**

* Fig. 1.—*Mycetes ursinus*, or howling monkey of Brazil.

49. *T.*—**How can the naturalist know** where the individual **is to be classed, after** he has determined **that it belongs to the** first sub-kingdom?

P.—Easily: suppose **that I have a specimen of a** monkey given me **to classify:** **it is** quite evident that it does not **belong** to the birds, reptiles, or fishes; **and must belong to** MAMMALIA, or animals that suckle their young; which is the first class of vertebrate animals. We have now to find out to which of the nine **orders of** Mammalia it belongs; and without **running** through all the peculiarities of **each,** I know that it should be placed in **the second order, among the** four-handed animals, or *quadrumana*, which are divided **into three genera—the monkeys, marmosets, and lemurs. It therefore belongs to the monkeys.**

50. *T.*—**How do you** know that the specimen **you have does** not belong to **the** lemurs or marmosets?

P.—Because **these two genera present** such distinct peculiarities **that it is impossible to make a mistake.**

[The pupil should explain what these peculiarities are.]

51. *T.*—**How** is it that the **vertebrate animals** have been subdivided into **so many parts, if they** all agree in respect **to their** general characteristics?

P.—Because, as I have explained **before,** [Question 26] they differ in some **important** particulars.

52. *T.*—Explain this more fully.

P.—If we examine the sub-kingdom **Vertebrata, we** shall find that there are **three distinct divisions** of animals: those **adapted for the earth,** the **air,** and the **water.**

53. *T.*—I thought that the vertebrate animals **were** subdivided into four classes; **how** is it that you only make three?

P.—I do not make three classes, but three divisions; and, as those that are adapted for existence upon **the earth** are divided into two—Mammalia and Reptilia, there are still four classes of animals; viz. 1, Mammalia; 2, Aves; 3, Reptilia; 4, Pisces.

54. *T.*—**Give me the** reason **that the vertebrate animals are** arranged **thus.**

P.—**The first** group—Mammalia, or animals that suckle their young—is ranged **first, because** the animals comprised **in this class** are superior in organization to the other three. They **are** formed for an especial purpose—residence upon the earth; while the birds and fishes have each their own peculiar element; and although the reptiles, strictly speaking, inhabit the earth, yet many of them are amphibious, such as alligators; they are also *cold-blooded* animals.

55. *T.*—What do you mean by *cold-blooded* animals?

P.—It has been found necessary to separate the quadrupeds into two distinct divisions, the *warm-blooded* and the *cold-blooded* animals. The former maintain a constant elevated temperature, or nearly so; are covered with hair, or something resembling it; bring forth their young alive, or are *viviparous*, and nourish them by suckling. The latter never have a uniform temperature, but one varying with the atmosphere, and seldom rising above it; are covered with scales; and are *oviparous*, or produce their young from eggs.

56. *T.*—How do birds differ from mammalia?

P.—The class **Aves**, or birds, are decidedly *oviparous*—constructed for propulsion in the air. The form of the body, the hollow bones, the light feathers, all demonstrate how fitted they are for the element they chiefly occupy. Can we say that they are devoid of some amount of intelligence? They are superior to reptiles in their organization, and therefore occupy the second class; and differ from mammalia chiefly in not suckling their young.

57. *T.*—Why should Reptiles be placed in the third class?

P.—Because they are intermediate between birds and fishes in their organization.

58. *T.*—Why are fishes placed in the fourth class?

P.—Because they inhabit the water, are oviparous, **not** so highly organized as the other classes, and possess distinctive characteristics.

[The pupil should state the peculiarities of each; thus, fishes respire the element they inhabit, by means of *branchiæ* or gills; the heart has only two cavities, one of which receives the blood from the system, and the other propels it through the gills, &c.]

59. *T.*—Do not some reptiles and fishes produce their young alive?

P.—Yes.

[The pupil should name the species that do so.]

60. *T.*—Are there **not** peculiarities in Mammalia, that render it almost necessary to separate them into another class?

P.—Yes, there are peculiarities, but not sufficient to warrant us to form another class. Thus, one tribe possesses the power of rising into the air, like birds, and another lives in the water, like fishes, but then they **agree** in all the essential characteristics of **the other** mammalia, while they differ materially **from** the classes with which they appear connected.

GENERAL **QUESTIONS ON** LESSON IV.

1. What is the best way to study Natural History?
2. Why **are** Vertebrata placed first?
3. How **can** you tell where an animal should be classed?
4. What is the difference between **a** monkey, a marmoset, and a lemur?
5. How is the sub-kingdom Vertebrata naturally divided?
6. Enumerate the four classes of vertebrate animals.
7. Give the reason that Mammalia is ranged before the other three classes, and why each is placed where it is.
8. What is the difference between warm-blooded and cold-blooded animals?
9. Explain the terms Viviparous and **Oviparous.**

LESSON V.

We have already seen **that** the Mammalia form the highest group in the animal kingdom, and were placed at the head of this kingdom, as Cuvier remarks, " Not only because this is the class to which we ourselves belong, but also because it **is** that which enjoys the most numerous faculties, the most delicate sensations, the most varied powers of motion, and in which all the different qualities seem together combined to produce a more perfect degree of intelligence,—the one most fertile in resources, most susceptible of perfection, and least the slave of instinct." In classifying animals, the naturalist aims at establishing that system which is most natural, therefore he examines those characters which are easily recognised and understood; and, on this account, selects the external appearance **of** each, so that those having the greatest resemblance are associated together. In order to do this, he examines the structure of the extremities, and the arrangement of the teeth, which, with other **peculiarities,** enables him to fix each **individual in** its proper place.

QUESTIONS.

61. *T.*—What is the use **of examining the** general structure of the **extremities of** animals?

P.—To enable us to learn something of their habits.

62. *T.*—How will **this give us a clue to** their habits?

P.—Because their extremities are adapted for the mode of life they lead. Thus, the **external** configuration of the orang-outang of Borneo at once indicates his fitness for climbing trees and clinging to their branches; and the general form of the lion denotes greater strength in front than behind; the **thick** neck, and broad chest and shoulders, are well adapted to sustain the weight of his prey; and his fore-limbs exhibit a beautiful arrangement **for strength and** seizure, the paws being **armed with most** powerful, hooked, sharp,

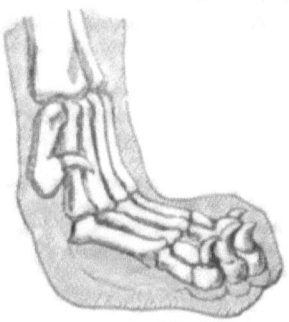

Fig. 2.

injured **during** progression or **other** motions. By **a** peculiar arrangement of muscles they **are** enabled to retract or draw back their **claws,** the same as a cat does; so you see **that** we are enabled at once, by examining the foot of an animal that can retract **its claws,** to decide that it belongs to a certain **class of animals.**

63. *T.*—Explain **how the lion** is enabled **to retract the claws.**

P.—You will understand the manner **in** which **they** are retracted much better **by** referring **to** this diagram, than **by a mere**

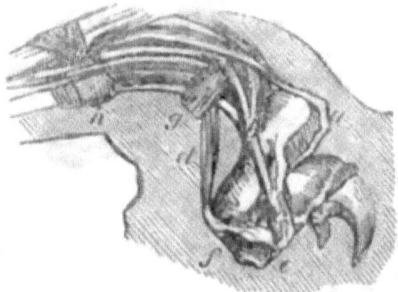

Fig. 4.

description. When **the retraction takes** place, the ends of **the** two **bones** (*f*) **are** placed **upon** the ground, between **which and** the bones, a pad of thickened skin is **interposed.** I cannot explain the action of the projection of the claws better **than** by drawing my hand forcibly backwards and curving the fingers, and then suddenly throwing it downwards, the arm being horizontal at **the** time.

64. *T.*—Does **not the perfection** of the organs **of touch influence us in** classifying animals?

---

* *Fig. 2.*—Front view of the paw of a lion, showing the claws projected.

† *Fig. 3.*—Profile outline of the paw of a lion, showing the bones of the foot with all the claws retracted, and **their** situation with respect to the muscles covering them.

* *Fig. 4.*—The mechanism in the foot of the lion. The claw is retracted, and supported on the last phalanx, which is grooved to receive it, and is kept in a retracted state by the tendon *a*, which passes from the extensor tendon upwards to the base of the third phalanx, and by the elastic ligaments *b, c.* The round tendon of the deep flexor (*d*) passes over the upper end of the last phalanx to *e,* and being strongly bound down at *g* and *h,* acts with great force.

P.—Yes, it forms an important part in classification.

65. *T.*—How is the perfection estimated?
P.—By the power of prehension or grasping possessed by the animal.

66. *T.*—Then all the Mammalia have not the power of grasping.
P.—Certainly not, the lower we descend the more it is wanting.

67. *T.*—If this be correct, we ought to divide the class Mammalia into two parts. How should we do this?
P.—Into animals having claws—*Unguiculated;* and animals with hoofs—*Ungulated.*

68. *T.*—Give me an example of each.
P.—The orang-outang is a very good

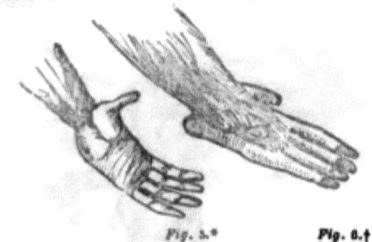

*Fig. 5.** *Fig. 6.†*

example of the former, and the ox or deer of the latter division.

69. *T.*—How can you determine the habits of an animal by examining its teeth?
P.—Because they vary in structure and arrangement, according to the food of the animal; and therefore the character of the teeth and extremities generally guides naturalists in determining the habits of animals.

70. *T.*—Does not the food exert its influence on other parts of the body? that is to say, can the naturalist ascertain the habits of animals by other parts of the body?

P.—Yes; the organs of the senses and digestion exhibit its habits in common with the teeth and extremities.

71. *T.*—Can you distinguish an herbivorous animal by its teeth?
P.—Yes; they have flat-crowned grinding teeth, with irregular ridges on their surface, for triturating their food.

72. *T.*—How can you distinguish, by means of its teeth, an animal that eats various kinds of food?
P.—The tops of the *molar* teeth or grinders are raised into flattened masses, like the end of a pestle, and are intended for bruising and crushing, as in man.

73. *T.*—How are carnivorous animals distinguished by their teeth?
P.—By the size of their *canine* teeth, which are very large, to enable them to seize firmly upon their prey.

[The pupil should give examples of the various teeth, such as those of the lion, boar, monkey, sheep, horse, &c.; and state the number, and classes of each.]

GENERAL QUESTIONS ON LESSON V.

1. Why does Cuvier consider Mammalia should be placed first among the vertebrate animals?
2. Can you learn anything of the habits of an animal by examining its extremities or teeth?
3. How can the knowledge of the form of the extremities of animals inform us of their habits?
4. What other reasons have we for classifying certain animals together?
5. Have all mammalia the power of grasping?
6. Describe the difference between unguiculated and ungulated animals.
7. Describe the difference in the structure of the teeth of herbivorous and carnivorous animals.

LESSON VI.

WE have seen that naturalists are guided by certain peculiarities in their classification of the Mammalia, and indeed of all objects of Natural History. Our purpose is not to enter into the peculiarities of the various orders of each class, but rather to show the

---

* *Fig. 5.*—Hand of Orang-outang. † *Fig. 6.*—Foot of Orang-outang.

principles of classification. The characteristics of each order, genus, and species, will be given in the Catechism on ZOOLOGY; and the remaining portions of Natural History, in those on BOTANY and GEOLOGY. Our present object is to consider the second class of vertebrate animals—*Aves*, or birds.

In classifying the birds, naturalists **attend to the form of the** extremities and **the bill**. In some birds, we see the bill and **claws sharp, hooked,** and powerful; as in **the eagle** and Egyptian neophron, **adapted for tearing the flesh and** holding the prey; in others,

Fig. 7.   *Fig. 8.†*   *Fig. 9.‡*

the beak is short and thick, suited for crushing hard seeds, as in the parrots and **loriets**; while **some** have long slender bills, or soft **short ones,** fitted for feeding upon insects. **The** bill varies in length, breadth, and direction, **as well as** shape. The feet also **differ** materially: thus we have perching, climbing, **wading,** and swimming feet. In addition to these means of classifying the birds, the naturalist has to call to his aid **the** appearance of the crests, eyes, ears, **mouth,** feathers, wings, and tail. The whole structure **of** this class of animals is peculiarly adapted for motion in the element the mass of them move in.

QUESTIONS.

74. *T.*—Is there anything peculiar in the structure of birds?

P.—Yes; the general adaptation **of** the bony framework to the purposes **of** life, and the covering of the body.

75. *T.*—Why is the body covered with feathers?

P.—Because they are bad conductors of heat; and therefore, when the birds are flying rapidly, the temperature of their bodies is not decreased too suddenly.

76. *T.*—Do they possess a complete double circulation?

P.—Yes, and are called warm-blooded animals.

77. *T.*—How is the body rendered **light?**

P.—By the interior of **the bones being** hollow, and containing **air, which lessens** their specific **gravity.**

78. *T.*—Can you distinguish a water-bird from another, and how?

P.—Yes: by **the form of its** feet, and other peculiarities.

[The pupil should name them.]

79. *T.*—Is there any very great difference in the form of a wading-bird's feet from those of a swimming-bird?

P.—Yes. The former have long slender legs, bare of feathers, and long straight toes; while the latter have short thick legs, and the toes united by a web, which forms a broad surface when expanded, so that the bird can propel itself by this means. The birds of prey have strong legs, armed with powerful, sharp, and hooked talons; the climbers have two toes behind and two in front; and the perching birds have **three** toes in front and one behind, **and the two** outer ones are united by a very **short membrane;** the toes **are long,** with **long claws** slightly curved.

80. *T.*—Have **naturalists** experienced much difficulty in the subdivision of the class Aves?

---

* *Fig.* 1. Head of Neophron percnopterus.   † *Fig.* 8. Head of Harpyia destructor.
‡ *Fig.* 9. Head of Pezoporous formosus.

P.—Yes, because there is a general conformity of type, and therefore it is difficult

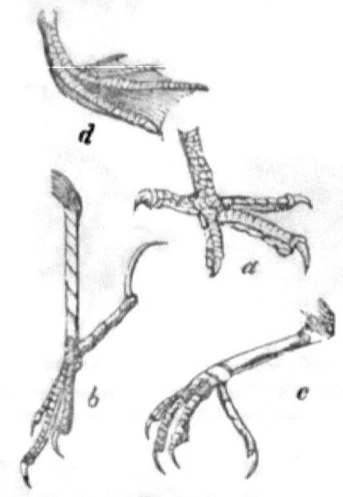

Fig. 10.*

to decide what characters are of greater or lesser importance; because there are not those prominent distinguishing characteristics that we find in the other classes of vertebrate animals.

81. *T.*—Are there any orders of this class possessing marked peculiarities?

P.—Yes, there are **six**; 1, ACCIPITRES, or birds of prey; 2, INCESSORES, or perching birds; 3, SCANSORES, or climbing birds; 4, GALLINÆ, or scratchers; 5, GRALLÆ, or stilt birds; 6, PALMIPEDES, or web-footed birds.

82. *T.*—**Give me** an example of the first order.

P.—The golden eagle, or condor vulture.

83. *T*—Give me examples of the second and third orders.

P.—In the second order we find the humming-birds, fly-catcher, thrush, jay, raven, sparrow, &c.; and in the third order, the cuckoos and macaws.

84. *T.*—Give some examples of the fourth and fifth orders.

P.—The fourth contains such birds as pigeons, pheasants, fowls, peacocks, &c.; and the fifth, the rail, snipe, heron, crane, and ostrich.

85. *T.*—Give examples of the sixth order.

P.—Here we find gulls, penguins, ducks, geese, swans, &c.

86. *T.*—Is there anything very peculiar in the anatomical configuration of birds, that assists naturalists in their classification?

P.—Yes; the form of the sternal apparatus, and the modifications of the digestive organs.

87. *T.*—Is there anything else?

P.—Yes, many things; but especially the modifications of the vocal organs.

GENERAL QUESTIONS ON LESSON VI.

1. **What peculiarities have** naturalists paid **attention to in the** classification of birds?
2. Is there any great difference in the beaks or bills of birds?
3. Why do the bills of birds differ?
4. Is there any difference in the feet of birds? If so, why?
5. Does the osseous, or bony structure of birds, differ from that of mammalians?
6. Why have birds feathers?
7. Are birds warm, or cold-blooded animals?
8. How are the various orders of birds distinguished?
9. How many orders **are there** of the class Aves?
10. What additional peculiarities assist the naturalist in the classification of birds?

LESSON VII.

WE have now to consider the third class of vertebrate animals—the Reptiles. There is this peculiarity in the class, that their form is more varied than that of any other. As their blood is imperfectly aerated, they only maintain a low degree of animal heat,

---

* *Fig.* 10.—*a*, foot of Egyptian neophron; *b*, foot of nuthatch; *c*, foot of thrush; *d*, foot of solan goose.

and are therefore termed cold-blooded **animals**. **Their** peculiar characteristics are—oviparous reproduction; low power of making heat; peculiarity of protecting-surface **by** means of scales, or hard plates, **and a** heart with three cavities, **one** of which receives the blood from the lungs; **another from** the **system generally; and the** third propels the blood which is mixed in it partly to the body **and partly to the lungs; so** that when each contraction of the heart takes place, only **part of the blood is affected** by the air, and the consequence **is, that** their motions are **sluggish, their sensations** dull, and their **digestion slow.**

QUESTIONS.

88. *T.*—**What** is **the** chief reason reptiles are separated from other animals?
P.—Because the conformation of their body is different, and also the circulation of their blood.

89. *T.*—**Is not the blood perfectly oxygenated?**
P.—**No; because the nutritive functions and power of circulation are feeble.**

90. *T.*—**Is** it possible **for reptiles** to suspend their respiration?
P.—Yes; because the smallness of the pulmonary vessels enables them to do so while submerged; and this is done without arresting the circulation of the blood.

91. *T.*—Why are reptiles **covered with** scales, or hard plates?
P.—Because, as they are not warm-blooded animals, they are only covered with a naked skin, which is not capable of **retaining** heat like those animals covered with fur, &c.

92. *T.*—**How are** reptiles subdivided?
P.—According to Cuvier, into four. 1. The TESTUDO, or tortoises. 2. The SAURIANS, or lizards. 3. The OPHIDIANS, or serpents. **4.** The BATRACHIANS, or frogs.

93. *T.*—Is this arrangement satisfactory to naturalists generally?
P.—No; and therefore they have adopted that proposed by M. Brongniart, viz.—1. The CHELONIANS, **or** turtles and tortoises. 2. The SAURIANS, or lizards. 3. The OPHIDIANS, or serpents. **4.** The BATRACHIANS, or frogs.

94. *T.*—Do reptiles incubate their eggs?
P.—No. In some genera of Batrachians they **have** merely a membranous envelop; and **in the snakes,** the young **are** tolerably advanced **in their** form when the egg is deposited.

95. *T.*—Have **not** naturalists adopted other divisions?
P.—Yes, **but as** they refer to other peculiar characteristics, and the more especially to extinct species, it does not belong to **this** part **of our** arrangement to consider them.

96. *T.*—Are reptiles easily distinguished **from the** other classes of vertebrate **animals?**
P.—Yes, **by their prominent peculiarities.**

97. *T.*—What **is the general** locality where reptiles are found?
P.—In thickets, caverns, **and** dark moist places.

98. *T.*—Is there anything peculiar in **the** fourth order, or *frogs?*
P.—They undergo a curious transformation, especially the loss of gills, upon attaining their perfect state.

99. *T.*—Explain **and** give account of these transformations.
P.—It is well known **to country** people who have been in the habit of seeing ditches

Fig. 11.*

and ponds during **the** spring, that there are little, round, bead-**like** masses, resembling

* *Fig.* 11.—Common Frog.

jelly, found floating in these places; some that look like bunches of grapes, the others like strings of beads. The first is the spawn of toads, the other of frogs; and these necklaces of beads (as it were) gradually get heads and tails, and grow on until they have legs, and lose the long tail they each had. The gills disappear, and they then breathe by means of lungs; and from vegetable they gradually ascend to insect food, which they swallow whole, slugs and beetles disappearing in large numbers.

GENERAL QUESTIONS ON LESSON VII.

1. What is the name of the third class of Vertebrate animals?
2. What peculiarity marks or distinguishes the class?
3. Are they warm or cold-blooded animals?
4. Why are Reptiles separated from other Vertebrate animals?
5. Can they suspend respiration?
6. Why are Reptiles covered with scales?
7. How many orders of Reptiles are there according to Cuvier, and how many according to other naturalists?
8. Where are Reptiles generally found?
9. State some peculiarities found or observed in the fourth order of Reptiles.
10. When and where do the transformations of frogs, toads, and others of this order take place?

LESSON VIII.

WE did not adopt the classification of some zoologists in our last lesson, and divide the Reptiles into two parts, so as to make a fourth class, called Amphibious animals, because the great Cuvier did not do so, and we wish to adhere to his system. GRANDFATHER WHITEHEAD is a zealous disciple of Cuvier, and does not desire to depart from his plan. There may be good reasons for separating the Reptiles, into those strictly inhabiting the land, and those that are amphibious; but although the AMPHIBIA are intermediate between Fishes and Reptiles, they are destitute of scales or hard plates; a good reason, some will say, that they should be divided from the Reptiles; but GRANDFATHER WHITEHEAD thinks differently, and therefore adopted the system of Cuvier. Perhaps, some day, he will give his reasons, in his " Lectures to Little-Folk."

We have now to consider the last class of the Vertebrate animals—Fishes. They have a double circulation, respire through the medium of water, and consequently, can live beneath its surface. Their structure is peculiar, because they have little or no weight to bear. Their bodies are formed for the purpose of easy propulsion, being of nearly the same specific gravity as the fluid they inhabit, and furnished with fins, by means of which, and the lateral movements of the tail and body, they are enabled to move without much effort. It is the texture of the fins that is so important in their classification, and therefore the proper arrangement of Fishes is a very difficult matter;

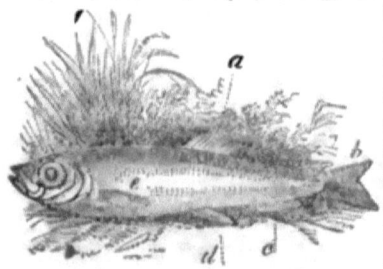

Fig. 12.*

but, nevertheless, we are enabled to divide them into two great divisions—*Bony* and *Cartilaginous* Fishes. The number of the fins varies in different groups, and assists in the arrangement of the orders and species.

---

* Fig. 12.—Whitebait. *a*, dorsal fin; *b*, caudal fin, or tail; *c*, anal fin; *d*, ventral fin; *e*, pectoral fin of one side.

QUESTIONS.

100. *T.*—Why are fishes called Oviparous animals?
P.—Because the species are reproduced from eggs, and the term signifies those born from eggs.

101. *T.*—Where can you procure these eggs?
P.—From the roe, which is a mass of eggs.

102. *T.*—Do any fishes bring forth their young alive?
P.—Yes; but the description of them is more suited to a Zoological catechism than this.

103. *T.*—What is the first order of Bony Fishes called?
P.—ACANTHOPTERYGII, or spiny-finned.

104. *T.*—What is there peculiar in the order?
P.—They have spinous rays in the first dorsal, if more than one, and spinous rays in the first part if there is only one. The anal fin has also its first rays spinous, and each ventral fin has generally one such ray.

105. *T.*—What do you mean by the ray of a fin?
P.—The ray is the rib; and when we say "the first ray of a fin," we mean the first rib of the fin, that is, nearest to the head of the fish.

106. *T.*—What do you mean by the rays being spinous?
P.—If the ray consists of a single bone, whether stiff or flexible, it is said to be *spinous*; but if composed of several bones or joints, then the ray is said to be *articulated* or *soft*.

107. *T.*—Enumerate the families of the first order of Bony Fishes.
P.—1, the Perch family; 2, the Gurnard; 3, the Maigre; 4, the Sea-bream; 5, the Menidæ; 6, the Scaly-finned; 7, the Mackerel; 8, the Ribbon-shaped; 9, the Lancet-fish; 10, Fishes with labyrinths in the pharynx; 11, the Mullet; 12, the Goby; 13, Fishes with wrists to the pectoral fins; 14, the Wrasse, or rock-fish; and 15, the Pipe-mouthed fishes.

108. *T.*—What is the second order of Bony Fishes called?

P.—MALACOPTERYGII ABDOMINALES, or soft-spined fishes, with ventral fins under the abdomen.

109. *T.*—How many families **are they** divided into?
P.—Five. 1, the Carps; 2, the Pikes; 3, the Sheat-fishes; 4, the Salmon or Trout family; and 5, the Herrings.

110. *T.*—What is the third order of Bony Fishes?
P.—The MALACOPTERYGII SUB-BRACHIATI, or soft-rayed fishes, which have the ventral fins under the pectorals, and the pelvis suspended to the shoulder bones.

111. *T.*—What do you mean by the term *Malacopterygii*?
P.—Jointed-fins.

112. *T.*—What families are contained in the third order?
P.—1, the Cod family; 2, the Flat-fish; and 3, Fishes with the ventral fins formed into a sucker.

113. *T.*—The third family of the third order of Bony Fishes is very peculiar; give me an example of the family.
P.—The *Echeneis remora*, or sucking-fish, which attaches itself to the bottom of ships.

114. *T.*—Why are these fish provided with this curious apparatus?
P.—To enable them to attach themselves to rocks and other places, and remain there to procure their food.

115. *T.*—What is the fourth order **of** Bony Fishes called?
P.—The MALACOPTERYGII APODA, or eel tribe, which all resemble the common eel.

116. *T.*—Give me some examples of this order.
P.—The conger-eel (*Conger vulgaris*), the muræna, and the gymnotus, or electric-eel.

117. *T.*—What is the name of the fifth order of Bony Fishes?
P.—LOPHOBRANCHII, or fishes with their gills in tufts.

118. *T.*—What peculiarities are observed in this order?
P.—The gills, instead of being in long

rows, like the teeth of a comb, are arranged in small rounded tufts; the body is covered with hard plates instead of scales; the jaws are united, except at the very end, **so that** they appear to have a tubular snout or nose, especially in the sea-horse; and the male is provided with **a** pouch, in which the female deposits the spawn, where the young **are** hatched, and retreat when alarmed.

119. *T.*—What is the sixth order of the Bony Fishes called?

P.—PLECTOGNATHI, or fishes with soldered jaws; so named because the bones of the jaw are immovable. The gills and gill-covers have a covering of thick skin.

120. *T.*—What is meant by CHONDROPTERYGII?

P.—Fishes with cartilaginous, instead of bony skeletons.

121. *T.*—What is the first order of this division called?

P.—CHONDROPTERYGII BRANCHIIS LIBERIS, or fishes with free gills, such as sturgeons.

122. *T.*—What is the name of the second order?

P.—CHONDROPTERYGII BRANCHIIS FIXIS, or fishes with fixed gills. These fish have the edges of the gills fixed, instead of being free at the edges, and the water enters through a number of small holes on each side of the head, as **in** the shark tribe.

GENERAL QUESTIONS ON LESSON VIII.

1. How are fishes divided?
2. What is the most important object to attend to, and guide us in the classification of fishes?
3. How are the young of fish and the species reproduced?
4. What do you mean by spinous rays?
5. What is the ray of a fin?
6. How many orders of Bony Fishes are there? Name them.
7. Explain the meaning of the various terms applied to each order?
8. Give some examples of each order?
9. How many orders of Cartilaginous fishes are there?
10. Name the orders, and their peculiarities?

LESSON IX.

WE have now to consider the second great division of the Animal Kingdom—the ANIMALIA MOLLUSCA, or soft-bodied animals. These animals present many peculiarities, being without an articulated skeleton, or back-bone, and without brain or spinal marrow. Their blood is of a bluish tinge, or white; and their muscles are attached to the integuments instead of to bones. Cuvier says, "that their organs of motion and of the senses have not the same uniformity in number and position as in the vertebrated animals; and the variety is still more striking with the viscera, particularly in relation to the position of the heart and respiratory organs, and even in the structure and nature of the latter; for some mollusca breathe the free air, and others the fresh or salt water." Some of the molluscous animals have naked bodies, while others are protected by shells. Cuvier divided the molluscous animals into six classes, which we have now to examine.

QUESTIONS.

123. *T.*—What is the first class of molluscous animals?

P.—The CEPHALOPODES, or head-footed animals.

124. *T.*—Why are they called thus?

P.—Because the animals in this class propel themselves by means of appendages connected with the head.

125. *T.*—Name some examples of this class of animals.

[Lesson IX.]   NATURAL HISTORY.   51

P.—The nautilus, and cuttle-fish.
[The pupil should name the peculiarities of both these examples.]

126. *T.*—What is the second class called?
P.—PTEROPODES, or fin-footed animals.

127. *T.*—State the peculiarities of this class.
P.—Cuvier says that, like the cephalopodes, they "swim in the ocean, but can neither fix themselves to any object, nor crawl on the ground, because they are without feet. They move from place to place by means of fins, placed like wings on each side of the mouth."

128. *T.*—Name the third class.
P.—They are called GASTEROPODES, or animals that move on their stomachs, such as snails and slugs.

129. *T.*—State something more about this class.
P.—It is divided into nine orders, containing many species, some of which are entirely naked; others have a concealed shell; but the greater number a complete covering—as snails, which shelters them from the attacks of other animals. Most of those that live in the water have an *operculum*, or little door, attached, which protects the animal when it has retreated within the shell.

130. *T.*—What animals with shells are arranged in this class?
P.—Those called *Univalves*; or molluscous animals with shells in one piece.

131. *T.*—What do you call the fourth class?
P.—ACEPHALES, or animals without heads. This is not strictly correct, as they only *appear* not to have heads.

132. *T.*—Give me an example of this order.
P.—Oysters, mussels, and all bivalve Molluscs.

133. *T.*—What do you mean by *bivalve* Mollusca?
P.—Soft-bodied animals, with shells in two pieces.

134. *T.*—How many orders are there in the class Acephales?
P.—Two. 1, *Acephala testacea*; and 2, *Acephala nuda*.

135. *T.*—What is the difference between them?

P.—The former have protecting shells; and the latter are naked, or without shells.

136. *T.*—What is the name of the fifth class of the Mollusca?
P.—BRACHIOPODES, or animals with arm-feet; but we do not know much about them, except that they have two fleshy arms, furnished with numerous filaments, which they can protrude from and draw within the shell when they please; the mouth is situated between these arms.

137. *T.*—What is the sixth class called?
P.—CIRRHOPODES, or animals with hair feet, like the barnacles (*Lepas*), which at-

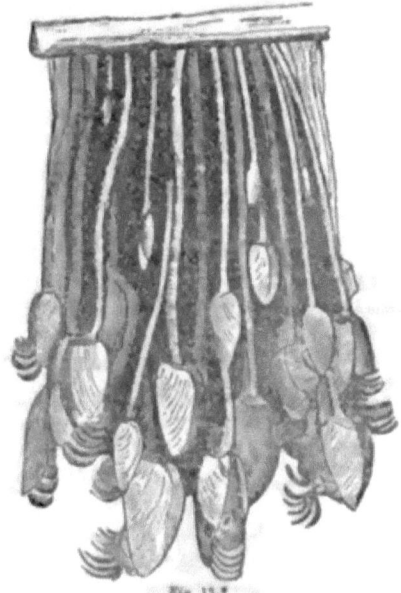

Fig. 13.

tach themselves to ships and posts by long fleshy stems. In this class we also have the acorn-shells (*balanus*). The principal part of the shell consists of a hard tube, with an opening at the narrower part, more or less closed by two or four valves.

GENERAL QUESTIONS ON LESSON IX.

1. What is the name of the second great division of the animal kingdom?

---

* *Fig.* 13.—Bunch of *Lepas Anatifera*, attached to part of a pier.

2. How do the Molluscous animals differ from the Vertebrate?
3. Name the various classes of Mollusca.
4. Give examples from each class.
5. State the peculiarities of the Molluscous animals.

6. What is the meaning of the terms applied to each class?
7. What is an *operculum*?
8. Explain what is meant by a *univalve* and *bivalve*.

LESSON X.

EACH great division of the Animal Kingdom presents some generality of form. We have observed the peculiarities of the first two divisions, and we have now to notice those presented by the third—ANIMALIA ARTICULATA, or animals with articulated bodies. That great naturalist, **Cuvier,** observed that "this third general form is as well characterised as that of **Vertebrata;** the skeleton is not internal, as in the latter; neither is it wanting, as in the Mollusca. The articulated rings which encircle the body, and frequently the limbs, supply the place of it; and as they are usually hard, they furnish all the necessary support for the muscles by which the body is moved; so that among the animals, as is the case of the Vertebrata, those which have limbs are able to walk, to swim, or to fly. Thus they have some general resemblance, more particularly in their internal organisation, although in most respects they differ from each other to the utmost degree."

QUESTIONS.

138. *T.*—In what respect do all articulated animals resemble each other most?
P.—In their nervous system.

139. *T.*—Is there anything peculiar in it?
P.—Yes, the brain, which is very small,

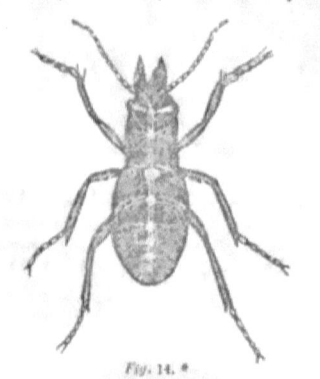

Fig. 14. *

is placed over the œsophagus or **gullet,** and supplies nerves to all the parts near to the head, and two chords which encircle the œsophagus are continued along the abdomen, and connected at intervals by ganglia, from which the nerves are sent to the various parts of the body and limbs.

140. *T.*—What office does a ganglion perform?
P.—It seems to act like a brain, conferring sensibility on the parts with which it is intimately connected.

141. *T.*—Are there any other peculiarities to be observed in the Articulata?
P.—Yes, their jaws are invariably lateral, and shut together like a pair of scissors—that is, horizontally, and not upwards and downwards; and besides this, we observe that they have not any distinct organ of smell.

142. *T.*—How are the articulated animals classed?
P.—Into four principal classes; 1. The ANNELIDES, or red-blooded worms. 2. The CRUSTACEA, or hard-coated animals; 3. The ARACHNIDA, or animals like spiders; 4. The INSECTA, or insects.

* *Fig.* 14.—Nervous system of Carabus Cinthrutus, showing the chain of ganglia connected by a double chord.

Lesson X.]   NATURAL HISTORY.   53

143. *T.*—Why have the Annelides been separated from the other three classes?

P.—Because they have red blood, and are the only invertebrate animals that have. The circulation is double, consisting of arteries and veins; almost all of them live in water, except the earth-worms. The body, which is more or less elongated, is always divided into little rings, whence the name (the Latin word *annellus* signifying a little ring), and they respire by organs which are either spread over the surface of the body, concealed internally, or developed externally.

144. *T.*—How are the Annelides divided?

P.—Into three orders, the first of which is called the TUBICOLÆ, or worms inhabiting tubes. Some of these animals form tubes of fragments of shells, sand, and mud, which are lined by a membrane; others form an uniform calcareous tube; and others have their tubes composed of membrane only.

145. *T.*—What is the name of the second order?

P.—The DORSIBRANCHIATA.

146. *T.*—Name their peculiarities.

P.—They have their *branchiæ* or gills equally distributed about the body, especially the middle portion. The Arenicola have beautiful little gills in tufts upon the

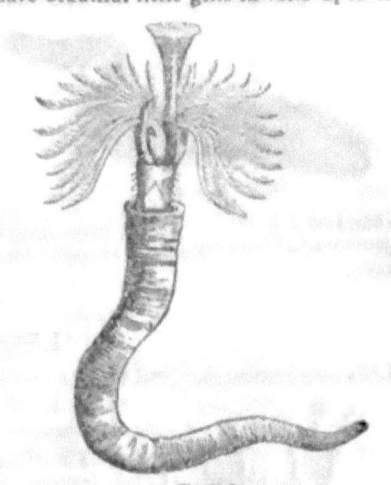

Fig. 15.*

middle part of the body, every fifth ring being larger than the others, and the feet and gills attached to it. In the same order we have the Nereids, and many other curious and interesting genera.

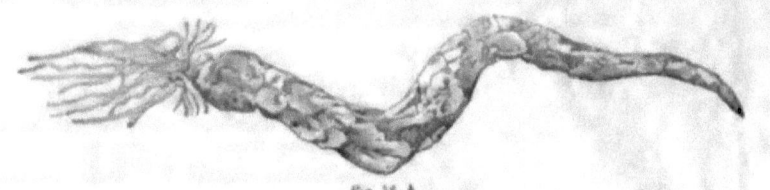

Fig. 16. †

147. *T.*—What is the name of the third order of Annelides?

P.—ABRANCHIA. This order of animals is destitute of external respiratory organs, and they seem to breathe from the entire surface of the skin, or, as in the leeches, by

Fig. 17. ‡

internal cavities. As some have bristles, which serve for the purpose of moving, and others are deficient of them, **they are** divided into two families.

---

* *Fig.* 15—*Serpula Contortuplicata,* with a portion of the body protruded from the calcareous shell.

† *Fig.* 16.—*Terebella medusa,* in its composite tube of sand and fragment of shells.

‡ *Fig.* 17.—*Arenicola piscatorum,* showing the respiratory tufts along the sides.

148. *T.*—What are these two families?
P.—The *Abranchia setigera*, provided with silky bristles, as the earthworm

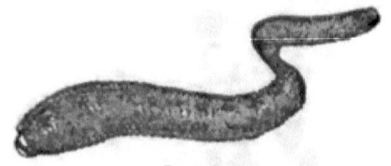

Fig. 18.*

tribe; and 2, the *Abranchia nuda*, or the *Abranchia* without bristles, such as the leech tribe.

GENERAL QUESTIONS ON LESSON X.

1. What is the name of the third great division of the Animal Kingdom?
2. What are articulated animals?
3. How many classes of articulated animals are there?
4. Describe the peculiarities of the first class, and give examples of each order and family?
5. Why have the Annelides been separated from the other classes?
6. Is there anything peculiar in the nervous system of the Articulata? If so, state the peculiarity.

LESSON XI.

LINNÆUS classed the Crustacea, Arachnida, and Insecta together, under the general name of Insects; but other Zoologists have thought proper to divide them. The second class of articulated animals is, properly speaking, the crustaceous or hard-coated animals. They have a great many genera and species, articulated legs, respire by branchiæ, or a kind of gills, sometimes enclosed, and in other species external to the shell; the circulation is double, and resembles that of the Molluscous animals; and the nervous system is of two kinds, which will be noticed in another Catechism.

QUESTIONS.

149. *T.*—How are the Crustacea divided?
P.—Into the MALACOSTRACA and ENTOMOSTRACA.

150. *T.*—Describe the peculiarities of the former.
P.—The shell of the animals is hard and calcareous; they have ten or fourteen legs, hooked at the tip; and some have fixed eyes, while others have theirs placed on a moveable piece.

151. *T.*—What is there peculiar in the second division?
P.—The shell is slender, and generally in two parts; the eyes are fixed, and frequently there is only one of these organs. The legs vary in number, have only one hook at the extremity, and appear more suited for swimming than anything else.

Fig. 19.†

* Fig. 18.—*Hirudo officinalis*, or leech.
† Fig. 19.—*A vertical longitudinal section of the common lobster (Astacus marinus)*.—*a*, mandibles and palpi; *b*, the stomach; *c c*, intestinal prolongation of the same; *d*, the outlet; *e*, the heart; *f g h i*, a system of great blood-vessels distributed to the posterior portion of the animal; *k l m*, great blood-vessels distributed to the sternal or anterior aspect of the body; *n n n*, lobes of the liver.

152. *T.*—How many orders are there in the first division?

P.—Five. The first is called *Decapoda* or ten-footed, all of which have ten feet, furnished with nippers; and the common lobster, which is included in the second family, is an excellent example of the order.

153. *T.*—What is the name of the second order?

P.—There is very little of interest in the second, third, fourth, or fifth orders, which are called *Stomapoda, Amphipoda, Læmodipoda,* and *Isopoda.*

154. *T.*—How is the second division of Crustacea divided?

P.—Into the *Branchiopoda* and *Pœcilopoda,* which have each certain peculiarities.

155. *T.*—What is the third class of Articulata?

P.—The *Arachnida,* or spiders.

156. *T.* State the peculiarities and reasons why they have been classified by themselves.

P.—They are destitute of wings, do not undergo any changes of form like insects, and differ in their nervous system.

Fig. 20.

157. *T.*—How are they divided?

P.—Into two orders. 1. The true spiders and scorpions, and—2. The small animals known as false scorpions, such as the *book-scorpion,* and the mites.

GENERAL QUESTIONS ON LESSON XI.

1. How are the Crustacea divided?
2. Describe the peculiarities of each division, and give examples from them?
3. Name the various orders of each division, and the reason they are divided from the others?
4. How is the Arachnida, or third class, divided?
5. Give examples from each order?

LESSON XII.

THE fourth class comprises those creatures called Insects whose peculiar and beautiful form, colour, and instincts, have captivated all enthusiastic naturalists. In a treatise like this, we can only take a glance at them—a mere transient glance. They undergo various changes during their brief existence, wonderful to behold, and yet typical of man's existence and future state. They are divided into twelve orders, each characterised by certain peculiarities which cannot be given here, but will be particularised in the Zoological Catechism.

QUESTIONS.

158. *T.*—What insects are found in the first order, or Myriapoda?

P.—Centipedes, which are destitute of wings, and have more than six feet.

159. *T.*—What is there peculiar to the second order.

P.—They have six legs, do not change their form, and have peculiar organs of locomotion at the sides or end of the body.

160. *T.*—What is the third order called?

P.—*Parasita,* or parasites, such as ticks, &c.

161. *T.*—What kind of insect do we find in the fourth order?

P.—The common flea (*Pulex irritans*) which every one of us is, no doubt, well acquainted with.

162. *T.*—What are the names of the fifth, sixth, and seventh orders?

P.—The fifth is called *Coleoptera;* the sixth, *Orthoptera;* and the seventh, *Hemiptera.*

163. *T.* What animals do we find in the fifth order?

P.—Generally beetles.

Fig. 20.—Acarus domesticus, or cheese mite, (highly magnified) attacking a piece of cheese.

164. *T.*—What kind of insects or animals in the sixth order?
P.—Such kind as cockroaches and earwigs.

165. *T.*—Give me an example of the seventh order.
P.—The bug tribes.

166. *T.*—Name the remaining orders.
P.—8. Neuroptera. 9. Hymenoptera. 10. Lepidoptera. 11. Rhipiptera; and 12. Diptera.

167. *T.*—Give the peculiarities of each.
P.—They shall be described when I know more of Natural History, especially Zoology.

GENERAL QUESTIONS ON LESSON XII.

1. Why are insects placed last?
2. Is there anything peculiar in their organisation?
3. How many orders are they divided into?
4. Give a familiar object under each order.
5. Name the peculiarities of each order.

LESSON XIII.

THE fourth, and last great division of the animal kingdom, is the radiated animals, or RADIATA. They are called thus because they generally agree in one respect—that of having the parts of which they are formed arranged round an axis or central point. Their organs of motion, when they have any, consist of moveable spines, or flexible papillæ, capable of inflation, attached to the skin. They are divided into five classes, according to their organization.

QUESTIONS.

168. *T.*—What is the last class of radiated animals called?
P.—*Echinodermata*, or bristly skinned animals.

169. *T.*—State their peculiarities.
P.—They have a digestive and a vascular system; a well-organized skin, and a nervous system which partakes of their general form.

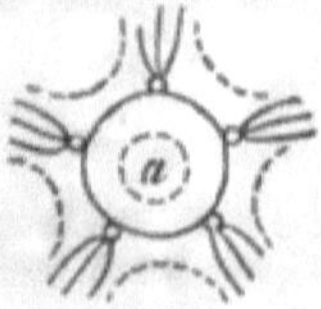

*Fig. 21.**

170. *T.*—How is this class divided?
P—Into two orders; those with feet, or vesicular appendages, serving as feet; and those without.

171. *T.*—What is the name of the first order?
P.—PEDICELLATA.

172. *T.*—Is there anything peculiar in **this** order?
P.—Yes; the skin is pierced with numerous small holes, from each of which protrude small tubes, terminating in suckers, which enable the animals to walk, or adhere to rocks.

*Fig. 22.**

173. *T.*—Are all the animals in this order alike?
P.—Not individually, but generally;

---

* *Fig. 21.*—Nervous system of Star-fish—*a* the mouth.

* *Fig. 22.*—The *Asterias aurantia*, showing the osseous plates and strong moveable spines.

[Lesson XIII.] NATURAL HISTORY.

therefore they have been divided into three families. 1. The *Asterias*, or **star-fish**. 2. The *Echinida*, or **sea-eggs**. **3. The** *Holothuriæ*, or sea-slugs.

174. *T.*—Describe the **star-fishes.**

P.—The mouth is on the underside, **and** the principal nerve surrounds it, **and sends** off filaments **to** each arm **or ray [see** *Fig.* 21]; the arms **or** rays are **five in number,** and in some species are covered with **osseous** plates, and the **sides furnished with strong** moveable spines.

175. *T.*—What **is** there peculiar about the sea-eggs?

P.—The **body is** enclosed **in a calcareous** shell, composed **of various segments,**

Fig. 23.

which fit closely together, and are arranged in alternate rows of plates, with tubercles to

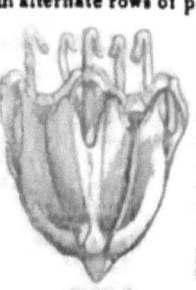

Fig. 24. †

which the spines are attached, and perforate the plates **for the membraneous feet to pass** through. The **mouth is** furnished **with five** flat, calcareous **teeth,** which are pointed with hard enamel. The whole dental **apparatus** consists **of** twenty-five pieces, moved **by** thirty-five muscles, which enable the animal **to** crush the **shells of the** fish on which it **feeds.**

176. *T.*—Can you tell me anything about that curious animal, the Sea-slug?

P.—The *Holothuriæ* **are sometimes called "sea-cucumbers," and have a number of**

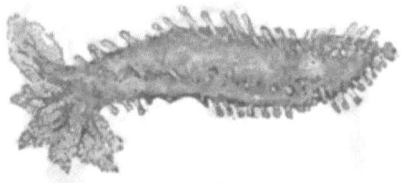

Fig. 25. *

curious looking tentacula distributed over their bodies, which they can retract **at** pleasure. They have a leather-like skin, with an aperture **at** each end, and **a** most complex structure.

177. *T.*—What is the second **order** called?

P.—APODA, or animals without **feet,** which are chiefly found in the **sand of the** sea-shore, and resemble the *Holothuriæ*, with the exception of their **skin, which** is devoid of tentacula, **and the want of feet.**

GENERAL QUESTIONS ON LESSON XIII.

1. What is the name of the last great division **of** animated nature?
2. Why are the radiated animals arranged last?
3. How **are the Radiata divided?**
4. What **is the meaning o' the term,** ECHINODERMATA?
5. Is there anything peculiar **in the** nervous system of this class?
6. What are the peculiarities of the **first order of** bristly-skinned animals?
7. **How** is the order divided?
8. State the reason the animals in this order have been separated from the others.

---

* *Fig. 23.—Echinus*, or sea-urchin; **the right** side covered with spines; the left has **them** removed to show the plates of the shell.

† *Fig. 24.*—**The** teeth of sea-urchin, **showing their arrangement.**

* *Fig. 25.—Holothuria*, showing the tentacula arranged **in rows on the** surface of the body, and the **tree-like respiratory** organ, or gill.

LESSON XIV.

We have the remaining four classes of the Radiated animals to examine, viz.—2. The Entozoa, or intestinal worms. 3. The Acalephæ, or sea-nettles. 4. The Polypi, or animals with many feet. 5. The Infusoria, or animalcules. The *Entozoa* are remarkable for being the inhabitants of the internal parts of other animals, especially the Vertebrata, but the other animals are scarcely ever affected with them. Some of them attain a large size, especially such as the tænia, which are often twenty feet long, and sometimes more than a hundred feet. The *Acalephæ* have been divided into the simple and the hydrostatic, and include all those animals. The *Polypi* are capable of producing new individuals, both by putting forth a kind of bud and by eggs, which are left to the mercy of the waters. The *Infusoria* are little known, although Ehrenberg, Pritchard, Owen, Grant, and others have written upon them, yet much remains to be discovered, as regards their organization, and still more in classifying them.

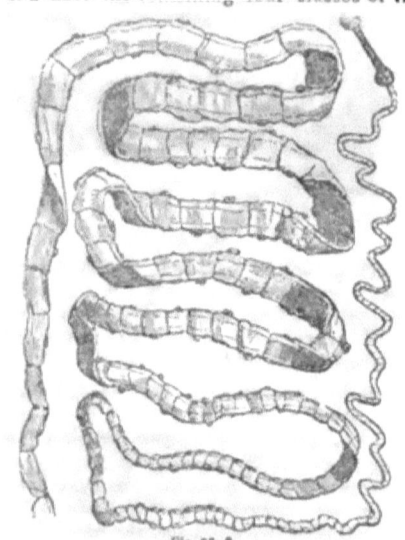

Fig. 26.

QUESTIONS.

178. *T.*—For what are the *Entozoa* remarkable?

P.—Inhabiting the interior of other animals, where they can only exist.

179. *T.*—Is there anything peculiar in their organization?

P.—Yes; they have no breathing apparatus, which shows that the nutriment they receive is aërated by animals upon which they are parasitic.

180. *T.*—Are the species of the *Entozoa* numerous?

P.—Yes; and they are divided into two distinct orders—the *Nematoidea*, or cavitied entozoa, and the *Entozoa Parenchymata*, which have the viscera obscure, the body being filled with a pulpy matter.

181. *T.*—Give me some examples of the order *Nematoidea*, and their peculiarities.

P.—The order *Nematoidea* comprises several genera which are remarkable for having no circulation that we can discover, and a simple nervous system which is only seen in some species, consisting of two cords extending from a ring round the mouth. The thread-worms and ascarides are familiar examples of this order.

182. *T.* Give me some examples of the second order, and state something about it.

P.—The order *Parenchymata* contains four families, and is remarkable for an absence of an alimentary apparatus, and no visible signs of a nervous system. The fluke found in the livers of sheep; the tape-worm (see *Fig.* 26*); and hydatids, are all examples of this order.

183. *T.*—What is supposed to be the use of the *Entozoa?*

---

* *Fig.* 26.—The *Tænia solium*, or solitary worm, exhibiting the alternating pores, head with suckers, and the narrow anterior, or neck part.

P.—From their habits being concealed from observation, we are unable to ascertain the part they play in the economy of nature.

184. *T.*—**Name** the peculiarities of the ACALEPHÆ, or sea-nettles?

P.—They float upon and swim **in the** water, propelling themselves by **alternate**

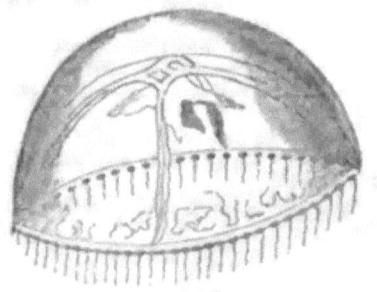

Fig. 27.*

contractions and dilatations of their gelatinous bodies. They do not appear to have any true circulation, and their bodies consist of a net-work of animal filaments, filled up with water, which exudes from their interstices when they are cast upon the seashore.

185. *T.*—What is there peculiar in the POLYPI?

P.—They have a visible stomach, and tentacula around their mouths, which vary

Fig. 28.†

in form and number; the body is always conical or cylindrical, and the viscera sometimes absent.

186. *T.*—How are they divided?

P.—1. Into the *Carnosi*, or fleshy polypi. 2. The *Gelatinosi*, or gelatinous polypi; and 3. The *Coralliferi*, or corals.

187. *T.*—Name some examples of **each.**

P.—The *Actinia Mesembryanthemum* **is** an example of the CARNOSI; the *Hydra viridis* of the GELATINOSI; and *Madrepores* of **the** CORALLIFERA.

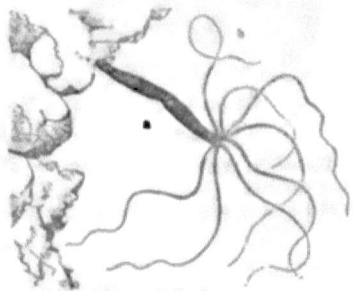

Fig. 29.*

188. *T.*—What is there peculiar **in the** INFUSORIA?

P.—The greater part of them have a gelatinous body, and very simple structure. They are very small, and require the aid of a microscope to study their organisation, as they differ somewhat in their structure. They have been divided into the *Rotifera* and *Homogenea*.

189. *T.*—What is there peculiar in the *Rotifera*?

P.—The body is oval and gelatinous, usually ending in a kind of tail; while the fore part has a singular apparatus of tubes, with teeth at the edges; and as they vibrate rapidly, they look like a number of toothed wheels revolving. We can discover a mouth, stomach, and intestine.

190. *T.*—What is supposed to **be the** use of this apparatus that appears **to revolve**?

P.—It has been stated to be **connected** with respiration; and as it does **not assist** in conveying the food, there is good reason to believe that it is connected with the function of respiration.

---

* *Fig. 27.—Thaumantias pilosella.*

† *Fig. 28.—Actinia mesembryanthemum.*

* *Fig. 29.—Hydra viridis,* a species of fresh-water polype.—*a* the body, containing a cavity (the stomach) in its interior; *b b* tentacula, whereby it lays hold of its prey.

191. *T.*—What is there peculiar in the *Homogenea?*

P.—There does not appear to be **any** mouth, viscera, or nervous system.

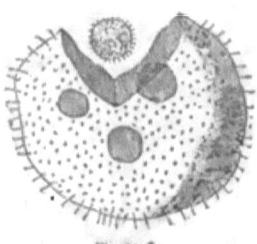

Fig. 30.*

192. *T.*—Give me **an** example **of an** infusorial animal.

P.—The ***Volvox*** *globator*, which revolves on its axis, and contains several small globes, each of which, it is thought, contains a numerous embryo race. When the *Volvox* **arrives at** maturity it bursts, and the globe escapes to perform like offices.

GENERAL QUESTIONS ON LESSON XIV.

1. **Name the** second and third **classes of** Radiata.
2. Name the fourth and fifth classes.
3. Give examples from each class.
4. Why have the classes been arranged thus?
5. What is an infusorial animal?
6. Into how many orders are the infusoria divided?
7. Give me **an** example of **an** infusorial animal.

RETROSPECT AND REMARKS.

Man, like the other animals, **is subject** to the law of death, but after his soul has left **its earthly** habitation, **it shall continue to** exist for ever. Some naturalists have excluded him from their system, **because he is too exalted in the scale** of creation to be classed with the "beasts that perish." Among **these, Aristotle, Ray,** Willoughby, Swainson, and others, maintain that **he** should not be **classed with animals, but hold a** distinct position. Let us see why he has been classed with animals. **It is argued that as he is suckled** at the breast of his mother, **he naturally belongs to the mammalia;** he **is placed among** unguiculated animals, because he **has nails upon his fingers and toes; and is classed with the apes because some of** them **have a hyoid bone, (a bone** situated **between the root of the tongue** and larynx, or windpipe). Respecting this, Swainson judiciously remarks—"**What can be a** greater violation of nature—all other considerations apart—**than to place a solitary species of** creature walking erect upon two limbs, among others which walk upon four?"

The various systems that have been put forth by naturalists from time to time, only tend to mislead **the beginner;** he gets within a labyrinth of them, where each is striving to prove how superior it is to all others. It is on this account that Grandfather Whitehead recommends his pupils to follow the system of Cuvier, until sufficiently grounded in **Natural History, and then to** read the others, at the same time making such observations **as** they may think necessary in a note-book.

M. Lamark errs in his **system,** by placing all animals with an internal skeleton in one division, and those with **an** external skeleton in the other division; because by such an arrangement, animals **with the** rudiments of an internal vertebræ will be classed with **apes, lions,** and other quadrupeds. As we have already remarked, Cuvier divides the **animal** kingdom into four **great divisions,** and bases his classification upon the organisation and nature of the animals themselves. It is true that there are objections to the

---

* *Fig.* 30.—The *Volvox globator*, exhibiting the minute hair-like cilia, and the small globes inside, with the young escaping.

RETROSPECT AND REMARKS.

entire adoption of the Cuvierian system, but it is no easy task to form any system that shall be perfect, for we have such vast numbers of animated beings, with distinct peculiarities to examine, understand, and classify, that it requires the undivided attention of a lifetime to arrive at correct conclusions. Suppose, for instance, that we saw a sprat, and were ignorant of its name and position in the animal kingdom, it is not an easy matter to fix upon the exact spot it should occupy in Nature's catalogue, for there are upwards of eight thousand varieties of fishes. We could, however, at once decide that it did not belong to quadrupeds, birds, or reptiles; and a *very little* further inquiry would determine that it belonged to the fishes, and not the amphibious animals. It does not require much study to decide that it should be classed with the bony fishes, and a little attention to other peculiarities of structure, such as the position or absence of the ventral fins, which we have already noticed, will enable us to place it in the second order of bony fishes; and then, by examining the scales, upper jaw, gills, &c., we know that it belongs to the fifth family of the second order.

It is quite evident that the primary types of nature are very few, the variations almost endless. Any person can tell a bird from a pig or quadruped, yet as there are nearly 7,000 species, it is not an easy thing to know a parrot from a barbet or other bird, unless by attending to the external characters we have pointed out in this Catechism, and the general organization.

Nature has arranged the animal, like the other kingdoms, with admirable precision, and her disciples or pupils can discover most of the groups by diligent observation and patient attention.

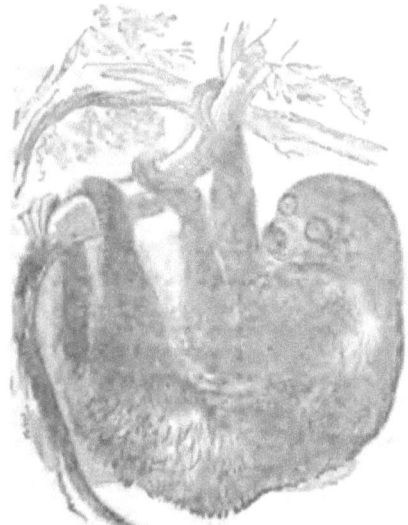

Fig. 31.

Could any sensible being mistake a cat for a sloth? Certainly not. The habits, form, and construction, all point out the difference. The cat is nimble, can retract the claws, has a long tail, &c.; the sloth is ill at ease on the ground, he moves slowly and awkwardly, he has not any tail; and the claws, which are bent towards the inside of the hand and sole of the foot, cannot be retracted. The sloth does not, like other animals, ramble upon the ground, soar into the air, or dive into the water; nor does he, like monkeys, live upon the trees he inhabits, but under them suspended from the branches. When in the trees his movements are not slow—on the contrary, pretty fast.

We have often mentioned VERTEBRATA, or *vertebrated animals*, in this Catechism; and perhaps some of my pupils will ask what a *vertebra* is. We explained that the back-bone or spine is made up of several pieces, each of which is called a *vertebra*; and if a naturalist has one of these pieces of bone given him to examine, he can determine what kind of animal it originally formed par

* *Fig.* 31.—The three-toed sloth, suspended from the branch of a tree.

of. I have no doubt that a great many of you have read or heard that Professor Owen, the great anatomist, was enabled to state the form and structure of an extinct bird of New Zealand, and even the kind of food it used, by examining some of the bones that were brought to England. We know he was correct, because since he examined the bones, other parts have been discovered, which verify his statements.

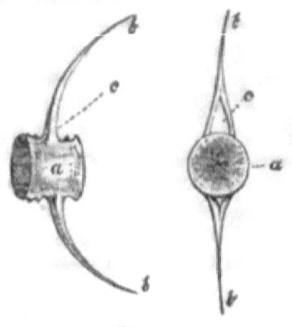

Fig. 32.*

A natural system should have such a thoroughly scientific basis, that it should connect all the links in the chain of relationship. We all know by observation that there is a scale in nature, and that each kingdom gradually merges into, or is blended with, the other. The difficulty is, therefore, to know where we are to draw the line of demarcation; hence the complexity of natural systems. It may be remarked that there are several Natural Systems, and that the pupil may request to be informed which is the best. GRANDFATHER WHITEHEAD considers the best Natural System to be that which approaches nearest to Nature's own plan, and exhibits a unity of classification; he has explained the difference between a natural and an artificial system in this Catechism.

To become a good Naturalist, it is necessary to observe things accurately and quickly, so as to be able to distinguish differences in the structure of animals almost at a glance. This will be acquired by practice; and I would advise my younger pupils to acquire the habit of observing all things closely and quickly, but not slovenly. Let them place a number of specimens of birds before them, such as swallows, swifts, sparrows, woodpeckers, &c., and endeavour to find out and describe the peculiarities of each, how they differ, and how they may each be distinguished; or let them examine the skeletons of a dozen quadrupeds, and exercise their minds in discriminating between one genus and another.

It is well to learn the habits and economy of animals, and make notes upon them in a book arranged alphabetically; the number of young they have, or eggs they lay; the changes the young undergo; giving examples of longevity, temper, &c.; food, how they capture their prey, and all interesting traits. Let the young read White's *Natural History of Selborne*, and endeavour to form such another history of the place they reside in. In after years, such a book will afford them many hours of amusement and instruction.

Cuvier has been blamed for arranging his animal kingdom upon anatomical principles, and severe remarks have been made upon his system for that reason. More than one author censures him for giving anatomical descriptions of the animals. Is it more difficult for a naturalist to study anatomy than an artist? Which is the more necessary —that the artist or the naturalist should make it their study?

The insect tribes—THE INSECTA—form the largest portion of the animal kingdom, having nearly 600,000 species; and yet, by attending to the principles of classification, naturalists have not any difficulty in assigning the proper place to each of them. We

---

* *Fig. 32.*—Side and front view of the vertebra of a salmon. *a*, the body; *b, b*, the processes; *c*, vertebral canal.

have only to look at the accompanying diagrams, to see how the external appearance of an ant differs from that of a bee; and if **we** examine a beetle—such as the Elm-destroying **scolytus, we** immediately **see how differently it is formed from either the ants,** the

Fig. 33.*   Fig. 34.†

bees, or **butterflies; in fact, the wings** are protected by **hard coverings, which** the others do not **possess; we could not, therefore,** place them in **the same order or** genus.

One thing is especially necessary for the naturalist **to remember; that the mere collecting** of specimens, **without any other object than that of acquiring a heap, as the** miser **does of gold, is useless, unscientific, and attended with many inconveniences, the least of which is—expense.**

Fig. 35.‡

Students should not be alarmed at the difficult looking **names employed in** Zoology, or indeed **any other science, they are necessary; and after reading them over a few times, they will become** almost **as familiar as** the names of their school**fellows. The best** way to master the dif**ficulty of reading and** speaking the technical names—if any exists—is to copy them **out** several times in a book, accent the syllables, then ask some scientific friend **to pronounce** the words, and write the **pronunciation** opposite **to them; thus—*formica rufa* (*fourmikha roofha*).** Do not let your only object be to learn a long list of scientific names **to astonish your friends,** but **endeavour rather to thoroughly understand what you do** learn. **Commence by getting a general knowledge of the great divisions of any one class of animals, such as the quadrupeds,** of which **there are about 1,200** species; learn **their peculiarities, names, orders,** tribes, families, &c.; **copy these names over** and over again, and persevere **in mastering** all the difficulties that **start up before you.** If one name appears more **difficult than another, underline** it with **red ink,** and **study that** more than the others. **When you have become acquainted** with their names **and** peculiarities, endeavour **to discover the reason each animal is classed** as described,

---

* *Fig. 33.—Ants, male and female—formica rufa.*
† *Fig. 34.—Bees; drone, queen, and worker.*
‡ *Fig. 35.—Scolytus destructor, or Elm-destroying scolytus, exhibiting the expanded wings and wing-covers of the insect.*

and if you appear doubtful about the matter, consult some books, or note it in your common-place book, so that you may consult some scientific friend upon the subject, when an opportunity occurs.

If you desire to be a naturalist, **if you** wish to excel your **equals** or betters, **if you** would gain **a wreath of fame**; **remember that the** worm of idleness will destroy **the** result of your previous labours, undermine **your** plans, and **eat away** the green leaves you have ordained for your brow. It has been said that "**it is** a mistake to imagine that only **the** violent passions, such as love and ambition, can triumph over the rest. Idleness, languid as she is, often masters them all; she, indeed, influences all our designs and actions, and insensibly consumes and destroys **both** passions and **virtues.**" Beware of her influences; live like a hermit; work like a slave; **bow to** experience; store your golden grains of knowledge; confirm reading by practice; and, whatever method you adopt, first draw out your plan, and then abide by its PRINCIPLES OF CLASSIFICATION.

GENERAL QUESTIONS ON RETROSPECT.

1. WHY have **some** naturalists excluded MAN from the animal **kingdom**?
2. Why have Cuvier, and **others**, included Man in the animal kingdom?
3. What objections does Swainson **urge** against Man being classed with **the** Mammalia?
4. Why is the system of Cuvier recommended by GRANDFATHER WHITEHEAD?
5. How does Lamark err in his classification?

[The pupil should, if sufficiently advanced, give the division proposed and adopted by M. Virey.]

6. How is **the classification of** Cuvier arranged?
7. Are the primary types of **nature very** numerous?
8. Can we readily distinguish **a cat from** a sloth?
9. Is there anything very peculiar about **a vertebra?**
10. **What** can we learn from the examination of a vertebra?
11. What **is the object** of Natural Systems?
12. What Natural Systems are the best?
13. Why has the arrangement of Cuvier been blamed?
14. Is anatomy essential to a naturalist?
15. Is there much difference between an ant, a bee, and a beetle?
16. State how these insects differ?
17. What should naturalists always have in view?
18. What are the best means to adopt to become a naturalist, or student generally?

III.—MECHANICS.

INTRODUCTORY NARRATIVE.

LESSON I.

A FEW miles from Keith, a little village in Banffshire, lived a poor man, who supported a large family by an occasional day's work, and the profits arising from the cultivation of a few acres of land which he rented; but although poor he was honest, and mindful of his duty towards his Maker. Early and late he was seen working in the fields, or busy about his house, which was situated on a high piece of ground, in the midst of groves of beautiful trees.

The country was truly picturesque, and from some points of the surrounding scenery

"The cottage chimneys, half conceal'd from view
By their embowering foliage, sent on high
Their pallid wreaths of smoke, unruffled to the sky."

Afar off, the river might be seen, like a glistening serpent, winding amidst the luxuriant trees that decked its banks.

Sometimes, when the labours of the day were not quite so severe, the father would instruct the elder children to read and write; but this was only in his leisure hours. Although his family was large, yet it was still further increased by another boy, who was born in the year 1710, and duly christened at the proper time—James Ferguson.

The history of Ferguson, written by himself, and prefixed to his *Select Mechanical Exercises*, published in 1778, (second edition,) is so instructive and interesting, that it will be better to give it in his own words.

When writing respecting the manner in which he acquired a knowledge of reading, he tells us that it was during the time his father was teaching his elder brother to read the *Scotch Catechism*.

"Ashamed to ask my father to instruct me, I used, when he and my brother were abroad, to take the Catechism, and study the lesson which he had been teaching my brother; and when any difficulty occurred, I went to a neighbouring old woman, who gave me such help as enabled me to read tolerably well before my father had thought of teaching me.

"Some time after, he was agreeably surprised to find me reading by myself; he thereupon gave me further instruction, and also taught me to write; which, with *about three months I afterwards had at the grammar school at Keith, was all the education I ever received.*

"My taste for mechanics arose from an odd accident:—When about seven or eight years of age, a part of the roof of the house being decayed, my father, desirous of mending it, applied a prop and lever to an upright spar, to raise it to its former situation; and, to my great astonishment, *I saw him, without considering the reason, lift up the ponderous roof as if it had been a small weight.* I attributed this at first to a degree of strength that excited my terror as well as wonder; but *thinking further of the matter,* I recollected that he had applied his strength to that end of the lever which was furthest from the prop; *and finding, on inquiry,* that this was the means whereby the seeming wonder was effected, *I began making levers* (which I then called bars); *and by applying weights to them different ways,* I found the power gained by my bar was just in proportion to the lengths of the different parts of the bar on either side of the prop. I then thought it was a great pity that, by means of this bar, a weight could be

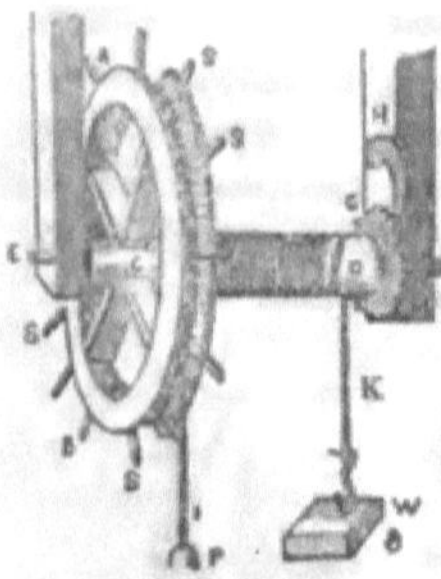

Fig. 1.

* *Fig.* 1.—"Let a b be a wheel, c d its axle, and suppose the circumference of the wheel to be eight times as great as the circumference of the axle; then, a power, p, equal to one pound, hanging by the cord i, which goes round the wheel, will balance a weight, w, of eight pounds, hanging by the rope k, which goes round the axle; and as the friction on the pivots, e f, or gudgeons of the axle is but small, a small addition to the power will cause it to descend, and raise the weight; but the weight will rise with only an eighth part of the velocity wherewith the power descends, and consequently, through no more than an eighth part of an equal space, in the same time. If the wheel be pulled round by the handles, z, g, the power will be increased in proportion to their length. g is a ratchet-wheel on one end of the axle, with a catch, h, to fall in its teeth."—*Ferguson's Lectures*, 10th *Edition*, p. 55.

raised but a very little way. On this, I soon imagined, that, by pulling round a wheel, the weight might be raised to any height by tying a rope to the weight, and winding the rope round the axle of the wheel; and that the power gained must be just as great as the wheel was broader than the axle was thick; and found it to be exactly so by hanging one weight to a rope put round the wheel, and another to the rope that coiled round the axle. So **that,** in these two machines, it appeared very plain, that their advantage was as great as the space gone through by the working power exceeded the space gone through by the weight; and this property, I also thought, must take place in a wedge for cleaving wood; but then—I happened not to think of the screw. *By means of a turning-lathe which my father had, and sometimes used, and a little knife, I was enabled to make wheels and other things necessary for my purpose.*

"I then wrote a short account of these machines, and sketched out figures of them with a pen, imagining it to be the first treatise of the kind that ever was written; but found my mistake when I afterwards showed it to a gentleman, who told me that these things were known long before, and showed me a printed book in which they were treated of; and I was much pleased when I found that my account (so far as I had carried it) agreed with the principles of mechanics in the book he showed me. And from that time my mind preserved a constant tendency to improve in that science.

"But as my father could not afford to maintain me while I was in pursuit only of these matters, and I was rather too young and weak for hard labour, he put me **out** to a neighbour to keep sheep, which I continued to do for some years; and in that time I began to study the stars in the night. *In the day-time I amused myself* **by making models** *of mills, spinning-wheels, and such other things as I happened to see.*

"I then went to serve a considerable farmer in the neighbourhood, whose **name was** James Glashan. I found him very kind and indulgent; but he soon observed that in the evenings, when my work was over, I went into **a field with a blanket about** me, lay down on my back, and stretched a thread with small beads **upon it,** at arm's length, between my eye and the stars; sliding the beads upon it till they hid such and such stars from my eye, in order to take their apparent distances from one another; and then, laying the thread down on a paper, I marked the stars thereon by the beads, according to their respective positions, having a candle by me. My master at first laughed at me; but when I explained my meaning to him, he encouraged me to go on; and that I might make fair copies in the day-time of what I had done in the night, he often worked for me himself."

One day, his master sent him with a message to the Rev. John Gilchrist, the minister at Keith, and Ferguson carried what he terms, in his Autobiography, his "star papers" with him, to show the clergyman, who was examining some maps. Mr. Gilchrist had some conversation with Ferguson, lent him a map to copy, and gave him a pair of compasses, a ruler, pens, ink, and paper for the purpose. He soon completed this **task, and** while on his way to the minister's, with the map and copy under his arm, he observed a man, named Alexander Cantley, painting a sun-dial on the wall of the school where he formerly had three months' instruction; and while staying to observe him, the schoolmaster came out, and asked Ferguson what he had under his arm. Ferguson showed him the map he had drawn, which pleased the schoolmaster very much, and the painter also praised the copy, remarking at the same time that it was a pity such a lad did not meet with notice and encouragement.

After he arrived at the minister's, and while conversing with him, a neighbouring gentleman (Thomas Grant, Esq., of Achoynaney,) called, and was so pleased with Ferguson and what he had done, that after asking him a few questions about the construction of maps, he promised that if he would go and live at his house, he would order his butler, Alexander Cantley, to instruct him. Ferguson thanked Squire Grant for his kindness, and promised, when the time of his servitude had expired, he would avail himself of the offer.

"When the term of my servitude was out," writes **Ferguson**, "I left **my** good master, and went to the gentleman's house, where I quickly **found** myself with a most humane, good family. Mr. Cantley, the butler, soon became my friend, and continued **so till his death. He** was the most extraordinary man I ever was acquainted with, or **perhaps ever shall see;** for he was a complete master of arithmetic, a good mathematician, a master of music on every known instrument except the harp, understood Latin, French, and Greek, let blood extremely well, and could even prescribe as a physician upon any urgent occasion. He was what is generally called self-taught; but, I think, he might with much greater propriety **have been** termed GOD ALMIGHTY'S scholar.

"He immediately began to teach me decimal arithmetic and **algebra;** for I had already learnt vulgar **arithmetic, at** my leisure hours, from books. **He then** proceeded to teach me the elements of geometry; but, to my inexpressible grief, just as I was beginning that branch of science, he left Mr. Grant, and went to the late Earl of Fife's, at several miles' distance. The good family **I was** then with could not prevail with me to stay after he was gone; so I left them, and went to my father's. He had made me a present of Gordon's *Geographical Grammar*, which, at that time, was to me a great treasure."

From a description contained in this book, Ferguson constructed a globe of wood—covered it with paper—delineated a map of the world upon it—and made a graduated horizon, and meridian ring of wood, covered with paper.

Finding that his father could not support him, he went into the service of a miller, who spent most of his time tippling at an ale-house, leaving the whole care of the mill to Ferguson, who was almost starved by his master, so that he was often glad to get a little oatmeal mixed with cold water to eat; and at the end of a year was obliged to return home, being **in a very weak** state from want of proper food. Having recovered his strength, his father **advised him to** go as a labouring servant to a neighbouring farmer, who practised as physician in that part of the country, telling him that the doctor had promised to instruct him. This proved a great temptation to Ferguson, who accordingly entered the doctor's service, but was so over-worked, that he was obliged to leave it at the end of three months, without receiving anything for his services, and so much disabled in his left arm and hand, that he despaired of ever recovering their use.

In his Autobiography, he complains bitterly of the conduct of Doctor Young, for not giving him any medicine while in his service, or visiting him after he left it, and attributes his recovery to some medicines sent to him by Cantley. While at his father's, in order to amuse himself, he made a wooden clock, the frame of which was also of wood; and the bell, on which the hammer struck the hours, was the neck of a broken bottle. Ferguson tells us that this clock kept time pretty well, and then adds:—
"**Having then** no idea how any time-keeper could go but by a weight and a line, I wondered **how a** watch could go in all positions; and was sorry that I had never thought of asking Mr. Cantley, who could very easily have informed me. But happening one

day to see a gentleman ride by my father's house, (which was close by a public road,) I asked him what o'clock it then was; he looked at his watch, and then told me. As he did that with so much good nature, I begged of him to show me the inside of his watch; **and** though he was an entire stranger, he immediately opened the watch, **and** put it into my hands. I saw the spring-box, with part of the chain round it, and asked him what it was that made the box turn round; he told me that it was turned round by a steel spring within it. Having then never seen any other spring than that of my father's gun-lock, I asked how a spring within a box could turn the box so often round as to wind all the chain upon it. He answered, **that** the spring was long and thin; that one end of it was fastened to the axis **of** the box, **and** the other end to the inside of the box; that the axis was fixed, and **the box was** loose upon it. I told him I did not yet thoroughly understand the **matter.** 'Well, my lad,' says he, 'take a long thin piece of whalebone, hold one **end of it** fast between your finger and thumb, and wind it round your finger; it will endeavour to unwind itself; and if you fix the other end of it to the inside of a small hoop, and leave it to itself, it will turn the hoop round and round, and wind up a thread tied to the outside of the hoop.' I thanked the gentleman, and told him I understood the thing very well."

From the scanty information he had thus acquired, Ferguson constructed a watch with wooden wheels, and made the spring of whalebone, enclosing the whole in a wooden case, very little larger than a teacup; but a clumsy neighbour, while looking at it, let the watch fall, and while endeavouring to pick it up, crushed it all to pieces **with** his foot; which discouraged him so much, that he never attempted to make such another machine again, especially as he felt convinced that he could never make one that would be of any real use.

When his strength was sufficiently restored, he carried his globe, clock, and copies of some other maps, besides that of the world, to Sir James Dunbar, of Durn, who lived about seven miles from his father's cottage. Sir James was much pleased with him, and desired that he would clean his clocks, which he did; and also painted two large globular stones that stood on the top of the gate of Sir James's house, with oil colours: the one representing a terrestrial, and the other a celestial globe. While at this house, he was introduced to Lady Dipple, sister to Sir James, and was requested to draw patterns for needle-work for her; and, soon after this, he obtained plenty of such employment from other ladies in the country; so that he was enabled, occasionally, to supply the wants of his poor father.

He still pursued his astronomical observations; and, as Sir James's house was **full** of pictures and prints, he commenced copying several of them with pen and ink; **and** by persevering, he was enabled, through the interest of Lady Dipple, to set up as **a** portrait painter in Edinburgh.

While in Edinburgh, he studied anatomy, surgery, and physic, intending to become a physician; but a visit to his **native place** put these thoughts out of his head, and he turned to portrait painting, **which he** followed for twenty-six years. He went to Inverness, and commenced his astronomical studies again; this was in 1739, the year he was **married,** a subject upon which he is remarkably silent; and, we may suppose, not without good reason, as he and his wife lived very unhappily together. It is related, that whilst Ferguson was delivering a lecture in 1770, on astronomy, before a large audience in London, his wife entered, and upset several pieces of his apparatus; but he merely looked at her, and said, "Ladies and gentlemen, I have the misfortune to be married to this woman." He made several orreries; and, in 1747, commenced publishing his works. The following year, he began to deliver lectures on astronomy, and, subsequently, on mechanics, hydrostatics, hydraulics, pneumatics, and electricity. He died in 1766, in the sixty-sixth year of his age, worth about £6,000 in property and cash, having received £50 a year from the Privy purse for many **years**. He was very properly elected a Fellow of the Royal Society for his scientific acquirements. We must acknowledge, that, however much astronomy, and the **other** branches **of** science, were indebted to his untiring perseverance and research, yet **he rendered most** essential service to **the study** of MECHANICS.

MECHANICS.

QUESTIONS AND EXPLANATIONS.

1. *T.*—WHAT **do you mean by Me**chanics?

P.—It is the Philosophy of Machinery, or the Theory of Powers or Forces, being a science which teaches us the proportion of the forces, motions, velocities, and even the actions of bodies upon one **another**, either directly or by means of machinery.

2. *T.*—What is the term mechanics derived from?

P.—From the Greek *meekanee* (Μηχανή), which signifies a machine.

3. *T.*—What do you mean by force?

P.—The power exerted on a body to **make it** change its position.

[The pupil should read **Q. 131, 132, and 133**, p. 24.]

4. *T.*—**What do you mean by a ma**chine?

P.—In **the** sense it is here employed, I mean any mechanical instrument by which force may be made **to act.**

5. *T.*—How is this accomplished?

P.—Machines can only convey the motion imparted **to** them to another body; they cannot **act of themselves**, but may regulate or modify **the** force employed, although they cannot produce it.

[Pupils should study Lesson X., p. 24, and then they will be better prepared to understand what is meant by motion, force, velocity, &c.]

6. *T.*—Explain what you mean by the term mechanical.

P.—Mechanical action is the result of the application of power or force acting upon a body. For example [Experiment 1], if I rub a metal button upon a brick for some time, **the** metal is reduced in thickness by the mechanical action of the particles of brick; again, [Experiment 2] if a tin can, with a small hole in the bottom of it, is filled with water, and placed about two feet above the brick we have just used, and allowed to remain there for some time, **the water** will act mechanically upon the **brick, and wear it away.**

7. *T.*—**Have not** some philosophers divided the science of mechanics, or as Dr. Wallis terms it, the " Geometry of motion," into two parts?

P.—Yes, into STATICS and DYNAMICS; but it is better to consider the subject as a whole, and not adopt this mode of dividing it.

8. *T.*—What is meant by Statics, and what is the term derived from?

P.—Statics is the doctrine of the equi**librium** of forces, and the term is derived **from** the Greek verb *stao* (Στάω), to stand.

9. *T.*—What is the word Dynamics derived from, and what is its signification?

P.—It is derived from the Greek word *dunamis* (Δύναμις), force or power, and literally means the theory of force and power.

10. *T.*—When **we** have to apply a machine, what are **the** chief things to be considered?

P.—1. The force which we have to overcome, sustain, **or** oppose. 2. The force which will enable us to overcome, sustain, or oppose the resisting force. 3. The machine by which the desired effect is produced, by transmitting the requisite force or power to the resisting force.

11. *T.*—What name has been given to the force we have to overcome, sustain, or oppose—or, in other words, the body which receives the power?
P.—It is technically termed the *weight*.

12. *T.*—Why is it called the weight?
P.—Because we can always obtain a weight of equivalent effect.

13. *T.*—What is the force which is employed to overcome, oppose, or sustain, termed?
P.—It is technically called the *power*, and communicates motion to the body.

14. *T.*—Then you would imply that the power sustains the weight.
P.—It is usual to say so, but this is not actually the case, because it is quite impossible for the power of an ounce to support the weight of two thousand pounds. We know it cannot do so, yet by employing a machine it *appears* to do so.

15. *T.*—How can you account for this?
P.—Every machine has certain fixed points, and it is so managed or contrived that the pressure caused by the applied weight or power, or both, shall be thrown upon the fixed points of the machine. It can be so arranged that the greater part of the weight shall be distributed among the fixed points, and that the remaining part shall not be greater than the power employed can sustain. Therefore we can now understand how one ounce *appears* to support two thousand pounds, and when we learn more about mechanic powers this **will be** more easily understood.

16. *T.*—What do you mean by mechanic powers?
P.—The **most** simple machines or instruments are termed the MECHANIC POWERS, which are, strictly speaking, only three in number: 1, the *Lever*; 2, the *Pulley* or *Cord*; 3, the *Inclined Plane*. All simple machines belong to one or other of these classes; and all complex machines, however large, are only made up of parts which are simple in themselves, and come under these three mechanic powers.

17. *T.*—Have these powers received any particular name from philosophers?
P.—Yes; they are called the **Primary** *Mechanical Powers*, from which all the rest are derived.

18. *T.*— **How** many other **mechanic** powers are there?
P.—Three: 1. The *wheel* and *axle*, derived from the *Lever*. 2. The *wedge*, from the *Inclined Plane*. 3. The *screw*, from the *Inclined Plane*.

19. *T.*—What are these powers called?
P.—The *Secondary Mechanical Powers*.

20. *T.*—How many mechanic **powers** are there?
P.—Three Primary and three Secondary; in all, six, from which are derived the elements of every kind of machinery.

GENERAL QUESTIONS ON **LESSON I.**

1. Explain what is meant by Mechanics.
2. What is the derivation of the word Mechanics?
3. What is a machine?
4. Explain the difference between mechanics and mechanical.
5. How has the science of Mechanics been divided by some philosophers?
6. Explain the meanings and derivations of the terms statics and dynamics.
7. What are the necessary things to bear in mind in the application of machines?
8. Define the terms weight and power.
9. What are mechanic powers, and **how** many are there?
10. How **are** the mechanic **powers** divided?

LESSON II.

FERGUSON is an admirable example for us all. The young should endeavour to imitate his zeal for study, his observing habits, humility, and perseverance; and the more aged, to avoid falling into some of his errors, and that love of *practical knowledge only*, which some persons extol so highly. In Ferguson's case, it was his misfortune, rather than his fault, to be an empirical mechanic: but, in the present age of cheap scientific literature, those who reject the theoretical part of mechanics altogether, have only themselves to blame. Dr. Playfair, in contrasting **theory** and practice, thus happily expresses himself:—" For a long time practice, standing still in the pride of empiricism, and in the ungrateful forgetfulness of what science **had** done in its development, reared upon its portal the **old** and vulgar adage, 'An **ounce** of practice **is** worth **a ton of theory.**' This wretched inscription acted like a Gorgon's head, and **turned to stone** the aspirations of science. Believe it not; for a grain of theory—if that **be an expression for science**—will, when planted, like the mustard-seed **of Scripture**, grow and **wax into the greatest of trees.** The pressure and difficulties **of the age, and the** rapid **advancement** of intellect in continental nations, have been the Perseus to cut off this **Medusa's** head from the industry **of** England, and to fix it on the shield of **Minerva,** who turns to stone such as still believe that science should be ignored by practice; **but,** reversing that **shield, wisely conducts those** who would go further under her guidance. It is **now** rare to find men who **openly** avow, although they actually entertain a belief in, a necessary antagonism between theory and practice. Theory is, in fact, the rule, and practice its example. Theory is but the **attempt** to furnish an intelligent explanation of that which is empirically ascertained to **be true,** and is always useful, **even when wrong. Theories are** the leaves of the tree of science, drawing nutriment to the parent stem **while they last, and, by their fall and** decay, affording materials for the new leaves which **are to succeed.**"

Ferguson saw his father **lift up the** ponderous roof **by means of a lever, and he tells us,** that *he did not consider* the reason, but that the fact **terrified him;** however, he goes on to relate, that he *thought further* **on the matter,** and inquired **if the theory he had** built up was well founded. To his great satisfaction, he discovered **that his ideas were correct.** How few children there are, even at double his age, that would have thought **further** of the matter, and inquired! Many grown-up people would have observed and **passed on,** without considering anything about the matter; and if they had, their false pride, in all probability, would have prevented them making any inquiries. Ferguson did not stop here, he commenced making experiments **with levers,** applying weights to them in different ways, and endeavouring **to** prove, practically, **that** which he believed theoretically. His experiments were successful**; and,** therefore, all that he knew was not like the knowledge acquired by **those who** make learning a labour—he knew what had cost him so much trouble **to** learn, **thoroughly,** theoretically, and practically.

QUESTIONS.

21. *T.*—What is **a Lever?**

P.—An inflexible **straight bar, or rod** of any material, which **turns on an axis, is** usually termed a lever. **It is one of the** most useful and extensively **employed mechan**ical powers.

22. *T.*—What is the principle **of the** lever founded on ?

P.—The theory of equilibrium, like that of all mechanic powers.

23. *T.*—What things have **we to con**sider as essential to the constitution of a lever ?

P.—Three: 1. The *power.* 2. The *fulcrum.* 3. The *weight.*

24. *T.*— What do you mean by the *fulcrum ?*

P.—It is the axis upon, or about which, the lever moves, and is generally termed the prop, but is technically termed the fulcrum.

25. *T.*—What is the use of the lever ?

P.—It enables us to overcome a **resistance, or move a weight, bearing on** one point, by **applying a** power to another.

26. *T.*—What are the parts of a **lever on** either side of the fulcrum called?
P.—The *arms.*

27. *T.*—**How many kinds of levers** are there?
P.—Three, which **vary** according **to** the relative situation **of the power,** fulcrum, and weight.

28. *T.*—**How are these levers distin**guished?
P.—Into **a** lever of the *first kind,* where **the** fulcrum **is** placed between the power and the weight; a lever of the *second kind,* where **the** weight is between the fulcrum and the power; and a lever of the *third kind,* where the power is placed between the fulcrum and the weight. *Fig.* **2 is an** example of a lever of the first kind. **A B**

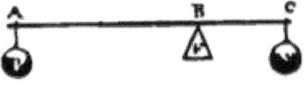

Fig. 2.

is termed the long arm of the **lever, and** B C its short arm. P represents **some** force, **such** as a hand drawing down the end **of the** long arm at A, and, as the **force** or power (P), is supposed to be weak **or** small compared with the resistance or weight (W), **the** long arm must **have a greater relative** length than the **one to which the weight** is attached.

29. *T.*—Give me some examples of levers of the first **kind.**
P.—When **a poker is** inserted between the bars **of the fire-grate to** raise the coals, we have **a** familiar **example** of a lever of this class. (*Fig.* 3.) **When** we use **a pin** to remove a periwinkle from its **shell, we** employ a lever of the first kind, **the** pin being the lever, and the shell the fulcrum. The brake of a pump is **a lever of the same** class, the piston and **the pump-rods being** the weight to be **raised, and the ful-**

crum, the point on which **it turns.** A common claw-hammer, employed to raise

Fig. 3.*

nails, is **a lever of the** first class; but, **in** this case, **the line of direction** of the power is perpendicular to **the** resistance. All instruments for cutting or holding, which are composed of two pieces crossing each other in the middle, **such** as scissors, shears, pincers, pliers, nippers, &c., are familiar examples; the pivot or **joint** being the fulcrum, **the resistance or weight the paper, grass,** &c. **to be cut or seized, and the power applied by the hand.** A common crowbar, **applied to** raise **stones or other** weights, **is another familiar** example; **the** fulcrum being **another stone** placed near to the one to be **raised, and** the power the man's hands **who raises it.** [See *Frontispiece.*]

Fig. 4.†

30. *T.*—Are levers always straight?
P.—No; they are sometimes curved, as in *Fig.* 5. The same advantage cannot be

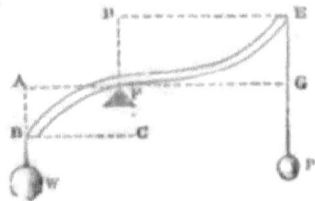

Fig. 5.‡

derived from **a bent lever as from** a straight

---

* *Fig.* 2.—A, the poker, or *lever;* B, the bar, or *fulcrum;* C, the coals, or *weight;* and D, the hand, or *power.*

† *Fig.* 4.—*a,* the hand, or *power;* n, the nail, or *resistance;* and *f,* the *fulcrum.*

‡ *Fig.* 5.—B E, a *curved lever,* supported by the *fulcrum* F. The *weight* W, is attached to B; and the *power* P, to E.

one of the same length. Let B E represent a curved lever, which is supported at F, having the weight (W) attached at B, and the power (P) applied at E. If we wish to find the momentum of the weight, we have only to multiply its weight by the ideal lines A F, or B C; and the momentum of power will be found by multiplying its weight by the ideal lines D E, or F G.

[See Q. 137 and 138, p. 25.]

31. *T.*—What you have stated leads me to suppose that levers do not always act in the same direction. Is this the case?

P.—Yes. All straight levers are supposed to have their powers or forces acting at right angles with them; but bent levers act obliquely, and not at right angles, which is the reason bent levers are not so advantageous as straight ones, because the obliquity in their action diminishes the **mechanical gain**.

32. *T.*—How is the mechanical advantage of the power and weight of a lever described?

P.—By a line drawn from the fulcrum, at right angles to the direction in the which the forces are respectively acting.

GENERAL QUESTIONS ON LESSON II.

1. What is the difference between theory and practice?
2. What is a lever?
3. What **is** essentially necessary **in a** lever?
4. Describe what is meant by a fulcrum?
5. What is the use of levers; and how many kinds of levers are there?
6. Describe and give examples of levers of the first kind.
7. How do levers of the first, second, and third class differ?
8. How is the advantage of the power and weight of a lever represented?

LESSON III.

FERGUSON tried many experiments with levers, to prove that the theories he had constructed were correct. It would be well for us, if we always followed his example in this respect. He applied weights to the levers in various ways, and was thus enabled to determine the advantages gained or lost. We must examine the principles of the lever experimentally, and endeavour to establish facts. One thing must always be borne in mind, that *what is gained in power is lost in velocity;* we cannot create either power or velocity; but we may substitute the one for the other.

QUESTIONS.

33. *T.*—Why is the power applied **at a** greater distance from the fulcrum of a lever, than that at which the weight bears?

P.—In order to overcome the resistance more effectually.

34. *T.*—Suppose that a pole, twelve feet long, resting in the centre upon a block of wood, is used as a lever, and that a weight of ten pounds is placed at each end, what will be the effect?

P.—Provided the pole is of uniform gravity, it will remain in a state of equilibrium, or in other words, it will be balanced; but if one end of the pole is heavier than the other, it will descend, and the lighter end be driven upwards.

35. *T.*—If one weight is removed, and a four pound weight placed there instead, the fulcrum being situated nearer to the ten pound weight than to the lesser one, what will be the effect?

P.—Possibly the same; because it will depend upon how near the fulcrum is placed. For example; if a weight of twenty pounds is placed on the short arm of a lever, at the distance of six inches from the fulcrum, it will require a weight of six pounds to be placed twenty inches from the fulcrum, to balance it.

36. *T.*—How do you know that this is correct?

P.—By experiment and calculation; besides, it is a general rule, that *the force of the lever increases in proportion as the dis-*

tance *of the power from the fulcrum increases, and diminishes in proportion as the distance of the weight from the fulcrum diminishes.*

37. *T.*—How can we find out, by calculation, the requisite power to employ?

P.—We must first of all establish certain points, and then act by rule. The points are—1. The respective lengths of the long and short arms of the lever. 2. The units of weight and distance.

38. *T.*—What do you mean by the units of weight and distance?

P.—If we fix ounces or pounds, or any other weight as the unit of the short arm of the lever, we *must* fix the unit of power of the long arm the same; and if we make the unit of distance of the short arm to be an inch, we *must* have inches as the units of length of the long arm.

39. *T.*—What is the rule you mentioned?

P.—A very simple one. Multiply the weight by its distance from the fulcrum; and multiply the power by its distance from the same point; if the products are equal, the weight and power will counteract each other.

[See Q. 35, above.]

40. *T.*—You have not told me yet how to calculate the power we must employ at the long arm of a lever, to balance a known weight attached to the short arm.

P.—That is easily done. Multiply the weight by the length of the short arm, and divide the product by the number of inches in the long arm, and the result is the power required. For example; a weight of 20 pounds, multiplied by 12 inches, (the length of the short arm,) gives us 240 as the product; now, if we divide 240 by 24, (which is the length of the long arm,) we shall have a quotient or result of 10, which is the number of pounds we must employ; therefore, it is evident, that the mechanical advantage is two to one, because the weight is twice that of the power.

41. *T.*—If we wish to use a lever to overcome a resistance, which is preferable, a long one or a short one?

P.—A short one; because it has to traverse a smaller space than the long one, and, consequently, does not fatigue the body so much.

42. *T.*—It is said to be a rule, *that a small weight, descending a long way in any given length of time, is equal in effect to a great weight descending a proportionally shorter way in the same space of time.* Will you give me an example of this, and state if it is correct?

P.—It is quite true; and it is on this principle that the see-saw acts. In this diagram we see that two boys are amusing themselves **with** a plank, which is balanced

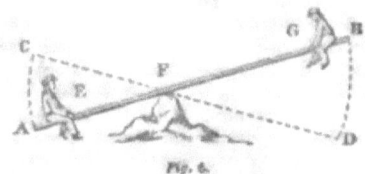

Fig. 6.

on a stone. The plank A B, is a **lever of the first class,** of which the stone F **is the** fulcrum. As the boy E is heavier **than** the boy G, it is necessary to place **him** nearer to the fulcrum. It is **easy to see** that the lighter **boy** traverses a greater space from B to D, than the heavy boy from C to A. Let us suppose that E represents a weight of ten pounds, **and** that G represents **a power of one** pound. If the power is **depressed to D, the** weight will be raised to C; **the space B D** bears the same proportion to C A, as the arm B F to A F. Therefore, if the B F is ten times A F, B D will be ten times C A, which proves that when the power G, of one pound, moves through ten inches, the weight E, of ten pounds, is only raised one inch.

43. *T.*—What does this prove?

P.—That the power expended is equal to the resistance overcome, which is the cause of my saying that it requires ten pounds of power to raise a weight of ten pounds; and that the machine was enabled to overcome this resistance with a small **power** by a succession of distinct efforts instead of only one.

44. *T.*—Can you give me a familiar example of the useful application of this knowledge?

P.—Yes; the common steelyard furnishes an example, when a small weight is made to sustain a large one. A lever is movable upon its pivot or fulcrum at *a*, while a scale is suspended at *c*, to receive the weight *b*, acting upon the arm *a c*, and this is kept in equilibrium by a movable weight *p*, on the other arm of the lever. As the weight *p* can **be slipped along the lever to any required point, it follows that the**

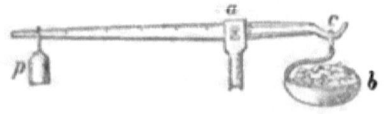

Fig. 7.

heavier the weight is, the further **must the movable weight be placed from the fulcrum** *a*, in order to balance the weight.

The common scale-beam **for weighing** is another example of this class, **and is** generally prefered to the steelyard, because the subdivision **of weights is more precise.**

GENERAL **QUESTIONS ON** LESSON III.

1. Why is **one arm of a** lever usually **longer than the other?**
2. **When a lever is** balanced in its centre, **and equal weights placed** at either end, **what takes place?**
3. **Give me a rule, to** prove that power **increases and diminishes** with distance.
4. **How can we calculate** the proper **power we require to employ?**
5. **Explain what is meant by units of weight and distance.**
6. **Why is a** short lever generally **better than a long one?**
7. **Explain how a see-saw acts.**
8. **Explain the principle of the** steel**yard.**

LESSON IV.

SUPPOSE that a line passed round a pulley, to the end of which a weight *p* was attached, and that some force was acting in the direction *a b*, equal to the weight *p*. By the

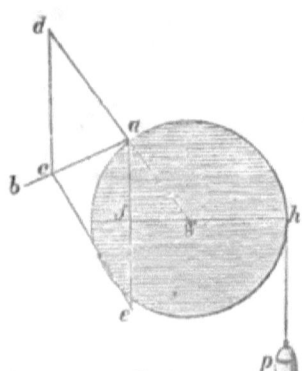

Fig. 8.

theory of the parallelogram of forces, we are enabled to decompose the forces meeting at *a*, and acting in the direction *a b*, into lateral forces; one of which acts in the direction of *d* from *a*, being a prolongation of the direction of the radius *g a*, while the direction of the other force *a e* is parallel with *h p*. If the pulley is fixed, the action of the force *a d* will be counteracted by the resistance, altogether, of the central point *g*; we may therefore take away the component force which is acting in the direction *a d* without disturbing the equilibrium; and we may replace the active force *a b*, by its component force acting in the direction *a e*. If the line *a c* represent the force *p* acting in the direction *a b*, then the line *a e*, will give the amount of the component force *P*, (*Fig.* 9) and without working out the relations of size between *a c* and *a e*, or *p* and *P*, we can easily see that *P* is larger than *p*. Therefore, without **disturbing the equilibrium, we may replace the force *p*,** acting in the direction *a b* by another **force *P*, acting at *a* in a vertical instead** of a lateral direction. Suppose that, instead of **the force *P* being allowed to act directly at** *a*, we make it act in any part of the line *a e*, we shall **find that the equilibrium will** not be disturbed. For example, let the force *P* act **at the point *f* in the line *a e*,** where it is intersected by the line *h g*, and we shall then **find that we have two rectangular** forces *p* and *P* in a state of equilibrium, at the ends of the line *f h* revolving round *g*, as in *Fig.* 9. The two forces **are unequal, as** their respective points **of action at *f*** and *h* are at unequal distances from the fulcrum g. We must now find out the relation which exists between the size of the forces p and P, and the lengths hg and fg. It will be seen that the triangles cae in Fig. 8, and afg are similar to each other, and therefore ac and ae are equal to fg and ag, and the lengths ac and ae are to each other as the forces p and P, consequently we may say that these forces bear an inverse ratio to the distances of their points of action from the fulcrum g. We can now see that a lever does revolve round a fixed point, as at g in Fig. 9.

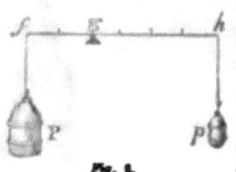

Fig. 8.

QUESTIONS.

45. *T.*—What is meant by the *static moment* of a force?

P.—It is the product obtained by multiplying the force by the arm of the lever, being that force which, acting at an arm of one unit on the opposite side of the fulcrum, shall preserve the state of equilibrium.

46. *T.*—Explain this more fully.

P.—If we suppose that the force to the right of Fig. 9 is equal to 6, and the arm of the lever equal to 4, the static moment of the force will be 4 multiplied by 6, or 24; then if the force on the left hand is to be in a state of equilibrium with the former, the static moment of the two must be equal, and the force acting on the left side of an arm equal to 2 must have a weight of 12.

47. *T.*—What do you mean by a lever of the second kind?

P.—It is a lever which has the weight placed between the fulcrum and the power.

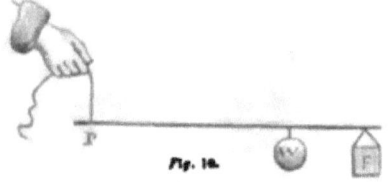

Fig. 10.

A familiar example of this kind of lever is a common wheelbarrow, the fulcrum being the point at which the wheel presses on the ground, the weight being the barrow and its load, while the power is represented by the two handles which the man lifts, and in proportion as he lengthens or shortens his hold on the handles, so is the power greater or less. [See *Frontispiece*.]

48. *T.*—Give me some other familiar examples of a lever of the second class.

P.—The oar which urges a boat forward is an excellent example; the blade forced against the water is the fulcrum, the boat the weight, and the man's hands the power. The rudder of a ship acts in the same manner. When we open a door, the hinge is the fulcrum, the air the resistance, and the person opening it the power. If we crack a nut we use two levers of the second kind, the hinge which keeps them together forming the fulcrum, the nut the resistance or weight, and the hand the power. The old sugar-chopper used by grocers is a very

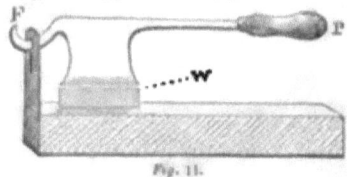

Fig. 11.

good example of a lever of this kind; the hinge being the fulcrum, the sugar the resistance or weight, and the handle the power. When a crowbar is placed underneath a stone, and the end of the bar raised, it becomes a lever of the second kind, the end resting on the ground being the fulcrum, the stone the resistance, and the upward movement of the man's hand the power. Two men carrying a sedan-chair is another example, each man forming the moving power and fulcrum with respect to each other, while the weight is the chair.

49. *T.*—What is meant by a one-armed lever?

P.—It is a lever which has one end fixed, and two forces acting in opposite directions on the same side of the fulcrum.

50. *T.*—Can you give me an example of this kind of lever?

P.—In this diagram we shall see that it has been applied to the boiler of a steam-engine. The valve p, which covers and closes the opening of the boiler, is forced up by the pressure of the steam, but this

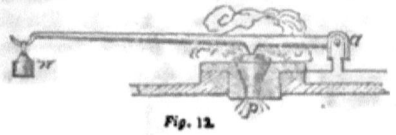

Fig. 12.

pressure is balanced by a smaller force (the weight w, which acts downwards), because it acts at a longer arm than the pressure on the under surface of the valve. In this case the fixed point of the lever a is the fulcrum.

51. *T.*—What is meant by a lever of the third kind?

P.—It is a lever with the power placed between the fulcrum and the weight or resistance (*Fig.* 13). The fulcrum is placed at the extremity of the short arm, at

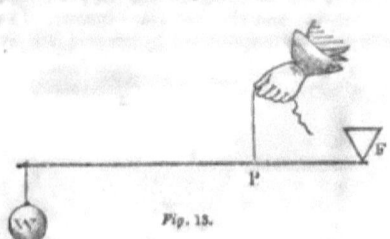

Fig. 13.

F; the weight w is suspended from the end of the long arm; and the power, P, is placed between them.

52. *T.*—Is this form of lever advantageous or not?

P.—What is lost in power is gained in velocity; therefore it is advantageous for some purposes, because a small power will cause the long arm of the lever to move over a great space.

53. *T.*—How is it that you tell me that power is lost in this kind of lever; and then say, that a small power will cause the long arm to move with greater velocity?

P.—I spoke comparatively, because we know that a greater power must be actually required than would be the case if the power was applied directly to the weight; and therefore this kind of lever is not used to overcome resistance, but to move a weight with great speed, or else for some particular purpose.

54. *T.*—Give me some familiar examples of levers of this kind.

P.—The treddle of a turning-lathe is one of the most common, the end which rests on the floor is the fulcrum; the foot of the man, which presses on the board near to the fulcrum, is the power; and the crank upon the axis of the fly-wheel, which is attached to the other end, is the weight. A man using a flail with two hands is another example. But the most interesting examples of the application of such levers are to be found in the structure of animals, particularly the arm and forearm of man;

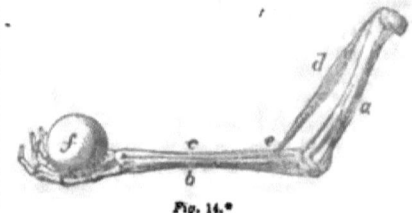

Fig. 14.*

and, although there is a mechanical disadvantage in the action of the *biceps*, yet there is a corresponding increase in velocity. The lower jaw also furnishes us

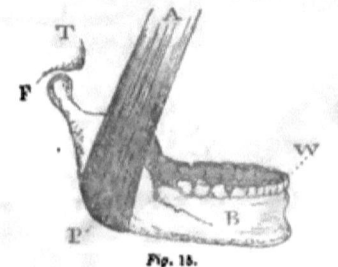

Fig. 15.

with an excellent example of the force exerted by muscular action, which, at times, cannot be less than three hundred pounds in man, and even more in large animals. Fig. 15 shows the arrangement of this kind of lever; A represents the *masseter* muscle,

---

* *Fig.* 14.—*a*, the *humerus*, or arm-bone; *b, c*, bones of the forearm; *d*, the muscle which bends the forearm, called *biceps flexor cubiti*, and is inserted at *e* into the posterior part of the tubercle of the *radius c*; and *f*, the weight.

which chiefly causes this force, and is attached to the lower jaw, B, at P. The fulcrum, F, is formed by the *condyle* or end of the bone, which rests against the temporal bone, T, while the weight or resistance is at W.

55. *T.*—Give me some examples of compound levers of the third class.

P.—A pair of shears, such as are used for shearing sheep, and a pair of tongs, are familiar examples. In both cases the action is the same; and here is a diagram

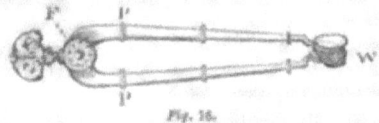

Fig. 16.

of a pair of tongs which will illustrate this. F is the fulcrum; P P, the parts where we lay hold of the tongs, represents the power; and the coal, W, is the weight or resistance.

GENERAL QUESTIONS ON LESSON IV.

1. Give an explanation of the decomposition of the forces acting upon a lever, by means of the theory of the parallelogram of forces, and explain how equilibrium is maintained.
2. Explain the meaning of the static moment of the force of a lever.
3. Define **a lever** of the second kind.
4. Give some **examples of levers of the** second class.
5. What do you mean by a one-armed lever?
6. Explain how a one-armed lever acts.
7. Define a lever of the third kind.
8. Is there any advantage to be gained in using levers of the third class?
9. Give some examples of third-class levers.
10. Are levers of the third class single or compound?

LESSON V.

If we wish to have a very long lever, or one possessing great mechanical power, it is easier to arrange a series of levers, so that the power acting on **the end of** the first lever shall raise the second, and that, depressing the end **of** the third, will raise a weight at the further end. For example, suppose that we wished to balance 1000 pounds by means of one pound, the distance of the power from the fulcrum must be 1000 times that of the weight, and as this would be very inconvenient, we employ three levers for the purpose of obtaining the same result. The relative length of the arms of each lever **is as ten** to one; and if we examine *Fig.* 17, we shall see that the levers are so **arranged, as to bear** upon one another. Thus, the power of one pound will balance the

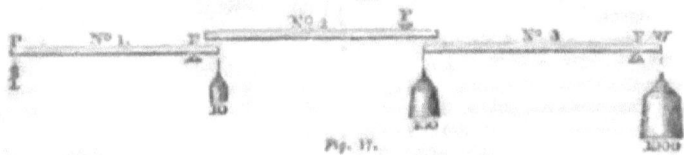

Fig. 17.

weight of ten pounds; and as the weight end of the first lever is placed under the power end of the second lever, it will exercise a force of ten pounds upon it. The second lever, being raised with a force of ten pounds, and having the same mechanical advantage as the first, will press down the weight end upon the power end of the third, with a force equal to 100 pounds. This force of 100 pounds, being applied to the power end of the third lever, will act upon the same principles as the others, and raise the weight end with a force of 1000 pounds.

In calculating the action of any compound system of levers, it does not affect the principles of calculation if some of the levers are of the first kind, and some of any other. The rule is, to "multiply the weight on any lever by its distance from the fulcrum, and multiply the power by its distance from the same **point;** if the products are equal, then the weight and power will balance each **other.**" **If we wish** to calculate the effect of the system given in *Fig.* 17, we must multiply **the length** of the long arm **by the power, and** multiply the short arm by the weight or resistance offered.

QUESTIONS.

56. *T.*—What is a *compound lever?*
P.—It is a lever composed of several simple levers connected together, so **as to** act one upon the other.

57. *T.*—How can the force of **a** compound lever be regulated?
P.—Very easily; because, as each lever acts with **a** power equal to the pressure on it of the **next lever** between it and the power, the **force may** be increased or decreased by **the kind of levers** employed, and their number.

58. *T.*—How can **you determine the** advantages of a compound **lever formed of** any number of levers?
P.—We must, first of all, call the **arms of** the various levers next to the power, *arms of power;* and those next to the weight, *arms of weight;* then we shall have prepared the way. Now, if the length of the arms **of** power and the **power** itself be successively multiplied **together,** we shall obtain **a** product equal **to the** continued product of the arms **of weight** and the weight, **when the power and weight are in** equilibrium.

59. *T.*—**What do you mean by the** *power of a machine?*
P.—It is the number which represents the proportion of the weight to the equilibrating power **of any machine.** Thus, if one pound sustains **a weight of** six pounds, the power of the machine **is** *six.* Again, if a power of three pounds supports a weight of eighteen pounds, **the** power of the machine is *six,* because 3 **is** contained in 18 only six times.

60. *T.*—There is one important thing that **we should** consider in all our experiments with respect to the lever—the weight of the **lever itself. Can** you tell me if this makes any **great** difference in its **effect?**

P.—If the centre of gravity of the **lever** be in the vertical line through the axis, its weight will only increase the pressure on the axis by its own amount, without causing **any** other effect.

61. *T.*—Suppose that the centre of gravity **of the lever be** on the same side of the axis as the weight, what will be the effect then?
P.—It will oppose **the** effect of the power; and, therefore, **a** certain amount of power must be allowed **for** its support.

62. *T.*—How can this amount of **power** be estimated?
P.—**By common** calculation. First, you find the moment of the weight of the lever collected at its centre of gravity, which **is** done by multiplying that weight by the distance from the centre of gravity to the fulcrum; therefore, we know that the moment of that part of the power which supports it, because it must be equal to it. Now we have only to find **out how much** of the power, multiplied by **double the** distance from its centre of **gravity to** the fulcrum, will be equal to the **weight of** the lever multiplied by the **distance from** the fulcrum to the centre of gravity.

63. *T.*—Suppose that the centre of gravity **of** the lever be at a different side of **the** axis from the weight, what will be the effect then?
P.—The weight **of the** lever will assist the power in sustaining the weight.

64. *T.*—How can you determine the amount of the weight thus sustained?
P.—Find out how much of the weight, multiplied by the distance from the weight to the fulcrum, is equal to the weight of the lever multiplied by the distance from the centre of gravity to the fulcrum.

GENERAL QUESTIONS ON LESSON V.

1. How should we act when a lever is required to possess very great mechanical power?
2. How is the action of a **system** of levers calculated?
3. What is a compound lever?
4. Is the power of a compound lever capable of being increased or diminished?
5. Explain what is meant by the power of a machine.
6. State how the variation in the centre of gravity of a lever affects its action.

LESSON VI.

THERE cannot be a doubt that science is vastly indebted to the lever, but yet its use is limited, **and its** action intermitting; and, therefore, **we must look** for further mechanical **assistance,** and, fortunately, we have not much trouble in obtaining it. You remember that Ferguson tried many experiments with levers; and then he thought that, by pulling round a wheel, the weight might be raised to any height by tying a rope to the weight, and winding the rope round the axle of the wheel; and, when he tried the effect of his theory, he found that it was correct. GRANDFATHER WHITEHEAD wishes his pupils to imitate Ferguson, **and make** some machines for themselves, and **try the** mechanical experiments he is going to perform for them. Ferguson **tells us**

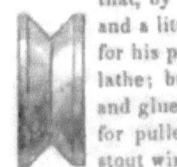

Fig. 18.

that, by means of a turning-lathe which his father had, and sometimes used, and a little knife, he was enabled to make wheels, and other things necessary for his purpose. It is not every one that can avail themselves **of a** turning-lathe; but they may get some old cotton reels, and, by sawing off **the two** ends and glueing them together (as in the annexed diagram,) very tolerable wheels for pulleys may be made; and by means of them, a few pieces of board, some stout wire, a pair of pliers, a knife, and a saw, **many** excellent *temporary blocks* may be constructed. In the frontispiece **is an** illustration of a man drawing a bucket up a well. The principle **is the** same **as the** *wheel and axle,* although the example is only one of the many varieties of this mechanical appliance, which possesses **so** many important advantages.

QUESTIONS.

65. *T.*—What is *the wheel and axle?*

P.—A more complicated form of the lever, **consisting** of a wheel or large flat cylinder, **with a** smaller cylinder passing through its centre, which has received the name of axle.

66. *T.*—Is the **wheel fixed to the axle,** or not?

P.—The wheel is sometimes fixed to its axle, so that both may move together about the same centre, and sometimes it turns **on** its axle; but we must not consider the wheel and axle as belonging to the latter variety in the **present** instance.

67. *T.*—**Has this** machine ever received any other name?

P.—Yes, it has sometimes been called "the perpetual lever," and sometimes the *Axis in Peritrochio.*

68. *T.*—Did you not tell me that a lever moved upon or about a fulcrum, or a fixed axis?

P.—Yes; and I have given **you** many examples to prove that it **moves** upon or about a fulcrum; and shall now **be** able to show that it moves about a fixed axis

Fig. 19.

[Experiment 3]. Take a straight piece of wood, bore a hole in its centre (*a*), and insert a piece of wire into the hole. If you push one end down (*b*) with your right hand, taking care to hold the wire fast with the other, you will cause the opposite end (*c*) to be raised, and *vice versâ*. Now, this is just the principle on which the wheel acts.

69. *T.*—How can a wheel act like the straight piece of wood?

P.—We have only to call the parts by other names, and you will immediately see that it is so. Let us call the wire at *a* the fulcrum, or fixed axis, and *b c* the arms of the lever; we shall now have two arms, spokes, or radii of a wheel, and we have only to multiply or increase the number, and we shall then increase the leverage, as in the case of the wheel by which a vessel is steered.

70. *T.*—What do you mean by the periphery of a wheel?

P.—It is the circumference or rim; the name being derived from two Greek words, *peri* (περι) about; and *fero* (φερο) I carry.

71. *T.*—What do you mean by the radii of a wheel?

P.—They are the spokes or arms, which radiate from a centre; therefore that part of a wheel which is situated between the centre and the circumference is said to be a radius. If we draw a line directly through the circle or circumference of a wheel, so as to touch both its sides, it is called the diameter, which is nothing more than two radii or semi-diameters joined together in the same line of direction. All the radii or spokes of a wheel are kept together in the centre by a cylindrical piece of wood, which serves as the common fulcrum for all the wheel, and at the circumference by the rim.

72. *T.*—Have all wheels their axes in the centre?

P.—No, some have not, and are called eccentric wheels; but we must leave the consideration of them for another time.

73. *T.*—What is the usual arrangement of a wheel and axle?

P.—The wheel is fixed to an axle or spindle, which revolves horizontally on its two ends, which are supported in some manner (usually by upright pieces of wood), and around this axle is coiled the rope, which sustains the weight, while the periphery of the wheel has another rope coiled round it, in a contrary direction, with the power suspended to it. [See *Fig.* 1, and description in foot note.]

74. *T.*—What is the fulcrum of the wheel and axle?

P.—The centre of the axle, which is common to the whole machine.

75. *T.*—How does the machine act?

P.—When the wheel revolves, of course the axle does the same; and as the rope is fixed to the axle, with the weight hanging at its end, it is wound round the axle, and so raises the weight.

76. *T.*—How can you balance this machine, or produce an equilibrium?

P.—By proportioning the two powers to the diameter of the wheel and the axle, so that the one power or weight may be made to balance the other power or weight. Suppose that the machine is made to move rapidly, it will then be found that the velocity of the power will be to that of the weight as the circumference of the wheel is to that of the axle; because it is quite clear that the power must sink through a space equal to the circumference of the wheel, before it can raise the weight through a space equal to the circumference of the axle. Now that we know this much, we have next to find the momentum, which is done by multiplying its velocity and weight together. It is therefore evident, that if the number of inches of the circuit of the wheel, multiplied by the number of pounds in the power, produce a sum equal to the product of the measure of the axle multiplied by the number of pounds in the weight, the machine will remain in a state of equilibrium.

77. *T.*—What does the effect of the wheel depend upon?

P.—The superiority of the radius, or diameter of the wheel to that of the axle. In *Fig.* 20, we observe that the weight (T) corresponds to the counteracting force (P) in an inverse ratio to the arms of the lever; that is, inversely to the radii (A B, and D C) of the wheel. Let us suppose that the radius (A B) of the axle, is four times less than the radius (D C) of the wheel, we may equipoise a weight of eighty pounds by a force of twenty pounds.

78. *T.*—Give me some examples of the

useful application of the principle of the wheel and axle.

P.—The *capstan* is, perhaps, the most useful of this class, and only differs from the windlass in having its revolving axis

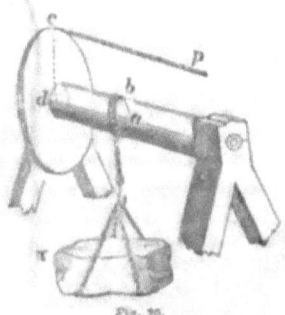

Fig. 20.

placed vertically. The circumference is pierced with holes, which receive long levers, by which it is worked by men, who walk round the capstan, and make it revolve by pressing the ends of the levers forward. The *tread-mill* is another variety. In this case the weight of several people treading on the circumference of a long wheel, causes it to revolve. The *paddle-wheel of a steam-boat* acts on the same principle; the water, which offers a resistance to the motion of the paddle-boards, is the power.

79. *T.*—Does it not sometimes happen that these machines will stop for a short time, and cause the weight to recoil?

P.—Yes; but, in order to prevent the recoil, it is usual to have a wheel, called a *ratchet wheel*, fixed to the axle (see Fig. 1), so as to allow it to turn in one direction; and, in order to prevent it going back, there is a catch placed at the side, which falls into the space between the teeth, and prevents the recoil.

80. *T.*—If we make a wheel larger in circumference, what will be the effect?

P.—It will lengthen the long arm of the lever, consequently we shall not require so great a power to overcome the weight on the short arm or axle.

81. *T.*—If this be the case, do we not gain by adopting this plan?

P.—No. We certainly gain a little as far as mechanical advantage is concerned; but then we lose it again, because the power has to descend through a proportionably greater space, in order to raise the weight through the same space in the same amount of time.

82. *T.*—Can you tell me how the very great inconvenience of having a large wheel on a very slender axle may be avoided, without diminishing the mechanical advantage?

P.—Yes; by employing a machine, which is called the Chinese wheel and axle, because it was introduced into this country from China. It consists of two cylinders,

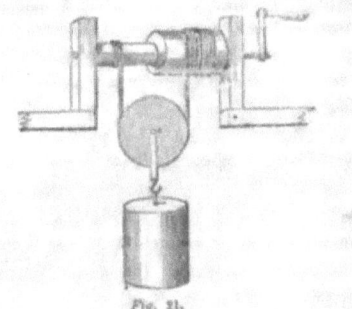

Fig. 21.

one larger than the other, turning about the same axis. The weight is attached to a pulley, which plays on a long cord, which is coiled round both axles in contrary directions. When the winch is turned, one end of the cord uncoils from the smaller cylinder, and is wound round the larger; thus the weight is elevated at each turn, through a space equal to half of the difference between the circumference of the two cylinders. Therefore the advantage of this machine, with its pulley, is in the ratio of the diameter of the larger cylinder, to half its excess above that of the lesser one.

GENERAL QUESTIONS ON LESSON VI.

1. Define the wheel and axle.
2. Are wheels always fixed to their axles?
3. What has the machine been sometimes called?
4. Explain how a wheel and axle resembles a simple lever.
5. What is the periphery of a wheel? what its diameter and radius?
6. Have all wheels central axes?
7. Where is the fulcrum of this machine placed?

8. How is equilibrium maintained with this machine?
9. Give the rule for finding the equilibrium of this machine.
10. How is the effect of this machine governed?
11. Do we gain or lose by increasing the size of a wheel?

LESSON VII.

BEFORE we can understand the pulley, we must consider what it consists of. Now, if we examine a pulley attentively, we shall see that it is nothing more than a wheel and axle, with the multiplied cord; so that, in fact, it is a compound machine. It is therefore evident, that we must understand what the multiplied cord really is, before we can consider the uses and mode of action of the pulley. The multiplied cord has sometimes been called the *funicular machine*, or rope machine, the term being derived from the Latin word *funis*, a rope. You observe that I rest the ends of this rope upon the backs of two chairs. [Experiment 4.] It is not in a straight line, and will not be so, whatever force may be employed in stretching it, because its own weight will prevent it. Suppose that I hang a pound weight in the centre of the rope [performs the Experiment], the chairs, which are the resisting points, are dragged towards each other; thus proving, that a very small force, if properly applied, will be sufficient to overcome a great resistance—a practical fact that seamen avail themselves of when bracing their sails. We know that ropes are not perfectly flexible, and that, as their strength increases, their rigidity is in proportion; if they were flexible, we should be able to dispense with the assistance of the pulley in many instances. For example, if

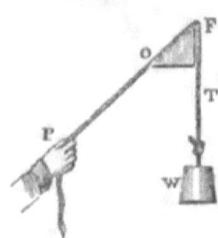

Fig. 22.

we could bend a rope over a sharp edge (F), as in *Fig.* 22, and the rope could be moved without friction, we should be enabled to transmit a force in any one direction, overcome resistance, or impart motion in another direction. The force P O, could be transmitted to T W, so as to support or overcome the resistance (W); or, a motion in the direction of O P could be made to produce another motion in the direction W T. But, as the cord is not perfectly flexible, the angle sharp, and friction exists, the force employed would cause the cord to snap; and, therefore, we find it is necessary to employ a curved surface for the cord to pass over. If the weight is only to be sustained, then a simple curved surface will answer the purpose; but if the cord has to move over the curved surface, it will be subject to friction, and corresponding wear; therefore, it has been found more advisable to cause the surface on which the rope runs to move with it, which is the case in the common pulley.

QUESTIONS.

83. *T.*—What is a pulley?
P.—It consists of a round thin disc or wheel grooved at its edges, called a *sheave*, turning upon an axis or pivot, passing through its centre at right angles with its plane, the whole being enclosed in a case called a *block*. The ropes and cords are called a *tackle*; and, when the whole machine is complete, and in working order, it is called a *block* and *tackle*.

84. *T.*—How are pulleys divided?
P.—Into fixed and movable.

85. *T.*—What are fixed pulleys?

P.—They are pulleys fixed to some place, such as a beam. The object of the fixed pulley is not to gain power, but to afford a more convenient mode of raising a weight; and as it requires the same amount of power to raise the weight as the amount of the weight itself, it is evident that it does not possess any mechanical advantage. [See men in frontispiece raising a cask with two fixed pulleys.]

86. *T.*—What are movable pulleys?

P.—They are of the same form as the fixed pulleys, but instead of being fixed or stationary, they sustain the weight, and are suspended by means of the cord that hangs under them. In Fig. 23 we have a representation of a fixed (A) and a movable pulley (B). C represents a hook inserted into a beam, and supporting one end of a cord, which passes under B, the movable pulley, and proceeding upwards, passes over the fixed pulley A, and descends to P, which is the power, acting against the resistance or weight W.

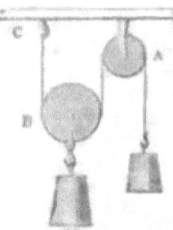
Fig. 23.

87. *T.*—What is the use of the fixed pulley in the machine you have described?

P.—To change the direction of the power.

88. *T.*—How is equilibrium maintained in a pulley?

P.—This may be explained by looking at Fig. 24, which represents a pulley (*c*) moving round a fixed axis or pivot, and the line stretched by forces acting in the directions *a b* and *d e*. If we could prolong these lines, they would meet at the point *f*, and it is therefore evident that if *f* were a point connected with the pulley, we could change the points of contact of the two forces, from *a* and *d* to *f*, without altering the action in any way; therefore we should have two

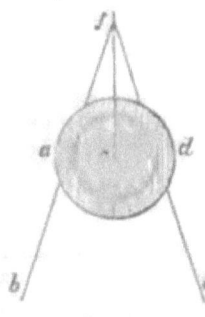
Fig. 24.

forces meeting at *f*, which could only be in equilibrium if their resultant were so. If the two forces meeting in *f*, and acting in the directions *f b* and *f e* are equal, their resultant will bisect, or cut into two, the angle *b f e*, and will then pass through the fixed central point *c* on the axis; the effect of which will be a state of equilibrium, but if one of the forces (*f b*) is greater than the other (*f e*), then the resultant will not pass through the axis, and equilibrium cannot be maintained.

89. *T.*—How can you estimate the pressure which the axis of the pulley has to sustain?

P.—Easily. It is evident from what we have learned before, that the pressure to be sustained is equal to the resultant of the

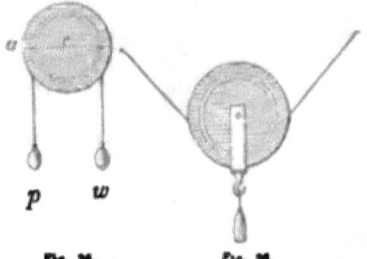
Fig. 25.   Fig. 26.

two forces. But if the directions of the forces be parallel, as in Fig. 25, the pressure upon the axis is equal to the sum of the two forces (*p* and *w*), and the weight of the pulley. [See Catechism I. Fig. 20.]

90. *T.*—How is a movable pulley maintained in equilibrium?

P.—By the forces which stretch the two ends of the cord being equal to one another, and causing their resultant to pass through the central point of the wheel. The action of this resultant is not stopped owing to the axis being fixed, but because there is a third power in the axis, in the direction of the resultant, which is equal and opposed to it.

91. *T.*—What is the third power you have mentioned?

P.—The weight (see Fig. 26), which is usually attached to a hook fastened to the block.

92. *T.*—What advantage does the movable possess over the fixed pulley?

P.—It halves the weight.

86　　　　　　　　　　MECHANICS.　　　　　　　　　[Lesson VII.

93. *T.*—How is this accomplished?

P.—The weight (W) hangs in the cord, and drags down each side of it equally [see *Fig.* 23], so that it has the same strain upon it at C as at P, consequently the weight (W) is divided between the two ends of the cords; which is the same as saying, that if the weight (W) is forty pounds, the end C of the cord sustains twenty pounds, and the end P the other twenty pounds.

94. *T.*—What is the principle upon which pulleys act?

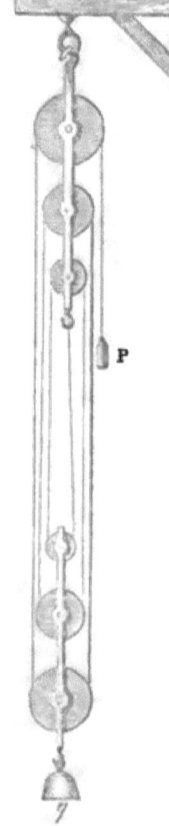

Fig. 27.

P.— By distributing the weight over the cord, so as to lessen the power required to overcome the resistance; and the facility afforded of changing the direction of the power.

95. *T.*—Then it appears that the cord really has more influence in the advantage gained by this machine, than the pulley.

P.—Certainly it has. The cord is the true power; for by means of it, the weight is distributed, and mechanical advantage gained.

96. *T.*—Cannot pulleys be increased in power?

P. — Yes, by combining several sheaves in one tackle. This may be done in various ways. For example, we may have a compound system of pulleys, consisting of three fixed, and three movable pulleys, the weight of which, attached to the common block of the three movable pulleys, is supported by the six lines which connect the upper and lower pulleys; and, therefore, as the weight is equally divided between the lines, each is drawn by one-sixth of the weight (*q*). Consequently, if sixty pounds weight is suspended to the bottom, each line would be drawn upon by a force of ten pounds. If we wish to keep this machine in a state of equilibrium, we must attach a weight (*p*) of ten pounds to the end of the line. Suppose that a person had to raise sixty pounds weight with this machine, it is evident that, by pulling at *p* with a force equal to ten pounds, this would be accomplished; therefore, we see the great advantage gained by employing this machine.

97. *T.*—It appears that the diminution of weight is in proportion to the number of pulleys used. Is this the case?

P.—Yes; and if we wish to calculate the expenditure of power or decrease of weight, we must multiply the number of movable pulleys by 2, and the product is the power required to be exerted. Thus, 3 movable pulleys multiplied by 2, gives 6; from which we know that a sixth of the weight is the power we require.

98. *T.*—What other varieties are there of a combination of pulleys?

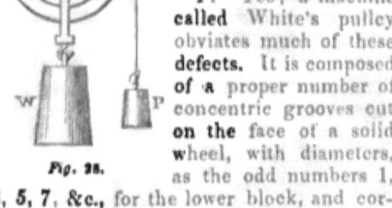

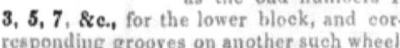

Fig. 28.

P.—We may have a system of pulleys with different cords so arranged, as to act successively on one another; indeed, the variety of tackles of pulleys is almost endless.

99. *T.*—Can you give me an example of a tackle which does away with much of the irregularity of action and friction, so common to pulleys generally?

P.—Yes; a machine called White's pulley obviates much of these defects. It is composed of a proper number of concentric grooves cut on the face of a solid wheel, with diameters, as the odd numbers 1, 3, 5, 7, &c., for the lower block, and corresponding grooves on another such wheel, with diameters as the even numbers 2, 4, 6, 8, &c., for the upper block. The cord passes successively over these grooves, as represented in *Fig.* 28, and is thrown off in the same manner as if every groove was a separate revolving wheel.

GENERAL QUESTIONS **ON LESSON VII.**

1. What **is** the funicular machine?
2. Why have pulleys round sheaves?
3. What is a pulley?
4. Describe the difference between fixed and movable pulleys.
5. How can you maintain equilibrium in a pulley?
6. Does the movable pulley possess any advantage over the fixed pulley?
7. How do pulleys act?
8. How can pulleys be increased in power?
9. What **is White's pulley?"**

LESSON VIII

The inclined **plane is** the most simple of all machines, and perhaps **the most familiar.** Roads and railroads often present instances of the application **of this** principle to practical and useful purposes. In applying this machine, it is generally supposed to be fixed, and the weight or load **to** be the movable body; but, sometimes, it is necessary to move the inclined plane **while** the body or load is partially fixed.

QUESTIONS.

100. *T.*—What is generally understood by the term, an *inclined plane?*

P.—It signifies a plane surface, perfectly smooth and unyielding, inclined in **such a manner,** that it **forms** some **angle with a horizontal** plane, **but** not **a right angle.**

101. *T.*—What do you **mean by a plane** surface being inclined, **and forming an** angle with a horizontal plane.

P.—If we look at *Fig.* 29, it will explain the difficulty, if there is any. A B represents the horizontal **plane, or** a surface that corresponds to the horizon, A D B is a right angle, formed by the line A D, being perpendicular to the line A B; A C represents the inclined plane, or sloping plane, which forms an acute angle (B A C) with the horizontal plane A B. Therefore, the inclined plane is represented by the lines A B **and** A C, uniting at A.

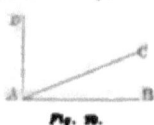

Fig. 29.

102. *T.*—What is the object of using the inclined plane?

P.—To raise weights to great heights, and overcome a great resisting force by the application of a lesser force or weight.

103. *T.*—How is **the advantage** gained by this machine estimated?

P.—By subtracting **the** perpendicular height **from** the length **of** the plane, and the product, **or excess of** length, shows the

Fig. 30.

advantage gained. Suppose the height, B C, of the inclined plane represented in *Fig.* 30, be one foot, and the inclined surface, B A, to be four feet; **then a** weight (W) of four pounds placed **on the** plane, will be balanced by a weight **of** one pound (P) hanging over **a** pulley **at** the end of the plane. It is evident that one-fourth of the power required to raise a great weight through the space B C, would impel it up the inclined plane from A to B. In all cases where this machine is used, allowance must be made for friction.

104. *T.*—Does the employment of the inclined plane afford us much advantage?

P.—In some cases, such as raising great loads to considerable heights; but like all other machines, what is gained in power, is lost in time or velocity.

105. *T.*—What have we to overcome in drawing a body up an inclined plane?

P.—Friction, and the gravity of the body, which always tends to make it occupy the lowest level.

106. *T.*—What do you mean by the *gradient* of an inclined plane?

P.—It is the proportion of the height to its length, and therefore the gradient may be said to be 1 in 100, or 1 in 50, as the case may be.

107. *T.*—What do you mean by the gradient being 1 in 100, or 1 in 50?

P.—It signifies, that the road rises 1 foot in height, for every 100 or 50 of its length, and therefore the additional load to be impelled up the inclined plane, will be the one-hundredth or fiftieth part of the weight to be impelled.

108. *T.*—Can you give me some familiar examples of the use of the inclined plane?

P.—Yes; the common chisel is an inclined plane, and the wood to be cut is the resistance or power to be overcome. Hatchets act in the same manner; planks placed in various positions for the purpose of wheeling barrows to heights, or rolling hogsheads to or from heights; ladders placed against houses or walls; flights of stairs; some kinds of printing-presses; the shovel, and many other things are familiar enough to most of us.

109. *T.*—Are not roads over hilly countries constructed on the principle of the inclined plane?

P.—Yes; and when a road has to be made to the top of a hill, it is usual to make it either wind round the hill, or ascend in a zigzag line. Carters usually make their carts describe a zigzag line of direction when ascending steep roads, because it saves their horses expending too much power.

GENERAL QUESTIONS ON LESSON VIII.

1. Are inclined planes always fixed?
2. Describe an inclined plane.
3. Are inclined planes advantageous or not?
4. Why do we use inclined planes?
5. In using the inclined plane, what have we to overcome?
6. Give some familiar examples of the inclined plane.

LESSON IX.

In our last lesson we considered the inclined plane as a fixed body; we have now to regard it in the condition of a movable body, or *movable inclined plane*. When we considered the inclined plane as a fixed body, the load or weight was movable; but in the present case we shall find that the load or resistance is fixed, and the inclined plane movable. In *Fig.* 31 you will see that we have an inclined plane (I, P), with a heavy weight (W) resting upon its small end (B). This will illustrate the double capacity of the inclined plane. For example, [Experiment 5,] if we drag the weight up the inclined plane by means of a cord, which is represented by the dotted line, we raise the weight from the level of B, C, to the height A. [Experiment 6.] We will now reverse the thing, and move the inclined plane by pushing it under the weight, and you now see we have moved the inclined plane through the space C, B, and the weight has been raised through the height C, A. In the former experiment it acts as an inclined plane; in the latter experiment it acts as a wedge.

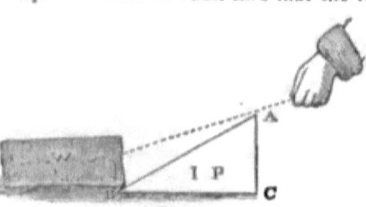
Fig. 31.

QUESTIONS.

110. *T.*—What is the *wedge?*

P.—It is a simple machine of **a triangular form, consisting of a solid mass of iron,** wood, or some other **hard** material, and is generally described **as** being composed of two inclined planes, united at their bases, or placed back to back, as represented in *Fig. 32,* B A being the line of union of their bases.

111. *T.*—Is the wedge always sloped on both sides?

P.—No; it is sometimes flat on one side, and sloped or inclined on the other, as B, A, C, in *Fig.* 31.

112. *T.*—What is the use of the wedge?

P.—It is generally employed to divide **solid bodies,** the edge A (*Fig.* **32**) being driven against them by force applied to the end D, B, C. *Fig.* 33 represents a wedge entering a piece of wood, and by employing repeated blows, you observe that it may be driven into the substance of the wood, so **as** to cause it to divide, as in *Fig.* **34.**

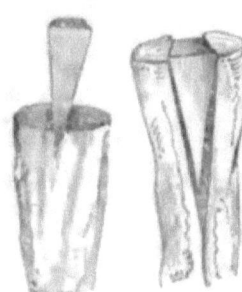

Fig. 33. *Fig. 34.*

113. *T.*—How does the wedge act, so as to divide the **wood thus?**

P.—When **the wedge** is urged by repeated blows to enter the substance of the wood, the fibres of the wood are compressed, and the point A (*Fig.* 32) is held fast **by** the two sides of the wood; eventually, **as** the blows are repeated, the point is driven still further in, and the space that at first scarcely admitted the point A, is obliged **to** separate, so as to allow D C to enter it.

114. *T.*—Is the wedge used for any other purpose than merely dividing solid bodies?

P.—Yes; it is used for raising ships in the docks, wedges being driven under their keels. It has been used **to** restore **an** inclined building **to** a perpendicular position. It is the principal agent **in** the oil-mill; the seeds from which the oil is to be extracted are placed between pieces of hard wood, and wedges are inserted between the bags, by allowing heavy beams to fall on them. The key-stone of an arch is a wedge; planes, knives, razors, nails, pins, needles, awls, and most cutting and piercing instruments **are** wedges. A most useful application of the wedge, is that of fastening large timbers together by means of a wedge-shaped mortice.

115. *T.*—How **can we** calculate the power of the wedge?

P.—We cannot do so satisfactorily, because the exact force applied will depend **upon** the number of blows, and the resist**ance** opposed by the sides; but we may **lay it** down as a rule, that in proportion as the angle is greater, so must be **the** power to overcome the resistance, which increases with **the** inclination, the **same as** in the inclined plane. Therefore, a **long** thin wedge has a greater power than **a** short thick one, because it does **not require** so great **a force** to be applied.

116. *T.*—How is it when **a** wedge is driven into **a block** of wood, that it is not generally **forced** out again by the wood?

P.—Because the friction, which is very great, acts upon the wedge in the same manner that a ratchet wheel does upon the wheel and axle. It is to this principle that nails owe their efficacy; for, if it were not for the friction which arises between their surface and the wood into which they are driven, they would recoil from their places.

GENERAL QUESTIONS ON LESSON IX.

1. What is the difference between **a fixed** and a movable inclined plane?
2. Give some illustrations of both.
3. Describe the wedge and its varieties.
4. How are wedges used?
5. To what may their action be ascribed?
6. Give some familiar examples of the useful application of the wedge.
7. Is it possible to estimate the power of the wedge?
8. Why are not wedges forced out of the substances into which they are driven?

LESSON X.

WHEN an inclined plane is coiled round a cylinder, we have a machine which has received the name of the screw. The screw consists of two parts, a solid cylinder with the inclined plane coiled round it, called the *male screw*, and a hollow cylinder with an inclined plane coiled round the inside (so as to receive the former one), called a *female screw*. The male screw consists of a projecting ridge winding round the cylinder, which is termed the *thread of the screw*, and is said to be spiral, but is really helical, being like a corkscrew, which is the helical thread of the screw without the cylinder. The difference between a spiral line and a helical line may be seen by the annexed diagrams, *Fig.* 35 representing the helical, and *Fig.* 36 the spiral line.

The hollow screw has a helical thread winding within it, corresponding to the spaces between the turns of the thread of the solid screw. By means of this arrangement, either screw may be made to revolve while the other is kept steady; and, therefore, any amount of pressure may be produced.

Fig. 35.   *Fig.* 36.

QUESTIONS.

117. *T.*—What is the *screw*?

P.—A solid cylinder with a projecting ridge, winding round it in the form of an inclined plane, which ridge or *thread* may present a thin sharp edge as in *Fig.* 37, or a square edge, as in *Fig.* 38, without affecting the principle of the machine.

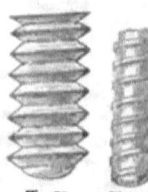

Fig. 37.   *Fig.* 38.

118. *T.*—Will you illustrate how the inclined plane, being **coiled round a cylinder**, forms a screw?

P.—Certainly; cut a piece of paper of the same shape as I P, in *Fig.* 31, and let the line B C be eighteen inches long, and A C six inches high, then black the edge A B. Wind this paper round a ruler, commencing at the part A C, and when it is all coiled round the ruler, you will observe a black line like the thread of a screw.

119. *T.*—It appears, then, that the screw is like a series of inclined planes coiled round a cylindrical axis. Can you explain this?

P.—If we examine *Fig.* 39, we observe that A B C D represents a cylinder divided into seven equal parts (*a, b, c, d, e, f,* B); if we draw lines from the perpendicular line A B, each equal to the circumference of the base, in a plane with the horizon and parallel to each other, and then join A *g* and *a h, b i, c k, d l, e m,* we shall form as many inclined planes as there are parts in the line A B. Now, if we roll these planes round the cylinder, so that the point *g* shall meet the point *a, h* with *b, i* with *c,* and so on, the longest lines of the inclined planes (A *g, a h, b i,* &c.) will form a continued helical line upon the cylinder, the same as the thread of a screw.

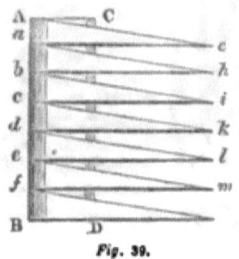

Fig. 39.

120. *T.*—Why is the thread of the screw called a helical line?

P.—The name is derived from the Greek word *elix* ("ελιξ), a whorl; and helical, therefore, signifies winding. One turn of this line is termed a *helix,* and several turns, or more than one, *helices.* No two points of a helix are in the same plane. [See *Fig.* 35.]

121. *T.*—If we remove the cylinder from the screw, and only leave the helical line, is there any mechanical advantage in the line itself?

P.—Yes, it is still a screw, as in the case of the common corkscrew (*Fig.* 35); and when it is inserted into a substance, acts as an inclined plane—1st, by the point of the helical line being smaller than the upper part; 2nd, by the line assuming a wedge-shape as it ascends; **3rd, by** the gradual ascent of the thread itself.

122. *T.*—How does the screw act?

P.—When the solid screw is inserted into the hollow screw, and is made to act vertically to raise a weight, it will be found that when the weight has been raised by one **turn** of the screw over one thread, or from *f* to *e*, in *Fig.* 39, that it has really been propelled up the inclined plane *m e*; consequently, the effect of the screw, independent of friction, will be as the length of the plane (*m e*) is to the height (*f e*). For example, if *f e* is a quarter of an inch in height, and *e m* is three inches, then a power equal to one pound, applied by the screw, would balance a weight of twelve pounds suspended from the nut.

123. *T.*—Can the screw be applied so as to act by itself?

P.—No, it is never used alone, but the power is always applied by means of a lever, inserted into, or passing through, the head of the screw [see *Fig.* 41], or through the nut into which the screw is inserted [see *Fig.* 40].

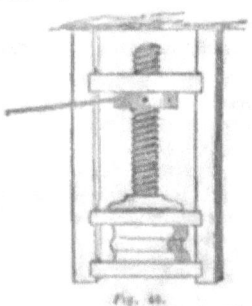

Fig. 40.

124. *T.*—If a screw is inserted into a piece of wood, does it not act alone, then?

P.—No; the wood corresponds to the hollow screw, and the screw-driver to the lever.

125. *T.*—How is the effect of the screw estimated?

P.—By the proportion between the space described by the power, and the space between any two of its threads, **in** one revolution of the screw. Therefore, the power applied to a long lever increases the effect of the machine, and hence it follows that, in order to increase the power of the machine, we must lengthen the lever, and decrease the distance between the threads of the **screw.**

126. *T.*—Is there no other way of increasing the power of this machine, because it frequently happens that it is inconvenient to have a very long lever, and if the threads of the screw are too thin, they are liable to break.

P.—There is a compound screw, invented by John Hunter, the great anatomist, which enables us to increase the efficacy of the machine, without diminishing its

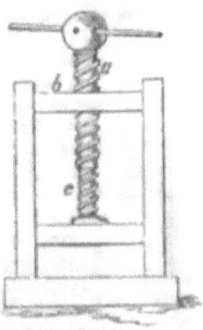

Fig. 41.

strength. This is accomplished by employing a large screw (*a*), which turns in a hollow screw placed in the beam (*b*). The lower extremity of the large screw contains a hollow screw, which is adapted to receive a smaller screw (*c*), and, therefore, while the larger screw passes forward, the smaller one is drawn back, and as both screws revolve together, each time a movement takes place, the beam (*e*) is pressed downward through a space equal to the difference of the distances between the threads of the large and small screw. For example, if the threads of the upper screw are $\frac{1}{8}$th of an inch apart, and those of the lower screw $\frac{1}{10}$th of an inch, then the same effect will be produced as if the simple screw was employed, the threads of which were only $\frac{1}{40}$th of an inch apart; because $\frac{1}{8}$, multiplied by $\frac{1}{10}$, are equal to $\frac{1}{80}$—the difference between the distances of the threads of John Hunter's compound screw.

127. *T.*—Is there any method by which we can combine velocity with power in the screw?

P.—Yes; by having a screw with two, three, or more threads, instead of one. Suppose that we had a screw with a very broad thread—say, for example, one inch —and that we wished to increase its velocity, we have only to form three threads in each, each one a quarter of an inch in width, with a space the one-eighth of an inch between them, and the thing is accomplished. This is a fact, and as the thing is applied to printing-presses, any curious person may see it for himself.

128. *T.*—Are not houses sometimes moved by means of the screw?

P.—Yes. It has been done in England, but is chiefly practised in America. The annexed diagram will explain the method. The building to be moved must be a detached one. Openings are made in the end walls, just above the ground, large enough to insert beams, about fifteen inches square, across the building (1); the end of each beam is supported on blocks of wood, fixed into the ground, and clear of the walls, and each beam made firm and tight by driving wedges between the beams and the upright block. When this has been done, the foundation is cleared away, and a clear space left. Then other beams (2) are placed under the first, and resting like them on blocks of wood, and by this means the front and back walls are supported, and now the whole foundation is exposed. The screws (3) are placed under the ends of the second beams (2), which are forced upwards by their means, and the weight of the whole building sustained by them. The ground underneath being all removed, set of grooved-ways, or beams (6), are placed where the end walls formerly stood, and the cradles (5), which are beams with a projection corresponding to the groove in the ways, are placed on them, both being previously well greased. Large beams (4) are placed over the cradles, between them and the beams (2) which support the ends of the house, and wedges driven in to render the whole tight and secure, which is also effected by additional blocks (7). The screws are now removed, and being placed horizontally, are made to act together against the cradles, and move them along the ways, at the rate of about four feet a day, to the place the house is to occupy. Then, by inverting the operations, the beams are removed, and the house firmly fixed, without sustaining any injury, and often without even moving as much as a chair from the house.

Fig. 42.

129. *T.*—What is the principle of the screw applied to?

P.—Various purposes. Among others, we may enumerate the cider-mill, oil-mill, common printing-press, napkin-press, bookbinder's press (see *Fig.* 40), patent cork-screw, vice, clamp, augers, gimlets, and many similar machines, which owe their efficacy to the principle of the screw. Common screws combine the principle of the wedge with that of the screw, for they are smaller at the point than at the lever end. There is another form which must also be mentioned—the endless screw. This is a solid screw, revolving on fixed axes, the thread of which is adapted to teeth on the circumference of a wheel.

GENERAL QUESTIONS ON LESSON X.

1. Describe the difference between a male and female screw.
2. Describe the difference between a spiral and a helical line.
3. Define a screw.
4. Describe the difference between a screw with a triangular thread, and one with a parallelogram.
5. How is the inclined plane referable to the screw?
6. What is the helical line, and what is the term derived from?
7. How can you estimate the effect of a screw?
8. Can the power of the screw be increased?

LESSON XI.

We have now duly considered the **leading** elements **of Mechanics, and even some of** the compound machines formed by uniting together two of the mechanic powers, as the lever and screw, and the lever with the wheel and axle. We have also examined the effect produced by combining some of **the** simple machines with each other, and thus producing systems of their own, **as with** levers or pulleys. In combining bodies to produce mechanical effects, we have certain laws to guide us, and certain objects to attain. One thing we must ever bear in mind, that **the** fewer parts there are in a machine, and the more simple its construction, the better.

QUESTIONS.

130. *T.*—**When** we undertake to construct **a machine,** what are the chief objects **we have** to consider?

P.—They are four. 1st. The strength or durability of the materials; 2nd. The arrangement of the parts of the machine in as simple a manner as possible; 3rd. The correct adaptation or fitting of one part to another; and, 4th. Ease, regularity, and uniformity of motion.

131. *T.*—What are machines generally constructed of?

P.—Iron, steel, brass, wood, or any durable materials.

132. *T.*—Do the materials differ greatly in their strength?

P.—Yes; but independent of the durability of the materials employed, it is necessary **to** pay attention to the positions in which they are placed, their form and bulk.

133. *T.*—What do you mean by the strength of **a** body?

P.—It is the force with which it resists the separation of its particles, and may be absolute or relative.

134. *T.*—What is the *absolute strength* of a body?

P.—It is the force by which the body resists being torn asunder when stretched lengthways. For example, when we pull the two ends of a piece of India-rubber apart; or when a great weight is suspended to the end of a rod, which has the other end fixed perpendicularly.

135. *T.*—Upon what does the absolute strength of a body depend?

P.—Its diagonal section; that is, a straight line drawn through it, so as to join the two opposite angles; and, in proportion to the diagonal section of the body, so is its absolute strength.

136. *T.*—What is the relative strength of a body?

P.—The force which it opposes to the process of breaking. In this case, the force is applied at right angles to the direction of its long axis, while one or both of its extremities are supported.

137. *T.*—How is the connexion between the particles of a solid body overcome?

P.—By breaking, tearing, twisting, or crushing **the** body.

138. *T.*—You said that the position of the materials employed in a machine affected their strength. Explain this.

P.—[Experiment 7.] You observe that I have a piece of thin wood, two feet long, in my hand—it is called a lath; and when each end rests on a block of wood or stone, as it does now—[places the ends of the lath on the stones,]—it will require twice the weight applied to its centre, in order to break it, than it will if only the centre is supported, and a weight suspended to each end; and four times the weight to break it, than it will if only one end is firmly fixed or supported, and the weight attached to the other. Observe, that when I attach a weight of one pound to its centre, that it bends, and if this is increased by adding another pound weight, perhaps the lath will be broken. [Experiment 8.] You observe, that I have moved the stones nearer, and that the lath does not bend so much as before, because the length of the lath between the stones is not so great as in the last experiment.

139. *T.*—Suppose that the distance between the ends of the lath was eight

feet, the lath being of **the same thickness as** in the present case, **what would be the** effect of placing it **on the stones without the weight?**

P.—It would bend with **its own** weight. As we shorten its length, we increase its strength, because the thicker and shorter a **beam is, the** stronger it will be ; and if a **beam is twice** as broad as another **of the same length, it will be twice as strong.**

140. *T.*—**Why does a beam increase in strength, when it increases in size ?**

P.—**Because it contains a greater number of resisting particles. If we double the depth of a beam we render it four times as** strong, **because** the number **of** fibres **are** doubled, **and the** lever is increased.

141. *T.*—**You** said that the form **of** materials employed required consideration. Explain this.

P.—We **know that the arch is the** strongest **form we can construct, and** this we learn **from** Nature, when **we** observe the roof of the skull, eggs, or cylindrical bodies.

142. *T.*—How is it **that the arch is the** strongest form ?

P.—Because the particles of which it is composed, bear upon each other like a **great** many wedges with their narrow ends **pointed** towards the **hollow part of the** arch, therefore the particles, or the concave or hollow **part, are** more compressed than on the convex **or** rounded part ; **consequently the more pressure we** apply to the upper or convex part in a perpendicular direction, the **greater** will be the compression and resistance to the weight.

143. *T.*—**How does bulk** influence **the employment of materials ?**

P.—**Because, after a body has attained a certain size, the** additional **increase of bulk only adds to** the weight without **increasing its power of** endurance, **for the** weight increases more rapidly than the strength ; **and** on this account **we are obliged to limit** the size of our machines, **which would not** be able to support their **own weight if made too** large.

GENERAL QUESTIONS ON **LESSON XI.**

1. What are the desirable **objects** in the construction of a machine ?
2. What materials are machines generally **constructed of?**
3. Are all materials of uniform strength ?
4. **What is meant by the** strength of a body, **and how is it classified ?**
5. How does position **affect the materials** used in machines ?
6. What influence has the form and bulk of materials on machines ?

LESSON XII.

A MACHINE **is made up of many parts, which are** so connected, as to be rendered available **for the particular purpose the** machine was designed for ; and the manner in which one mechanic power acts upon another, may be changed to suit certain particular purposes. Power may be transmitted **by belts, as in** *Fig.* 43, where it is obvious that **the** wheel c is turned by the belt B B, which receives its motion from A ; but, **as it is** smaller, the velocity is **increased.** The motion of machinery may be **regulated so as to** produce a uniform velocity ; **or** a quick motion **may be** transformed **into a slow** motion, or *vice versa ;* **motion** may also be made to **alternate** by means of eccentric wheels, or wheels **that have the axis** nearer to the circumference than the centre.

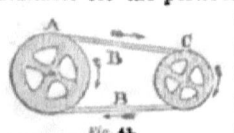
Fig. 43.

QUESTIONS.

144. *T.*—What are the chief **agents in** the transmission of power ?

P.—Toothed wheels, bevel wheels, shafts, and pulleys, which are arranged according to the direction of the motion required to be conveyed. *Fig.* 44 enables us to understand how the change of direction is effected by beveled wheels placed at various angles; and *Fig.* 45 exhibits another method of changing the direction by means of a

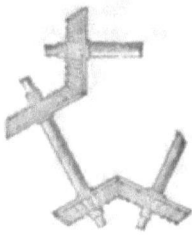

Fig. 44.

crown wheel, which works into an ordinary pinion, whose axis is at right angles to its own.

145. *T.*—What is meant by a cog wheel?
P.—It is a wheel with projecting teeth; the term *cog* being used for all large teeth.

146. *T.*—What is a shaft?
P.—A long and large axle, attached to some part of a machine, which enables us to transmit **power to a** great distance. Small shafts are called spindles.

147. *T.*—**What is** a pivot or gudgeon?
P.—The end of a shaft, axle, or spindle, upon which it turns and rests.

148. *T.*—What is a crown wheel?

Fig. 45.

P.—A wheel, with teeth placed at right angles to its circumference (see *Fig.* 45.)

149. *T.*—Is **not the motion** of machinery sometimes irregular?
P.—Yes; and **it may proceed** either from irregularity in **the principal** mover, variation in the amount **of pressure** or the load, or defect in the **proper transmission** of force, and friction.

150. *T.*—How can friction cause **the** irregularity of motion; and how may friction **be** prevented?
P.—Friction causes the irregularity, by destroying **the** proper adaptation of the various **parts** by wearing away, as in the axle of a **wheel,** which revolves with great rapidity; and, **in order to** diminish this, a plan has been adopted for subdividing the friction, by making the axle to revolve **on**

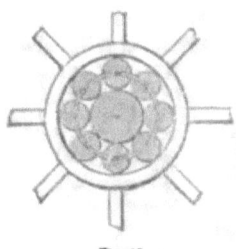

Fig. 46.

two or more wheels, which are therefore termed friction wheels, as in *Fig.* 46.

151. *T.*—How may the irregularities **of** machinery be generally remedied?
P.—By having a reservoir of power **to** each machine, which will enable the prime mover to give a more equal motion. This is accomplished by the fly-wheel, which may be seen attached to mangles, turning-lathes, &c.

152. *T.*—Then **it** appears **the** power is capable of being accumulated **and** concentrated. Is this the case?
P.—Yes. We see **this in the** grocer's handmill, which has a **fly-wheel** attached.

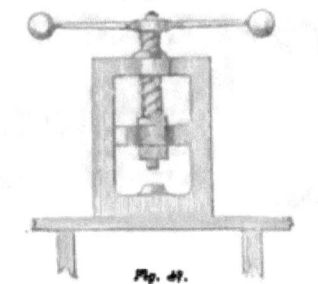

Fig. 47.

The coining-press (*Fig.* 47) said to **have** been invented by Briot, the Mint Master to Louis XIII. of France, is an excellent example of the effect of the concentration of force. A man causing the screw to descend with great force, makes a good impression of the **die** upon the metal at one stroke, by whirling the balls at the end of the horizontal bar.

153. *T.*—**Can the** force of machinery **be** regulated?
P.—**Yes; by** employing a cog-wheel,

called the governor wheel, which regulates the velocity of the machine with which it is connected. Thus, in the steam-engine it acts upon the valve; in the water-mill upon the shuttle; and in the windmill, upon the sail-cloth. In the steam-engine it consists of two heavy balls, A A, attached

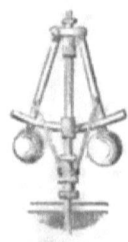

Fig. 48.

to the ends of two rods, which play upon a point at B, and as they rotate upon C, and separate by the centrifugal force, a ring above B is depressed, which acts by means of a rod upon the valve and closes it, thereby diminishing the speed; and as the balls fall or are at rest, **the** valve is opened, and the speed **again** established by supplying more steam.

154. *T.*—What is **a** crank?

P.—A mechanical contrivance, **by means** of which a revolving motion **is changed** into an alternate motion.

155. *T.*—How is this effected?

P.—[Experiment 9.] I have a piece **of** iron wire, which you observe is straight. I will now bend it so as to form a crank

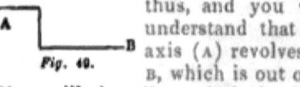

Fig. 49.

thus, and you will easily understand that while the axis (A) revolves, the **part** B, which is out of the **same** line, **will** describe **a** circle (makes **it do so** by twisting the wire between the **finger and** thumb). Now if a piston or rod **is attached** to the **part** B, its motion **cannot be the same as the** axis, but must **rise and fall, or** be alternate.

156. *T.*—I thought that cranks were used to make alternate motions change into revolving motions. Explain this difficulty.

P.—Sometimes they are employed for that purpose, and **are** double, being made

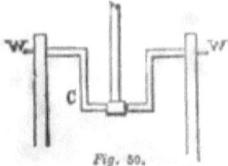

Fig. 50.

to turn **two** wheels as in *Fig.* 50, but the same **arrangement** may **be** retained, and only **one crank used,** which is the same as turning the **handle of an** organ, the piston or rod being represented by the hand. Now **as** the piston's motion is alternate, or falls and rises, the crank converts that motion into a rotary one, and conveys it to the wheels. We observe this in turning-lathes and steamers.

GENERAL QUESTIONS **ON LESSON** XII.

1. How is motion **transmitted to** machinery?
2. Can motion be changed in its direction?
3. What is the difference between a crown wheel and a bevelled wheel?
4. How may friction be partially prevented?
5. Is force susceptible of accumulation?
6. What is the governor wheel?
7. What is the use of a crank?
8. Are cranks single or double?

IV.—CHEMISTRY.

INTRODUCTORY NARRATIVE.

LESSON I.

RATHER more than seventy-three years ago, there resided in the old corporate town of Penzance—which is situated on the north-western shore of Mount's Bay, in Cornwall—a carver in wood, who has left some specimens behind him in the town, to testify that he was a skilful workman. On the 17th December, 1778, his family was increased by the addition of a fine boy, whose name was afterwards intimately connected with Chemistry, and will ever grace the calendar of science—Sir Humphry Davy.

INTRODUCTORY NARRATIVE. [Lesson I

Biographers inform us that Humphry Davy **received the** rudiments of **a** classical education at a seminary in Truro, and that he was afterwards **placed** with a surgeon and apothecary, at Penzance. Instead of **paying** proper **attention to his** medical studies, Davy was always making **experiments in the garret of his master's** house, frequently alarming the **whole household by his detonations;** or rambling about the country, so that his master was obliged **to part with him.** When **fifteen** years of age, he was placed with Mr. Borlase, **another** surgeon **in** Penzance; but **his** mind was too much occupied with other subjects to allow him to follow his medical studies. He laid down an extensive plan of study for himself, which embraced the learned languages, natural philosophy, botany, geometry, anatomy, metaphysics, history, chemistry, &c.; and so **great was** his application, that in three years he had made considerable proficiency in **all these** branches of learning.

The fascinating science of Chemistry was peculiarly suited to the taste of Davy, **and** we are informed that he pursued the study of it with the greatest ardour. He was not furnished with expensive apparatus to enable him to prosecute **his** investigations, but he managed to convert the phials **and gallipots belonging to his master, the** pots and pans used **in** the kitchen, and many **other things, to the** purposes he required.

His **first** original experiment is said to have **been the** examination of the air contained in the bladders of sea-weed, which resulted in his discovering that these plants **have** the property of purifying **the air** contained in water, **the same as** other plants **have of** purifying the atmosphere.

Mr. Gregory Watt, the son of the **celebrated James Watt,** being in delicate health, was advised to try the air of Penzance, **and, while lodging with Mrs.** Davy, he discovered the talent of her son, and his devotion **to Chemistry. One day,** soon after Mr. Watt became his mother's lodger, young Davy was leaning on the gate **in** front of the house, when Mr. Gilbert, afterwards the President of the Royal Society, passed with some friends, one of whom remarked that Davy was much attached to Chemistry. This attracted Mr. Gilbert's attention towards Davy, and after some conversation with him, he was so pleased with his talents that he offered him the use of his library, and whatever he required for his studies. In 1798 Davy was introduced to the celebrated Dr. Beddoes by Mr. Watt and Mr. Gilbert, and as that physician had just established at Clifton, near Bristol, **what** he **called a Pneumatic** Institution, for investigating the **medical properties of the** different gases, **he offered** Davy, who was scarcely twenty years **of** age, **the superintendence of the institution, which was accepted at once.**

The **following** year Dr. Beddoes published a work, **called** *Contributions to Physical and Medical Knowledge, principally from the West of England,* **and among** them we find some essays by Humphry Davy on " **Heat, Light, and the Combinations** of Light," with a new " Theory of Respiration ;" on the " Generation **of Oxygen Gases,"** and the " Causes of the colours **of Organic** Bodies."

His attention **was then turned to** the existence of **silica in** various plants ; and in 1800 he published a work, called *Researches, Chemical and Philosophical, chiefly concerning Nitrous Oxide, and its Respiration,* in which he detailed all the experiments made with **this and** other gases. This work created a great sensation, and was the means of **introducing** him to Count Rumford, and also establishing his reputation as a chemist **and** philosopher.

In 1801 Davy came to London, and delivered his first Lecture at the Royal Institution, **to which he was** appointed Professor of Chemistry, **on 31st** May, 1802. The

Board of Agriculture appointed him Professor of Chemistry in 1802, and engaged him to deliver a course of lectures *On the Connexion of Chemistry with Vegetable Physiology*, which were highly appreciated, and he therefore continued to lecture at the meetings of the Board for ten successive years, on subjects connected with agriculture, which were published at the request of the Board in 1813.

In 1803 he was elected a Fellow of the Royal Society; in 1805 he was made a member of the Royal Irish Academy; and, in 1806, he was elected Secretary to the Royal Society, and chosen to deliver the Bakerian lecture before the Society, in which he made known the results of his inquiries into galvanism and electricity. The following year he discovered *potassium, sodium,* and *boron*; and, in 1808, *baryam, calcium,* and *strontium*. In 1810 he obtained the prize of the French Institute, and during that and the following year he delivered two courses of lectures before the Dublin Society, for which they voted him £1150; and Trinity College, Dublin, conferred the degree of D.C.L. on him.

On the 8th of April, 1812, the Prince-Regent knighted him; and, on the 11th, he was married to Mrs. Apreece, a widow of fortune. The following year he was elected Corresponding Member of the French Institute, and Vice-president of the Royal Society.

The most important of his discoveries was made in the year 1815. The many dreadful accidents and great loss of life frequently occurring from the explosions in coal-mines, occasioned by the *fire-damp*, induced some of the proprietors of mines to form a committee at Bishop-Wearmouth, for investigating the causes of these frequent disasters, and to consider the best means of preventing their occurrence in future. Sir Humphry Davy's assistance was requested, and he immediately set out for the collieries, where he obtained specimens of the fire-damp, for the purpose of analyzing on his return to London; and also made some experiments, with a view to adopting a system of ventilation. After examining the fire-damp, and trying numerous experiments, he discovered that the carburetted hydrogen gas, or fire-damp, would not explode when mixed with less than six, or more than fourteen times its volume of air; and that, when the gas did explode, the explosion could not pass through apertures less than one-seventh of an inch in diameter. Satisfied with these results, he constructed his *safety-lamp*, which is generally termed by miners "*The Davy*." It is a simple oil-lamp, enclosed in a long cylinder cage of wire gauze, which contains about four hundred holes in the square inch. The wick is trimmed by a bent wire, passing tightly through a small tube in the body of the lamp, so that the wick can be kept burning without unscrewing the cylinder, an act that would endanger the lives of the miners. The air that passes through the wire gauze is sufficient to support combustion, which produces enough carbonic acid and nitrogen to prevent the fire-damp causing any explosion. When the air is foul, or charged with fire-damp, the flame of the lamp becomes extinguished, and the interior of the wire gauze cylinder is filled with a green flame, therefore the miner should withdraw, otherwise by continuing in the place too long the gauze will be destroyed, and an explosion take place. When the lamp is removed to a purer air the wick becomes

Fig. 1.*

---

* *The Davy*, or Miner's Safety Lamp.

relighted, and the green flame disappears. The coal owners of the northern districts rewarded Sir Humphry Davy for his valuable discovery by inviting him to a public dinner in 1817, and presenting him with a service of plate worth £2000.*

In 1817 Davy was elected an Associate of the Royal Academy; and was created a baronet in 1818, while absent on the continent. On the 30th November, 1820, he was elected President of the Royal Society, (in the place of Sir Joseph Banks, who had died,) and he continued to fill the office till 1827, when he resigned it in consequence of ill health. Immediately after this he proceeded to the continent, where he continued to prosecute his philosophical researches, contributing the results of his investigations to the *Transactions of the Royal Society*. His chief residence was at Rome, but, in consequence of an alarming attack of paralysis, he was obliged to leave for Geneva. Proceeding by easy stages in company with Lady Davy, he arrived at La Couronne on the 29th of May, 1829, and repaired to an inn overlooking the Lake of Geneva. After he retired to rest he was attacked with **apoplexy,** and expired early on the 30th May, 1829, in the fifty-first year of his age.

Sir Humphry Davy published *Chemical and Philosophical Researches; Elements of Chemical Philosophy; Electro-Chemical Researches; Elements of Agricultural Chemistry;* and a great many pamphlets and papers in the various leading scientific journals. His last works are *Salmonia*, and *The Last Days of a Philosopher*, the latter being published after his death.

Those who have seen Sir Humphry Davy must remember his gentlemanly deportment and quiet manner. His head, which was small, was set off by an ample and elevated forehead, and light-brown hair. His eyes, which were remarkably penetrative, were light hazel. His nose aquiline, the mouth rather large, and marked by a thoughtful expression, which imparted a fulness and prominence to the under lip, and complexion fair. He was about five feet seven inches in height, with a large, well-formed chest, slender neck, and small feet and hands.

A simple monument in the burying-ground of Geneva, which is without the walls of the city, marks the grave which received the remains of Sir Humphry Davy, on the 1st of June, 1829. When we reflect upon the career of this remarkable man, we are struck with the perseverance he displayed, and his thirst after knowledge; no difficulties seemed to deter him; on the contrary, they only appeared to stimulate him to greater exertions. Although studious in his habits, he was, nevertheless, particularly fond of the amusements of fly-fishing and shooting, few persons being able to excel him in either sport. Viewed as a scholar, and a philosopher, he is greatly to be admired; his writings display great force, judgment, and extensive knowledge; his discoveries were most important to the scientific advancement of the age, and the well-being of his fellow creatures. Thousands of people were saved through the invention and adoption of his safety-lamp—another instance of the many obligations that society is under to CHEMISTRY.

---

* The Davy Safety-lamp was improved by the Rev. W. Thorp, of Womersley, in the West Riding of Yorkshire, in the year 1849. 1. By introducing the Argand or solar burner, with a circular wick. 2. By admitting the air from the bottom of the lamp. 3. By having an adjustment outside the lamp, to regulate the wick. 4. By having an iron chimney based with glass, introduced into four or five chambers of wire gauze. The advantages of this new invention are therefore—1. Increased light. 2. The lamp only requires trimming once a week. 3. The oil does not fall out if laid on one side. 4. It is more easily cleaned. 5. It burns the cheapest oil. 6. It is much safer than the old lamp.

CHEMISTRY.

QUESTIONS AND EXPLANATIONS.

1. *T.*—WHAT is Chemistry?
P.—It is that science which enables us to discover the nature and properties of the elements of matter, their action upon each other, and their combinations; the proportions in which these elements unite, the mode of changing compound bodies into simple ones, or single bodies into compound; and the laws which govern their action.

2. *T.*—What is the term chemistry derived from?
P.—It is of doubtful derivation; but is probably derived from the Coptic root, *chemi*, which means *obscure* or *secret*.

3. *T.*—Do you remember the general properties of matter?
P.—Yes; extension, impenetrability, mobility, extreme divisibility, gravitation, porosity, and indestructibility.

[The pupil should be requested to define these terms, and, if not able to do so, should consult Cat. 1.]

4. *T.*—What are the secondary properties of matter?
P.—Opacity, transparency, softness, hardness, elasticity, colour, density, solidity, fluidity, and others of a similar kind.

[These terms should be explained to the student, according to their general acceptation. Thus, *coal* is *opaque*; *glass* is *transparent*; *clay soft*; *iron hard*, &c.]

5. *T.*—What do the various phenomena of chemistry chiefly depend on?
P.—The modifications of attractive and repulsive force, exercised on particles of matter placed at insensible distances from each other.

6. *T.*—Inform me what are the attractive agents?
P.—1. *Cohesive attraction*, or *the attraction of aggregation*. 2. *Chemical attraction* or *affinity*.
[See Lesson VIII., p. 21.]

7. *T.*—What are the repulsive agents?
P.—1. *Caloric*. 2. *Light*. 3. *Electricity* and *Galvanism*.
[See Lesson IX., p. 22.]

8. *T.*—When we change a compound body into simple ones, what is the process termed?
P.—*Decomposition* or *analysis*, which chemists have divided into *simple* and *compound*, or *single* and *double decomposition*. Thus, when a body composed of two substances is decomposed by means of a third body, which acts simply, it is called *single* or *simple decomposition*. If the intervention of the third body causes two new compounds instead of one, the operation is then called *compound*, or *double decomposition*.

9. *T.*—What is the term analysis derived from?
P.—The Greek word *analuo* (ἀναλυω), *I dissolve*, and therefore means the resolution of a substance into its component parts. Analysis was first scientifically pursued by Bergman of Sweden.

10. *T.*—When two simple bodies are changed into a compound body, what is the process termed?
P.—*Synthesis* or *composition*, which is directly opposed to analysis.

11. *T.*—What is the term derived from?
P.—Two Greek words, *soon* (συν), *with*, and *tithemi* (τιθημι), I place.

12. *T.*—Give me examples of analysis and synthesis.
P.—If I decompose water by galvanism, and cause the evolution of oxygen and hydrogen gases at the opposite poles, I examine it analytically; but if I explode these two gases and cause them to recombine so as to form the water, which had previously been decomposed, I examine it synthetically.

13. *T.*—You have made use of the terms simple and compound bodies several times. Explain their meaning.
P.—A *simple body*, or element, is a substance that cannot be further decomposed or resolved into any other kind of matter, for example, the gas oxygen. A *compound body* is composed of two or more substances, differing in their nature and properties; thus, *chloride of sodium* or common salt, is

composed of a *gas* called *chlorine*, and a *metal* called *sodium*.

14. *T.*—Explain the difference between integrant and constituent particles.

P.—*Integrant particles* are the smallest particles into which a body can be mechanically divided, and resemble each other and the mass which they originally composed. *Constituent particles* are those which form the integrant particles of a complex body, differing from each other and the mass which they form. For example, the particles of iodine, and those of silver in a mass of iodide of silver, are the constituent particles of that body.

GENERAL QUESTIONS ON LESSON I.

1. What is chemistry?
2. Give the general and secondary properties of matter, and examples of each.
3. What are the chief chemical agents?
4. Explain the difference between attraction and repulsion, and give examples of each.
5. Define analysis and synthesis, their derivation, and examples of each.
6. What is the difference between a simple and a compound body?
7. What is an integrant particle?
8. What is a constituent particle?

LESSON II.

THE student in Chemistry should endeavour to imitate the great Davy, by constructing rude and extemporaneous forms of apparatus for himself. It is not necessary to have expensive apparatus for the elementary part of the science; indeed, with a few simple things the student may perform the greater portion of the experiments required. Let him procure a few Florence flasks, such as salad oil is sold in, five or six gallipots or tea-cups, four or five common plates, a basin, a dozen phials, a glass funnel, a pestle and mortar, some glass tubing of different sizes, two dozen large corks, a few wine-glasses, an iron saucepan, a triangular file, a yard of brass tubing one-eighth of an inch in diameter, and a foot one quarter of an inch in diameter, some long glass jars, copper and iron wire (o to O), a few blocks of wood, and a brass stop-cock, if possible. If to these we add a common blowpipe, a piece of platinum foil and wire, he will be in possession of nearly all the apparatus required; but occasionally we shall have to construct extemporaneous apparatus for his use, which a few shillings will pay for. It is a positive advantage to a student to be thrown upon his own resources, as it gives him a habit of thinking and observing. If he is ingenious and careful, he will contrive to convert many things to his use, that others would throw away. Let him save all the broken window glass, and cut it into long, thin strips; they will serve to evaporate solutions

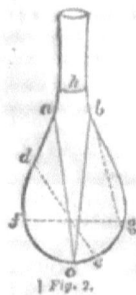
Fig. 2.

upon, or act as stirring rods; some of the glass should be cut into pieces varying from 2 to 6 or 8 inches square, as they are useful for covering solutions in small vessels, and many other purposes. The feet of wine-glasses, &c. may also be used for covering solutions; the bottoms of broken tumblers will frequently serve as evaporating dishes; stoppers of all kinds are useful, and should be kept to fit bottles, &c., by grinding them with a little sand and water. Very good evaporating dishes may be made by *slightly* scratching a Florence flask with a file, and then passing a red-hot iron wire in the direction required. For example—in the directions *a c* and *b c* in *Fig.* 2, which will enable us to have dishes with very tolerable lips (*a* and *b*) for pouring fluids from them. As these flasks are sometimes apt to be broken when used as retorts, the pieces should be saved, as dishes may be formed from them by following the same plan in the directions *f g, d e*, and *b g*. The neck *h* may be converted into a small test-tube, by means of a blow-pipe, and a red-hot wire. A common tobacco-pipe makes a tolerable temporary blow-pipe; and a common flower-pot an excellent extemporaneous furnace; but these are matters we must leave for the present, to consider affinity or chemical attraction, which is the basis of Chemistry.

QUESTIONS.

15. *T.*—What is chemical affinity?

P.—It is that property of matter which causes heterogeneous or dissimilar bodies to combine, and form compounds frequently quite different from the substances which compose them. For example [Experiment 1], I will dissolve these copper filings, or this piece of copper wire, in a little sulphuric acid (oil of vitriol), and allow it to crystallize, and then we shall get a salt commonly called *blue stone* (sulphate of copper), which is quite different from the acid, or the metal in its appearance or properties. Caustic vegetable alkali will corrode the flesh, and so will oil of vitriol; but when these two are united, we get a salt called sulphate of potash, which may be swallowed with safety.

16. *T.*— Why did you call potash a vegetable alkali?

P.—To distinguish it from soda the mineral, and ammonia the volatile alkali.

17. *T.*—It appears, then, that change of form and properties are results of chemical combination. Is it so?

P.—Yes. *Two solids will produce a fluid.* [Experiment 2.] I have a lump of solid ice, and a lump of salt, another solid; and when I place these two together, they will combine and form a fluid [places them in contact.] You observe that we have produced a quantity of brine by our experiment, therefore the form of the substances are altered. Again, *solids will produce a gas.* [Experiment 3.] Here are a few grains of gunpowder, and you will see that, when I place the end of this heated wire on them, they will explode, and become converted into a gaseous form. *Two gaseous bodies will form a solid;* thus, if we mix the vapour of ammonia with hydrochloric acid **gas, dense** white fumes will be produced, **which** then collect in flakes and fall on the sides and bottom of the jar; this product is muriate of ammonia or sal ammoniac. *Two gases will produce a liquid.* [Experiment 4.] I have some olefiant gas in the jar which is marked O, and an equal volume of chlorine gas in the jar marked **C**, and if you observe closely you will see an oily compound produced, when the two gases are mixed [mixes them]. You see it collects in large drops on the sides of the jar in which they were mixed, and the gases are being gradually absorbed. This oily compound is called chloride of olefiant gas; but we have other matters to consider before we can describe all about the gases.

18. *T.*—Are there not other changes of form?

P.—Yes; but the consideration of them would occupy too much of our time.

[The pupil should be required to give some examples of those changes of form and quality. For example, *a liquid and a solid form a liquid* (salt mixed with water). *Liquids produce gases* (nitric, and hydrochloric acids, &c.]

19. *T.*—**Are all** bodies affected in the same manner?

P.—No; the **attractive** force is exerted with different degrees **of** force between different bodies; sometimes it acts very feebly, sometimes with great energy, and at other times we cannot detect its existence at **all.**

20. *T.*—How do you know that all bodies are not similarly affected?

P.—By experiment. [Experiment 5.] Here is a piece of camphor, and you will see that when it is placed in this wine-glass, containing alcohol, it will dissolve. [Places the camphor in the alcohol, and it dissolves.] Now, if some water be poured into the glass the camphor will be separated, because the alcohol combines with the water. In this case combination and decomposition both takes place, the water combines with the alcohol, and decomposition of the camphor and alcohol is the result.

21. *T.*—Has not this combination been called by some particular name?

P.—Yes; Bergman named it *single elective affinity.*

22. *T.*—Why did he call it *elective* affinity?

P.—Because a substance chooses or elects one substance from several others in preference, and to the exclusion of the rest, and then combines with it. The particles of a certain body, having an affinity for the particles of another body, will unite with them, but if **they** have not **any affinity** for another body **they** will not **combine.**

23. *T.*—Give me an illustration of this.

P.—[Experiment 6.] Here is a small piece of **gold, which** I will place in this wine-glass, **and** then pour some *aquafortis* (nitric **acid**) upon it. [Does so.] You observe that no change has taken place ; **but** when the gold is removed and some potash added, chemical combination is **the result, and** nitrate of potash, or saltpetre, is formed. In this experiment we see that the acid had a stronger affinity for the potash than the gold, in fact, its affinity for gold is imperceptible.

24. *T.*—Then you think that **some** substances have a stronger affinity for one substance than for another ?

P.—Undoubtedly; and if you **refer to** the following tables you will **see that** it really is the case.

I. Sulphuric Acid.	II. Oxygen.
Baryta.	Zinc.
Strontia.	Lead.
Potash.	Copper.
Soda.	Mercury.
Lime.	Silver.
Magnesia.	
Ammonia.	

Now, **if we look at** Table **I. we see** that sulphuric acid has an affinity for ammonia, and the result is sulphate of ammonia ; but then, if we add magnesia to the solution, decomposition will take place, and sulphate of magnesia will be the result. This proves that the acid has an affinity for all the substances placed below the lime, and will combine separa**tely** with each, but that the bases of the salts formed may be decomposed or separated from the acid by adding any of the substances above it to the solution, until we arrive **at** baryta, and then we find that the other substances do not exert any power **over** the affinity of baryta and sulphuric acid. The **same** thing occurs in Table II. with **regard to** oxygen, **and** the various metals placed underneath it.

25. *T.*—Are there any laws by which **the** phenomena of chemical attraction are regulated ?

P.—Certainly. 1st. The **force is** said to e exerted in different degrees **by** various bodies. 2nd. As it operates on **the** molecules of bodies, it is found that its action is promoted by any method which assists the mechanical division and intermixture of the minute particles. 3rd. Chemical combination is generally attended by alteration of temperature, and sometimes emission of light. 4th. Opposite states of electricity are observed between bodies which have an affinity for each other. 5th. Chemical combination consists of the combination **of a** certain number of the molecules or atoms **of** one body, with some definite number **of atoms** of the other body combining **with** it. 6. Chemical attraction takes place either by simple or compound affinity. 7. All compound bodies uniting with other bodies without undergoing decomposition, act as simple bodies.

GENERAL QUESTIONS ON LESSON II.

1. Is it necessary to have expensive apparatus for the study of chemistry ?
2. Define chemical affinity.
3. How many kinds of alkalies are there ?
4. **Does** chemical affinity change the form and quality of bodies ?
5. Is **the** force of chemical attraction the same for all bodies ?
6. What are the laws regulating chemical attraction.

LESSON III.

We do not require to study **Chemistry very** deeply to discover that an alteration of temperature generally takes place when bodies combine. *Heat* is evolved when sulphuric acid (oil **of** vitriol) is mixed with water, or when lime is slacked. The production of *cold* takes place only when heat is rendered insensible by the conversion of a solid into a fluid, or a liquid into a gas. [Experiment 7.] Thus, by combining three parts of sulphate of soda, and two parts of diluted nitric acid, eighty degrees of cold is produced. [Experiment 8.] If we mix two parts of pounded ice with one part of chloride sodium (common salt), we shall cause the mercury in a thermometer to sink to five degrees, when surrounded by the mixture. This effect will always be produced, whatever may be the temperature the thermometer was occupying previous to the experiment; the mercury will never fall lower.

Before entering into the consideration of other matters, it will be necessary to examine some **of the phenomena attending** combustion: **Firstly.** Because they are intimately connected with heat; Secondly. Because they are so **frequently** witnessed, and so little understood by **the** chemical student.

QUESTIONS.

26. *T.*—What is COMBUSTION?
P.—The phenomena exhibited by burning substances, which are attended by heat and light, and the production of new compounds.

27. *T.*—Will any substance burn?
P.—No. It must be a combustible substance.

28. *T.*—Suppose that we heat a piece of iron, and make it what is commonly termed red-hot, is not that combustion?
P.—No; although it emits light and heat it does not *burn*, it is only *incandescent* or ignited.

29. *T.*—Then what do you mean by combustion? Give me an example.
P.—The body experimented upon *burns* or consumes in combustion; but, when rendered incandescent, it cools again, and remains unaltered, or nearly so. For example, [Experiment 9] take a piece of charcoal and set it on fire; it will burn and waste away, and finally leave a residue of white ash. We know that it has been consumed by combustion, and heat has been evolved; we feel the heat, and therefore know such is the case. When we heat a bar of iron, heat is evolved, but the iron does not consume, because its temperature is not kept up by the heat evolved in its union with the oxygen of the air.

30. *T.*—How is it that the **charcoal is** destroyed, and the iron is not?
P.—The charcoal is *not destroyed*, **but** altered in form. There is not any such thing **as** destruction in Nature. Matter never ceases to exist, although its form alters, for annihilation is contrary to the laws of Nature.

31. *T.*—How do you know that substances are altered in form, without being destroyed?
P.—By experiment. [Eperiment 10.] If I place a piece of heated charcoal under a glass jar it generates a gas called *carbonic acid*, which is known by adding some lime-water, the result of which is a white precipitate of carbonate of lime.

32. *T.*—Do the substances which burn support combustion?
P.—No, they neither support it, nor burn, unless when assisted by a supporter of combustion, which will not burn of itself, although it supports combustion.

33. *T.*—What is the chief supporter of combustion?
P.—Oxygen gas.

34. *T.*—How do you know that it supports combustion?
P.—Because, if a lighted candle is plunged into this gas, the taper burns more brilliantly, but the gas itself is not ignited. If the same candle is plunged into a jar of coal gas the gas is ignited, and the candle extinguished.

35. *T.*—Is it not possible to burn **iron,** and other bodies of a like nature?
P.—Yes; we can burn the most incombustible bodies by means of the oxyhydrogen blowpipe, even tobacco-pipes, pipe-clay, &c.

36. *T.*—When I placed a lighted candle under a glass jar, the jar became covered with moisture, and then the candle went out. What was the reason?
P.—The moisture was water, caused by the hydrogen of the candle uniting with

E 3

part of the oxygen of the air within the glass. Then the carbon of the candle united with a part of the oxygen of the air, and formed carbonic acid gas, which is not a supporter of combustion; and as the oxygen, the chief supporter of combustion, was withdrawn, the candle went out.

GENERAL QUESTIONS ON LESSON III.

1. Can we burn any substance?
2. What is the difference between combustible and incombustible substances?
3. What is incandescence?
4. Can substances be destroyed?

LESSON IV.

WE have seen that the oxygen of the air is a supporter of combustion, **and hence it** follows, that in order to maintain combustion, a fresh supply of air must be established, and the smoke allowed to escape. It is therefore evident, that combustion, after all, is nothing more than a process of *oxidation*, or combination of oxygen with the body consumed. Now combination is not merely mixing, it is more; it is the intimate and close union of substances. For example, [Experiment 11] **we** have some oil in this bottle, and when I add some water to it, you will see that **the two** substances mix, but they do not combine, because when they have stood a short **time**, the oil will separate itself from the water. [The bottle is allowed to stand, and the oil is **then** seen floating on the top of the water]. I will **cause** these two bodies to *combine*, by adding another substance—potash, and then we shall get **a** soapy compound, differing from the oil, the water, or the potash.

The elevation of temperature generally promotes the chemical action of bodies, but nevertheless, the effect will depend, in certain cases, on the degree of heat adapted for particular purposes. For example, if we expose mercury in a proper vessel, and in **contact with the** air to a heat of 680° Fahrenheit, it becomes converted into the red **oxide of mercury.** If we expose the red oxide of mercury to 980° Fahrenheit, the **mercury will be** reproduced in its metallic state, and a gas given off, which is oxygen. **This naturally** leads us to reflect, what caused the red oxide of mercury to resolve **itself** into the metal, mercury—and the gas, oxygen? Heat. It could not have been effected by any other means than heat. We therefore learn that heat is an important agent in chemical combination.

When elements unite with elements, chemists regard the union as combinations of the *first order*—as acids and bases. When these combine, to form *salts*, we have combinations of the *second order*. When we find *double salts* resulting from the union of salts with salts, we regard them as combinations of the *third order*. Bodies do not generally combine chemically, otherwise than in fixed proportions; hence every body, the result of chemical combination, generally contains fixed proportions. For example, water always consists of one atom of hydrogen, and one atom of oxygen.

[The pupil should read Lessons III., IV., and V., of *Natural Philosophy*, before entering upon the question of this Lesson.]

QUESTIONS.

37. *T.*—What is the atomic theory?
P.—It is the theory which explains the manner in which the atoms of bodies combine chemically in certain proportions to form new substances. For example, we know that an atom of hydrogen and an

atom of oxygen combine and form water, the atomic weight of which is 9; hence it follows that the relative weight of the atom of hydrogen to the atom of oxygen is as 1 to 8, which is the same as saying that the atom of hydrogen weighs one grain, and the atom of oxygen eight grains.

38. *T.*—Then I suppose that is the reason water is always said to be composed of 1 volume of hydrogen and 8 volumes of oxygen?

P.—You are correct. It is nothing more than saying, water is composed of so many measures of each gas, instead of volumes.

39. *T.*—Do not some bodies combine in all proportions?

P.—Yes; for example, gold and silver, water and alcohol, and water and sulphuric acid. Other bodies combine in all proportions to a certain point, but cannot be made to combine after that; for example, water will dissolve and hold in solution any salt, (as alum or Epsom salts,) but after it has dissolved a certain portion, it is said to be saturated, and cannot dissolve any more. Some bodies unite in several definite proportions; for example, 14 parts of nitrogen will combine with 8·16, or 24 parts of oxygen, but will not combine with any intermediate proportion. Certain bodies unite in only one proportion, as chlorine and hydrogen.

40. *T.*—Have all bodies the same kind of atoms?

P.—No; simple bodies have simple atoms, and compound bodies have compound atoms. For example:—

OXYGEN.   SODIUM.   NITRATE OF SODA.

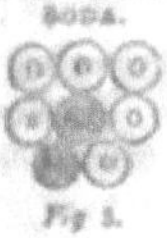

Fig. 3.   *Fig.* 4.   *Fig.* 5.

Figs. 3 and 4 **are diagrams** representing simple atoms of oxygen and sodium (*natrium*), but *Fig.* 5 represents **the** compound atoms of nitrate of soda.

41. *T.*—Have these atoms any weight, that you say the atomic weight of water is 9?

P.—We do not know anything of the *absolute* weight of atoms; they are too small to weigh; therefore we can only determine the *relative* weight of atoms, but it is certain that atoms have some weight.

42. *T.*—How can you determine the relative atomic weight of bodies?

P.—By fixing a particular number, as the atomic weight of any one substance, and then determining the atomic weights of other bodies, according to the proportions by weight in which they unite. For example, let us assume that the atomic weight of hydrogen is equal **to** 1, the atomic weights of other bodies may then be found; thus 100 parts of sulphuretted hydrogen contain 5·9 parts of hydrogen and 94·1 parts of sulphur. We suppose that there are an equal number of atoms of hydrogen, and the same of sulphur, therefore we have the proportion of 5·9 : 94·1 equal to 1 : 16. Thus we know that the atomic weight of sulphur is **16**, if that of hydrogen is 1.

43. *T.*—Has the knowledge of the relative weights of the atoms been usefully applied?

P.—Yes; the relative weights of the atoms of bodies, and their chemical equivalents, are expressed by the same **numbers.**

44. *T.*—Who invented the **atomic** theory?

P.—Dalton, in 1804. He supposed the atoms of bodies to be spherical, and invented symbols to represent the manner in which he thought they combined together. Thus, hydrogen was represented by a circle with a dot in the centre; nitrogen, by a circle with a vertical line drawn through the centre; oxygen, by a plain circle; and carbon, by a black sphere.

45. *T.*—How did he classify the combinations of atoms?

P.—Those substances containing only 2 atoms he called *binary* compounds, those having 3 atoms, *ternary* compounds, those with 4 atoms, *quaternary*, &c.

46. *T.*—Is it probable that the **disposi**tion or arrangement of the atoms of **solid** bodies can influence their form?

P.—Certainly. When a solution of any salt is set aside to crystallize, and the process goes on slowly, *regular* crystals are obtained; but if it is too sudden, the crystals are *irregular.*

47. *T.*—How does this prove that form depends upon the arrangement of the atoms?

P.—If they are arranged suddenly and without order, the same salt that always crystallizes in octahedral crystals, will be amorphous from *a* (α) without, and *morphe* (μορφη) form, or devoid of regular forms. For example, I have eight balls here, and can arrange them into many forms, thus:—

a	b	c	d	e
ooo	o	oo	o	oo
ooo	ooo	oo	oo	oooo
oo	ooo	oo	oo	oo
		o	oo	ooo

Fig. 6.

but it is possible to make them assume more figures than those I have formed, and as it is probable that all the atoms of bodies are not the same size, we can easily understand how the form of bodies is altered by the arrangement of their atoms.

48. *T.*—Explain how this affects their form.

P.—I have four apples here, 1, 2, 3, 4; and if I place them upon the table, as in *Fig.* 7, and draw four lines round them, I

Fig. 7.

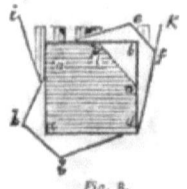
Fig. 8.

shall have a figure like that represented by *a, b, c, d,* in *Fig.* 8, which has its four sides equal. Suppose that I remove the apple marked 2 from within the square, and place a nut in the spot marked 5 in *Fig.* 7, and then draw a line (*ln*) so as to touch the apples 1 and 4, and include the nut, the form will be similar to the shaded part within the square. If we substitute two large cricket-balls for the apples 1 and 2, the figure will be wedge-shaped, like that within the lines *i c, c d, d k,* and *k i;* but, if we put the balls where 2 and 3 are, the figure will be **similar to** that enclosed by the lines *ah, hg,* **gd,** *df, fe,* and *ea*. Let us suppose that the apple marked 2 is removed, and replaced by a pear; provided it is the same **size,** the form will not be altered. It is thus with the atoms of some crystals, they may be removed, and replaced by other atoms, without altering the form of the crystals; hence we infer that certain atoms are isomorphous.

49. *T.*—What do you mean by the term *isomorphous?*

P.—The term is derived from two Greek words, *isos* (ισος) equal, and *morphe* (μορφη) form, and signifies of the same form. For example, the phosphate and biphosphate of soda are of the same form as the arseniate and binarseniate of soda, and only differ in the one salt containing phosphorus, and the other arsenic.

GENERAL QUESTIONS ON LESSON IV.

1. What is the difference between a mixture and a combination?
2. How are chemical combinations classified?
3. Explain the atomic theory.
4. Have all bodies atoms resembling each other?
5. Can we weigh atoms?
6. To what purpose has the knowledge of the relative weights of the atoms of bodies been applied?
7. Explain the terms amorphous and isomorphous.
8. How does the arrangement of atoms influence the form of bodies?

LESSON V.

There are some facts connected with the atomic theory which are worthy of remark. We observe that certain substances, having different forms and qualities, are composed of the same materials. How is this to be accounted for? The atomic theory comes to our assistance, and seems to say that it is the arrangement of the particles or atoms. For example, the cyanic and fulminic acids are isomeric compounds of carbon, oxygen, and nitrogen. From this we learn that the same elements may be grouped in different ways, which is the same as saying that having a dozen bricks it is possible to place them in other positions than one above the other, but that their position does not alter the materials. It is not absolutely imperative that pewter (an alloy of tin with lead and antimony) **should** be made into measures, the same materials will form dish-covers, hot-water plates, dishes, &c.; and so it is with the atoms of certain materials, as they are placed in groups, differing from each other in arrangement, so will the compounds they form differ in their qualities, properties, and appearance. **Some** bodies consist of the same elements, in the same ratio, and yet differ in their equivalents.

QUESTIONS.

50. *T.*—What is the derivation and meaning of the word isomeric?

P.—It is derived from two Greek words, *isos* (ισος), equal; and *meros* (μερος), part; and is applied to those substances which contain the same elements, in the same proportions, and yet differ essentially in their chemical qualities.

51. *T.*—How does the atomic theory solve the problem of the isomeric state of bodies depending upon the grouping of their atoms?

P.—Simply by demonstrating the arrangement of the atoms. If we take twelve square pieces of wood we can easily see how this is effected. For example, we see that

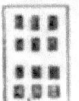

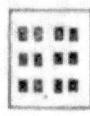

Fig. 9.　*Fig.* 10.　*Fig.* 11.　*Fig.* 12.

in *Fig.* 9 the atoms are arranged in groups containing six in each; in *Fig.* 10 each group contains 3; in *Fig.* 11 each group consists of two; and, in *Fig.* 12, the atoms combine in groups of three. [See Question 47.]

52. *T.*—You said (Q. 41) that atoms have weight—How do you know that they have?

P.—Although we cannot weigh them, because they are so small, yet it is certain that they must possess some degree of weight. If we take the common puff-ball fungus in our hands, we are sensible that it possesses weight; when it bursts, and scatters its fine dust, we discover that each particle is about $\frac{1}{1000}$th of an inch in diameter. Now it would be as absurd to attempt to define the weight of one of **these** particles, as it would be to weigh the perfume emitted from a grain of musk, and yet, if these particles did not possess weight, the puff-ball, or the grain of musk, could not have weight.

53. *T.*—Have the atomic weights, or, **as** they are sometimes called, the chemical equivalents of the elementary bodies, been determined?

P.—Yes; and arranged into groups.

54. *T.*—How are the elementary bodies arranged?

P.—They are divided into the non-metallic and metallic groups. The non-metallic elements are divided into *gazolytes*, or bodies which are permanently gaseous; *halogens*, or bodies which produce salts when combined with the metals; and *metalloids*, or bodies resembling metals in their chemical relations.

55. *T.*—**How are the elements** expressed in chemistry?

P.—**By symbols, which** were selected by **Berzelius, from Latin** names, because that **language is known to** all civilized nations.

56. *T.*—What is the use of symbols?

P.—They enable us to express the composition of a definite chemical compound in a concise manner, by using the initials of the elementary bodies, and numbers annexed to them, denoting the number of atoms of the several constituents existing in the compound.

57. *T.*—Suppose that a symbol has not any number affixed—what does it mean?

P.—That only one atom of the substance exists in the compound.

58. *T.*—Is there any particular method of arrangement observed in expressing chemical formulæ by symbols?

P.—Yes. Electro-positive substances, such as metals and salifiable bases, precede electro-negative substances, such as oxygen and acids, in the formulæ. Oxygen is frequently expressed by a dot, placed over the symbol of the body with which it is in combination. Thus, oxide of lead is written **Pb**; silica, Si; and sulphuric acid S; **we** therefore learn that the lead contains one atom, the silica two atoms, and the sulphuric acid three atoms, of oxygen. When a compound contains proximate and ultimate elements, the mode of union is expressed by means of points, commas, + signs, and brackets. For example, crystallized sulphate of ammonia (one atom of ammonia, one atom of sulphuric acid, and two atoms of water) is $NH^3 + SO^3 + 2 HO = NH^3 SO^3$, $2 HO = \overset{...}{N} \overset{..}{S} H^2$. The dots under the symbol of a body denote atoms of hydrogen; and commas, or strokes leaning from right to left, atoms of sulphur—as, when we express the tersulphuret of molybdenum, thus, $\overset{'''}{Mo}$. A number placed on the right and upper part of a symbol, expresses the number of atoms of the substance denoted by the symbol — thus, SO^3 means one atom of sulphur, and three atoms of oxygen.

59. *T.*—Why do you place the number above the symbol, instead of below, which is more usual with chemists?

P.—Because it is more easily read than when placed below.

60. *T.*—What do the numbers placed before symbols mean?

P.—A number placed before several symbols multiplies them all as far as the next + sign, or comma; or, if the number is placed before a bracket, it multiplies all the numbers or symbols within the brackets —thus, $KO + 2 CO^2 + HO = KO$, CO^2, $HO = K\overset{..}{C}^2$ if, means, that one atom of potash, two atoms of carbonic acid, and one atom of water, unite to form bicarbonate of potash, and $8 (CaO, SeO^3) + KO^1, 2 S, {}^1O^3 + 16 Aq.$, gives the composition of apophyllite; $2 HO$ means two atoms of hydrogen, and two atoms of oxygen.

61. *T.*—What is meant by a stroke over a symbol?

P.—Berzelius used it to express the vegetable and animal acids—thus, $\bar{T}$, signifies tartaric acid, and $\bar{F}$ formic acid.

62. *T.*—Why have some symbols a stroke under them?

P.—It is an abbreviation sometimes used to denote two equivalents of a substance; thus, $\underline{Fe}$ instead of $Fe^2 O^3$, or it may be written $\underline{Fe} O^3$.

63. *T.*—Have not certain compounds particular symbols appropriated to them?

P.—Yes; water is written Aq; cyanogen, Cy; tartaric acid, $\bar{T}$; citric acid, $\bar{C}$; acetic acid, $\bar{A}$; Morphia, M; &c.

64. *T.*—How is the water of crystallization expressed?

P.—By attaching an h to the symbol of the substance; thus $\bar{A}h$ denotes the hydrate of acetic acid.

GENERAL QUESTIONS ON LESSON V.

1. How is it that certain substances, composed of the same materials, possess different qualities and forms?

2. Explain the meaning of isomeric, and give its derivation.

3. How do we know that atoms have weight?

4. How are the elementary bodies arranged and expressed?

5. Do symbols express the elementary bodies in a satisfactory manner?

6. Give illustrations of the various symbols.

LESSON VI.

WE have found how certain substances may be expressed by abbreviating them, and as every beginner in chemistry is somewhat alarmed by seeing so many great h's, o's, and other letters, combined with +'s and figures staring him in the face, we must take this opportunity of recommending that the symbols—which are, in fact, the alphabet of chemistry—be practised by the pupil with a piece of soft chalk on a slate or board. If a little attention is given to the subject, an hour's practice will overcome the difficulty. It is said that chemistry has a great many hard names, but, really, it does not abound with more than any other science, and after all, they are very simple. For example, we meet with the words *oxide*, *chloride*, *bromide*, &c., but they only mean the combination of metals with these substances, and it is not more difficult to understand them than saying a *syrup* of orange, mulberry, &c., or an *essence* of lemon, verbena, &c. "Oh, but **are not** those long names, *protoxide*, *bi-chloride*, &c., very disagreeable and difficult?" says a lazy juvenile. No; they are really very easy. Let us see what they mean. *Proto* means first, and therefore a *protoxide* is a single oxide; *deutoxide*, **or** *binoxide*, a double oxide; *tritoxide*, or *teroxide*, a triple oxide, &c.; and when **the base** is saturated with oxygen (still not acid) it is called a *peroxide*. All the **difficulty** attending these names will be removed by remembering that each name has a prefix, which explains the meaning; thus *proto* means 1; *sesqui*, 1½; *bi*, *bin*, *deuto*, *di*, 2; *ter*, *tris*, 3; *quadro*, 4; *quinto*, 5; &c.

As we shall meet with some other names of a peculiar kind, it will be better to examine their meaning first. We shall find that acids ending in *ic* form salts with bases that end in *ate*—at least, such is a general rule; for example, sulphur*ic* acid and potassa form sulph*ate* of potash. Acids ending in *ous* form salts that end in *ite*; **thus**, phosphor*ous* acid and potassa form phosph*ite* of potash. When we meet with words terminating in *uret*, we know that the simple non-metallic substances are in combination with each other, with a metal, or with a metallic oxide; thus, carbur*et* of iron means a combination of carbon with iron. The names of most metals end in *um* —as sodi*um*, platin*um*, &c.—and alkaline bases, when expressed in one word terminate in *a*, as magnesi*a* and potass*a*. The prefix *hypo*, means less; thus *hypo*-sulphuric acid means an acid with less oxygen than the sulphuric, and more than the sulphurous. **The** prefixes *hyper* and *per* signify more; thus, *hyper*-nitrous, and *per*-chloric acids, means acids with more oxygen than the nitrous and chloric.

QUESTIONS.

65. *T.*—Name the first group of the elementary bodies, and give the equivalents and the symbols at the same time.

P.—The first group, the *gazolytes*, contains three elementary bodies, viz.:—

	Symbol.	Equiv.
Hydrogen	H.	1
Oxygen	O.	8
Nitrogen	N.	14

66. *T.*—**What substances are** found in the second group?

P.—The *halogens* consist of **four** bodies, viz.:—

	Symbol.	Equiv.
Bromine	Br.	78·4
Chlorine	Cl.	35·4
Fluorine	F.	18·7
Iodine	I.	126

67.—Name the metalloids.

P.—This group contains only four bodies, viz.:—

	Symbol.	Equiv.
Boron	B.	10·9
Carbon	C.	6
Phosphorus	P.	31·4
Sulphur	S.	16

68. *T.*—Name the metals.

P.—They are fifty in number, viz.:—

Name.	Symbol.	Equiv.
Aluminum	Al.	13·7
Antimony (*Stibium*)*	Sb.	129
Arsenic	As.	75.2
Barium	Ba.	68·6
Bismuth	Bi.	106·4
Cadmium	Cd.	55·8
Calcium	Ca.	20·5
Cerium†	Ce.	46·3
Chromium	Cr.	28·1
Cobalt	Co.	29·6
Copper (*Cuprum*)	Cu.	31·8
Didymium	Di.	49·6
Erbium	?	?
Glucinum	G.	17·7
Gold (*Aurum*)	Au.	199
Iridium	Ir.	98·7
Iron (*Ferrum*)	Fe.	27·2
Lanthanum	Ln.	96·1
Lead (*Plumbum*)	Po.	103·8
Lithium	Li.	6·4

* The names within brackets are the Latin names of the elements.

† The elementary bodies printed in *italics* are rarely met with, and are unimportant.

Names of Metals—continued.

Name.	Symbol.	Equiv.
Magnesium	Mg.	12·7
Manganese	Mn.	27·6
Mercury (*Hydrangyrum*)	Hg.	101·4
Molybdenum	Mo.	48
Nickel	Ni.	29·6
Niobium	?	?
Osmium	Os.	99·6
Palladium	Pd.	53·4
Pelopium	?	?
Platinum	Pt.	98·7
Potassium (*Kalium*)	K.	39·2
Rhodium	R.	52·1
Ruthenium	Ru.	51·7
Selenium	Se.	40
Silicium	Si.	14·8
Silver (*Argentum*)	Ag.	108·1
Sodium (*Natronium*)	Na.	23·2
Strontium	Sr.	44
Tantalium	Ta.	185
Terbium	?	?
Tellurium	Te.	64
Thorium	Th.	59·6
Tin (*Stannum*)	St.	59
Titanium	Ti.	24·3
Tungsten (*Wolframium*)	W.	95
Uranium	U.	217
Vanadium	V.	68·6
Yttrium	Y.	32·2
Zinc	Zn.	32·2
Zirconium	Zr.	22·4

69. *T.*—Will these equivalents enable us to find the composition of the compounds of these elements?

P.—Yes. We can learn that by finding out the weight of the atoms of its ingredients, from the groups we have examined, and adding them together: thus, Oxide of Copper is expressed by Cu O; and, as we know that the equivalent of copper is 31·8, and that of oxygen 8, we add them together, and that gives us the atomic weight of oxide of copper—viz. 39·8.

70. *T.*—Can we find the composition of any compound as easily?

P.—Yes. For example, Peroxide of Manganese is represented by $Mn\,O_2$, and by adding 27·6, the equivalent of manganese, to 16, which is equal to two atoms of oxygen, we get 43·6 as the product, which is the atomic weight. Let us take sulphuret of bismuth for another example; the symbol for this is Bi^2 and S^3, and, by the same rule, we find that its equivalent is 260·8.

[The pupil should be requested to explain the meaning of the following symbols, and to give their equivalents—viz., $Cu^2\,S$; $Pb\,S$; $Cd\,S$; $H\,S^5$; $As\,Fe^3$; $Zn\,O$, $S\,O_3$, 7 HO.]

71. *T.*—Have not some chemists proposed the adoption of other terms, instead of sulphuret and phosphuret?

P.—Yes, Professors Graham and Hoffmann propose using the terms sulph*ide* and phosh*ide*.

GENERAL QUESTIONS ON LESSON VI.

1. Explain the meaning of the various prefixes to chemical names.
2. When the names of acids end in *ic*, how do the names of their salts terminate?
3. When acids end in *ous*, how do the names of their salts terminate?
4. How do the names of most metals and alkalis end?
5. Give the symbols and equivalents of each group of elementary bodies.
6. How can we find the equivalents of compound bodies?

LESSON VII.

WE have already noticed some of the peculiarities and properties of heat (p. 22), but as some of the processes in connexion with the science of chemistry are under great obligations to this agent, we must notice some other properties belonging to it. Heat or Caloric is the great agent of repulsion, as its particles repel each other. It causes bodies to expand, and pass from a solid to a liquid, and from a liquid to a gaseous form, and we are enabled to observe the changes of temperature by availing ourselves of this property. Thus we measure the degrees of heat by means of a thermometer (*Fig.* 13), an instrument constructed for materials which readily expand

CHEMISTRY.

by heat. We have already learned (p. 22) **how heat is** communicated, and it has been found by experiment that certain bodies **are** better conductors than others, hence they have been divided into *conductors* and *non-conductors*, and their relative conducting power has been **given** by Despretz **as** follows:—

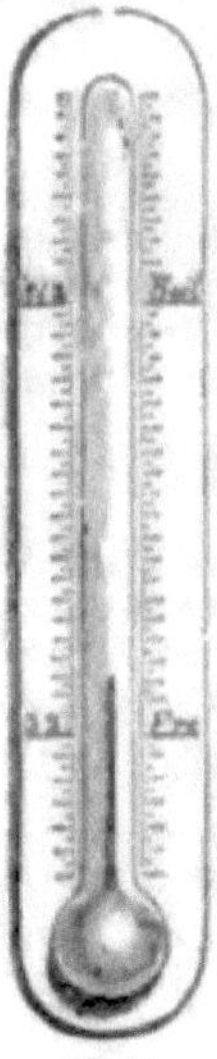

Gold	1000	Tin	303.9
Silver	973	Lead	179.6
Copper	898.2	Marble	23.6
Platinum	381	Porcelain	12.2
Iron	374.3	Fine Clay	11.4
Zinc	363		

From this **we** learn that metals are the **best** conductors; liquids and æriform fluids are very imperfect conductors of caloric. When a solid becomes a liquid, **a** certain amount of heat becomes latent, that is to say, it is, as it were, squeezed out and disappears; and **when** a liquid becomes a solid, a corresponding effect is produced. Latent heat varies according to the substances operated on; for example, the heat of fluidity in

Bismuth	550°
Tin	500°
Zinc	493°
Bees-wax	175°
Lead	162°
Spermaceti	145°
Sulphur	143°
Water	142°

Fig. 13.

All bodies expand by heat, and contract on cooling.

QUESTIONS.

72. *T.*—When we place a vessel containing water upon the fire, how is the heat diffused?

P.—By *convection*—that is, the heated particles ascend, or are *carried* to the top of the vessel.

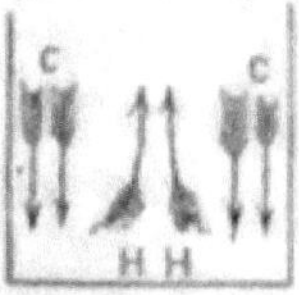

Fig. 14.

73. *T.*—Why does the water roll about and bubble up when it boils?

P.—Because the particles of which it is composed, are constantly put in motion by the contending currents, and the escape of steam.

74. *T.*—What currents are they of which you speak?

P.—An *ascending hot current* in the centre of the vessel (H H, *Fig.* 14), and a *descending cold current* on each side of the vessel (C C, *Fig.* 14).

75. *T.*—When we wish to measure high degrees of heat in chemical experiments, how do we manage?

P.—If the temperature is very high, like that of furnaces, we use one of Daniell's platina pyrometers, but if only for boiling liquids, we use a cylindrical thermometer, graduated on the glass tube to 572° Fahrenheit, which may be fitted into a cork, and thus be adapted for any vessel, or allowed to float in the liquid.

76. *T.*—What are the chief effects produced by heat?

P.—Expansion, liquefaction, **va**porisation, evaporation, and burning or ignition.

77. *T.*—How do you know that expansion is caused by heat?

P.—By experiment and observation. The iron rim of a cart **wheel** is expanded by heat before it is put **on**, and then when water is thrown over it, it cools and contracts, thus binding the spokes and circumference together.

[See Question 14, p. 6; and Question 38 and 39, p. 13.]

Fig. 15.

78. *T.*—Then this knowledge is practically applied?

P.—Certainly; in laying down railways, building iron bridges, and constructing all works of the kind where metal is much employed, provision is made for expansion?

79. *T.*—How do people know how much to calculate for the expansion?

P.—By referring to tables of the expansion of various bodies, and remembering that the degree of expansion is in the direct ratio of the increase of temperature, and that when the heat decreases, the body will contract again to its former size. MM. Lavoisier and Laplace investigated the subject, and the following is the result:—

English flint glass	$\frac{3}{1248}$*
Common French glass	$\frac{1}{1417}$
Glass without lead	$\frac{1}{1152}$
Steel, untempered	$\frac{1}{927}$
Steel, tempered	$\frac{1}{807}$
Soft iron	$\frac{1}{810}$
Gold	$\frac{1}{682}$
Copper	$\frac{1}{584}$
Brass	$\frac{1}{535}$
Silver	$\frac{1}{524}$
Lead	$\frac{1}{351}$

80. *T.*—What causes liquefaction?

P.—The repulsive agency of the caloric, which drives the particles of bodies capable of assuming the liquid form so far apart, that their cohesion is diminished, and they are rendered easily movable on one another in any direction.

81. *T.*—What is vaporisation?

P.—The rapid conversion of a solid or liquid into an aeriform state, as when water is converted into steam by boiling it. Now water boils at 212° under ordinary atmospheric pressure, but when this is removed it boils at a lower temperature. Steam is invisible, colourless, and transparent, which may be proved by looking at the spout of a tea-kettle, when it will be found that the first half inch from the spout appears unoccupied, but that the rest of the space in front is occupied by what is generally called steam, which is in reality condensed vapour. Steam is 1696 times greater in bulk than water; therefore, one volume of water will yield 1696 volumes of steam.

* The fractions show the amount of expansion in length of the rods of the various bodies passing from 32° to 212.°

82. *T.*—What is evaporation?

P.—The dissipation of a liquid by its conversion into vapour. It may be spontaneous, or caused by the application of heat.

83. *T.*—How is spontaneous evaporation produced?

P.—Partly by the temperature and partly by the solvent power of the atmospheric air forming a solution of the body. Ether, alcohol, and volatile oils are examples of the class of bodies that undergo this change.

84. *T.*—What is the object of employing heat to cause evaporation?

P.—To drive off the fluid from the substance held in solution; for evaporation is generally used for the purpose of obtaining salts from aqueous solutions; because when the fluid is valuable, as alcohol, for example, then the process of distillation is employed. When we wish to evaporate any solution, we employ a stand like that

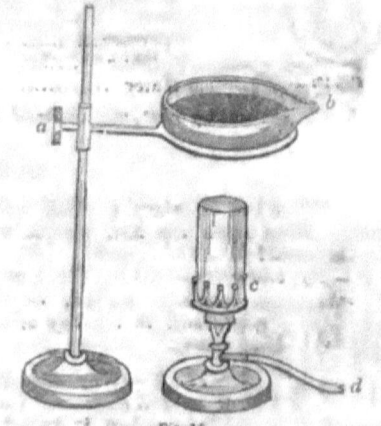

Fig. 16.

in *Fig.* 16, which has a movable slide (*a*), so that we can raise or lower the evaporating basin (*b*); the heat is supplied by means of an argand gas-burner, (*c*), supported on a heavy base, and furnished with a flexible tube of vulcanised India-rubber (*d*). If gas cannot be procured, a common argand oil-lamp, or a spirit-lamp will do.

85. *T.*—Is it necessary to employ a great heat for evaporating purposes, such as you have described?

P.—No. A very convenient method is to use an iron saucepan filled with sand, which is heated by resting it upon some bricks, and placing an argand lamp, similar to the one in *Fig.* 16, under it. This is preferable for glass or earthenware vessels, and is called a *sand-bath*. Sometimes the evaporating dish is placed over boiling water in another vessel, which is called a *water-bath*. A very convenient manner of evaporating small portions of fluids, is to hold a small slip of glass over the flame of a spirit-lamp, as in *Fig.* 17. Occasionally an evaporating dish is held over a spirit-lamp by means of a pair of tongs (*Fig.* 18) bent near the points. These tongs are very useful, being frequently

Fig. 17.

Fig. 18.

required for lifting small crucibles from sand-baths, or furnaces, &c.

86. *T.*—What is ignition?

P.—This scarcely requires explanation, because nearly everybody knows that bodies become luminous when exposed to a high degree of heat (800° in the dark, and about 1000° in the daylight), and radiate caloric without undergoing any great marked chemical change. When the body looks red hot it is said to be ignited; but when it appears paler, or what is called *white* hot, it is said to be *incandescent*.

87. *T.*—What is distillation?

P.—It is the condensation of the vapour of a liquid or solid, by means of a particular kind of apparatus. For example, in the preparation of alcohol and distilled waters, the common still is used. The materials to be distilled are placed in one part called a retort, which has a pipe connected with its narrow end; this pipe passes through cold water contained in a tub or other vessel, and as the pipe (or *worm*, as it is technically called) is coiled within the tub, every part of it is exposed to the refrigerating action of the cold water, which requires to be renewed occasionally. It may be conducted on a smaller scale by using a common glass retort, which may be fitted with a stopper, being then called

Fig. 19.

tubulated, as (*a*) in *Fig.* 19. The neck of the retort is inserted into a flask immersed in a basin of cold water, and the heat maintained by a lamp (*b*) placed under the retort.

GENERAL QUESTIONS ON LESSON VII.

1. How is caloric measured?
2. What changes may be ascribed to caloric?
3. Give the relative conducting power of bodies?
4. Give examples of the degrees of the heat of fluidity?
5. What is meant by convection?
6. Explain the phenomena of the bubbling and continued motion of boiling water?
7. How are high temperatures measured?
8. Give practical illustrations of expansion, liquefaction, vaporisation, evaporation, ignition, and distillation?

LESSON VIII.

WHEN we look around us, and see the many improvements made in objects that are daily brought under our notice, we are struck with the great benefits conferred upon us by Chemistry. The luxuriant crops of the farmer, the improvements in dyeing, bleaching, soap and candle-making, flax-dressing, smelting, photography and daguerreotyping, baking, brewing, distilling, calico-printing, and sugar-refining, are all familiar instances of the obligations we are under to Chemistry. We must not forget the improvements made in the manufacture and colouring of glass, the discovery of gun-cotton; the separation of wolfrum from tin, by Mr. Oxland's process of roasting; electro-gilding and silvering, the electric telegraph, the **Bude** light, porcelain manufacture; and the preservation of wood, canvass, &c., by Sir **W.** Burnett's chloride of zinc; they furnish **us with admirable** examples of the **application** of Chemistry to useful purposes, benefitting mankind by its results, and turning **our thoughts to** Him who developes the faculties of invention.

Before commencing the investigation of the elementary bodies, **we** must notice **some** of the **apparatus** and processes required. *Rectification* is performed by the aid of heat, **and is only the** repeated distillation of **any** product obtained by distillation, but as it **requires a lower** temperature than distillation, the more volatile parts only are raised **and pass into the** receiver, while the impurities remain behind. According to the **process** and the results, so it has received its name; thus, when the liquid is distilled **from any** substance it is called *abstraction;* when the product is re-distilled from the **same** materials, or another supply of the same materials, it receives the name of *cohobation;* and when the object is to increase the strength of the fluid by leaving the watery part behind, as in the case of spirits, the process is called *concentration* or *dephlegmation*. *Sublimation* is another process required to be performed; the product is called **a** *sublimate*. It consists in driving off certain volatile parts of substances, and condensing them again **in a** solid form, which is done by employing a common crucible with a cone of paper over it **in some** cases; in others, two flasks placed mouth to mouth may be used.

In determining the weight of bodies, the **Apothecaries** or Troy weight **is** commonly used, according to the following table:—

Pound [*libra* lb.]*   Ounces [*uncia* ℥]   Drachms [*drachma* ʒ]
1   =   12   =   96
                    1   =   8
                                    1

Scruples [*scrupulus* ℈]   Grains [*granum*, gr.]
288   =   5,760
24   =   480
3   =   60
1   =   20

And a common Apothecary's balance with the necessary weights, is all that is required.

Liquids are measured by the following table, in which it will be seen that *drops* are not recognised, as they are very liable to vary in quantity from various causes. Graduated glass measures of different sizes are used for measuring:—

Gallon [*congius* C]   Pints [*octarius* O]   Fluid ounces [*fluid-uncia* f℥]
1   =   8   =   128
                   1   =   16
                                 1

Fluid drachms [*fluid drachma* fʒ]   Minims [*minimum* ♏]
1,024   =   61,440
128   =   7,680
8   =   480
1   =   60

---

* The Latin names for the various weights and measures, and their distinguishing signs, are inserted between brackets. The Latin names are given in the singular.

QUESTIONS.

88. *T.*—What do you mean by the specific gravity of a body?

P.—It is the ratio of its weight to the weight of an equal bulk of another body, taken as a standard [Experiment 12.] If we fill one egg-cup with water and another with mercury or quicksilver, we shall find that although they both occupy the same space, yet the mercury is $13\frac{1}{2}$ times heavier than the water, and hence we say that the density of mercury is greater than that of water. [*See* Q. 55, p. 15.]

89. *T.*—How is the density or specific gravity of a body ascertained?

P.—It depends upon the nature of the body. That of *fluids* is easily obtained. For example, take a small bottle with a narrow neck (*Fig.* 20), and weigh it carefully. Then fill it with pure water up to a certain mark (*a*), and weigh it again. Now empty the bottle, dry it well, and fill it up to the same mark with any fluid—say, for example, beer —and weigh it again; then divide the weight of the fluid, (the beer) the specific gravity of which is required, by the weight of the water, and the product will indicate the specific weight. By employing a vial that holds exactly 1,000 grains of water,* much time and trouble in calculating is saved, because we only require to weigh the liquid contained in the bottle, and its weight expresses its specific gravity.

Fig. 20.

90. *T.*—Is it necessary to be particular with respect to the temperature of the fluid to be weighed?

P.—Yes; because we know that liquids are extremely expansible when heated; therefore, if one fluid (water) is weighed at 60°, and the other (spirit) at 70°, it is probable that you will not have weighed an equal volume of each, because when they are both reduced to the same temperature, it will be found that the one that stood at 70° will occupy less space. It has, therefore, been found convenient to weigh all bodies at a fixed temperature, such as 60° Fahrenheit. Let us see how the 1,000 grain bottle acts. [Experiment 13.] I have the bottle here; it is filled with distilled water, at 60°, and you see how correct it is, for it weighs exactly 1,000 grains. [Weighs it, then empties the bottle and dries it]. We will now fill it with sulphuric ether, and weigh it. [Does so, and the bottle is found **to be** too light]. You see that it requires 270 grains to be placed in the same scale with the bottle to balance the 1,000 grains weight; therefore we say that the specific gravity of the **ether** is 0·730. Let us fill the bottle with sulphuric acid instead of the ether, and observe what takes place. [Does so, and the bottle weighs down the 1,000 grains weight.] You see that we must add 875 grains to the scale with the weight in it, consequently the specific gravity of the acid is 1·875.

91. *T.*—Is not the specific gravity of fluids ascertained by some other means than weighing them?

P.—Yes; by means of the hydrometer or areometer, which consists of a hollow glass tube, with a scale in the inside (*a*) so arranged that it denotes the specific gravity of lighter fluids by a scale with the degrees proceeding from the bottom to the top, and of heavier fluids by the degrees proceeding from the top to the bottom; the end of the tube is blown out into two hollow balls (*Fig.* 21), the lower one containing mercury, **so** as to balance the instrument. Now, if we place this instrument in a vessel containing a fluid, **and** find that it marks 80 on the scale, we learn that 80 parts **of** the fluid weigh as much as 100 of water; the specific gravity is therefore that of water as 100 to 80, or $=\frac{100}{80}$ or 1·25.

Fig. 21.

92. *T.*—How can you ascertain the specific gravity of a solid body?

P.—First weigh the body in the air; then suspend it from the pan of a common balance (*Fig.* 22, *b*), by a fine thread, and

---

* These bottles may be procured for 1s. 6d. each, of Messrs. Horne, Thornwaite & Wood, 123, Newgate-street, London, from whom any of the apparatus used by GRANDFATHER WHITEHEAD may be purchased at a moderate rate, and of the best quality.

immerse it in pure water at 60°; weigh it, and as it weighs less than when in the air, the opposite pan will fall. Remove weights from the pan a until the equilibrium is restored, and the weight removed will be the weight of the bulk of water displaced by the body immersed. Now divide the weight of the body in the air, by the weight of the water displaced, and the quotient will be the density of the body experimented upon, water being = 1. We need not be frightened at seeing the specific gravity of any body stated to be 9 (as uranium), it only means that it is

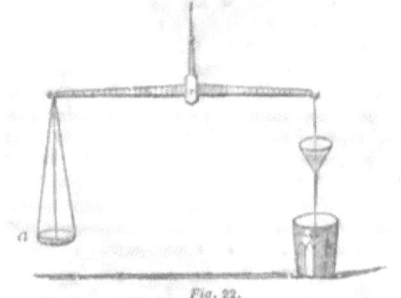

Fig. 22.

nine times heavier than an equal bulk of water.

93. T.—How can we ascertain the specific gravity of a gaseous body?

P.—To do this we must have an air-pump. We then take a flask with a stop-cock attached to it, and weigh it when full of air; **this gives the** weight of the **air.** Then we exhaust the air by means of the air-pump, and weigh it again, so as to find the weight of the flask. We have now only to fill the flask with the gas, the specific gravity of which we have to ascertain, and weigh the flask, and then we learn the weight of the gas. For example, suppose that the flask full of air weighed 60 grains, and the empty flask 54 grains; that leaves 6 grains as the weight of the air; and if the flask full of gas weighed 72 grains, it **is** evident that the gas weighs three times as much as the same bulk **of air, or the gas is** = 18, and the air = 6.

94. T.—How are bodies reduced to the state of powder for chemical purposes?

P.—By pulverisation, trituration, levigation, and granulation.

95. T.—How are these processes performed?

P.—*Pulverisation* is the reduction of solid, friable, **and** brittle bodies, **to a state** of powder, **and is** generally performed **by** means of pestles in mortars. *Trituration* is performed **by** a rotatory motion of the pestle, and has the effect of making the powder very fine indeed. *Levigation* resembles trituration, **only** the process is assisted by using a liquid that does not dissolve the body operated upon, such as water, spirit of wine, lard, honey, &c. When a painter uses a muller and slab to mix his paints, he levigates them. *Granulation* is used to divide metals, and **is** performed by melting and stirring them **quickly** until cold, or pouring them through **a** bundle of damp straw, which is shaken while held over a basin of water.

96. T.—What are the means used to separate substances?

P.—Sifting, washing, or elutriation, and filtration.

97. T.—Explain the processes of **sifting,** and elutriation.

P.—*Sifting* is used to separate **the finer** particles of powders from the coarser, **and** is usually performed by means of wire **or** hair-cloth **sieves.** *Elutriation* **or washing** is used to separate the finer **parts of** powders from the fluids with which **they** are sometimes mixed. This may be done by using a glass syphon (*Fig.* 23,) taking care to insert the short leg b into the vessel containing the fluid, until it nearly touches the bottom, then closing the end of the long one with your finger, suck up the fluid by means of the arm c, until both legs are full, and on removing the finger the fluid will flow from a into a vessel placed **to** receive it. The liquid may also be drawn off by capillary attraction. [See Q. 107, p. 22.]

98. T. — What is filtration?

P.—It is used to separate solid bodies **from** fluids, the object being to get a clear liquid. For this purpose, take a square piece of white blotting paper, A B C D, (*Fig.* 24), double it over, first

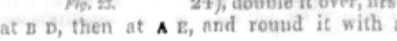

Fig. 23.

at B D, then at A E, and round it with a

pair of scissors at A and B, so as to make it look like the black part in the figure, then fold it again upon itself, until it **looks** like the letter V ; open it out, place it in a funnel, moisten with distilled water and pour the liquid *gently* into the filtering paper. If the fluid does not pass through readily, in consequence of the paper adhering to the sides of the funnel, place a straw between the paper and the funnel.

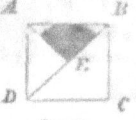

Fig. 24.

99. *T.*—What is digestion ?
P.—It is the process of obtaining the soluble parts of substances by the aid of heat. A glass matrass (*Fig.* 25) with a piece of wire twisted round it to suspend it over a spirit-lamp, is used for the purpose. When the vapour of the liquid in which the substance is digested is valuable, as alcohol, the cork of the flask is fitted with a long open glass tube, so that the vapour becomes condensed in the tube and returns again to the matrass, and on this account the process is called *circulation*.

Fig. 25.

100. *T.*—What is decomposition ?
P.—The separation of the component parts of substances, and may be the result of the greater affinity of certain particles of the compound, for the decomposing agent; or it may be caused by heat, electricity, or galvanism, separating the particles.

101. *T.*—What is precipitation ?
P.—The throwing down or separation of a solid substance, from the liquid which holds it in solution, caused by some other body; *precipitant* is the body which produces it, and the *precipitate* the body thrown down. The process is usually performed in tall glasses like champagne glasses.

102. *T.*—As it is necessary sometimes to have a greater heat than that obtained from a common fire, how is this to be procured ?

P.—By a very simple apparatus. Take two common earthenware flower-pots, without any flaw, and twist some iron wire tightly round the upper part of each, then make three or four holes (*d*), in the lower part of one (*a*), and place **it** on three or four stones so as to raise it above the ground, as in *Fig.* 26. Have a piece of sheet iron pierced with holes *c*, fitted to this pot, and a chimney *p*, made of sheet iron fitted to the other pot *b*, which should be somewhat larger than the one just described. The chimney should be about 2½ to 3 feet long, and 3 inches in diameter. When the heated charcoal is placed above the perforated sheet iron *c*, and the pot with the chimney covered over it, as in the *Fig.* above, we have an excellent temporary furnace. A little practice with this furnace will soon enable any one to regulate the quantity of air required for the purpose of maintaining combustion. Crucibles should be purchased.

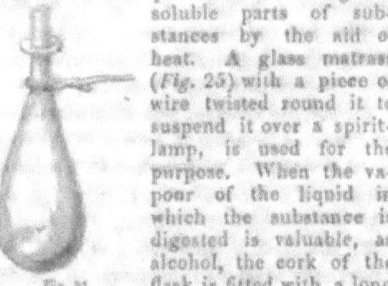

Fig. 26.

103. *T.*—Have we not another method of obtaining an intense heat on a small scale ?

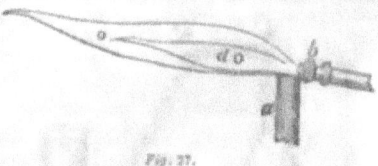

Fig. 27.

P.—Yes, by means of the blow-pipe. The flame consists of an inner deoxidizing or reducing flame *d o*, and an outer oxidizing flame *a*. With a gas-jet and blow-pipe, or even a candle, and a common tobacco-pipe, and a piece of charcoal, we may deoxidize metals, or reduce their metallic oxides to the metallic form.

GENERAL QUESTIONS ON LESSON VIII.

1. Can you describe to me the processes of rectification, sublimation, and abstraction ?
2. What are the weights made use of by chemists ?

3. Describe the specific gravity of a fluid, a solid, and a gas.
4. Describe the signification and processes of pulverization, trituration, levigation, and **granulation**.

5. **Describe** the processes of sifting, elutriation, **and** filtration.
6. What **means** have we of obtaining a greater heat **than** that furnished by **an** ordinary fire?

LESSON IX.

Now that we have become acquainted with the general principles and leading points of chemistry, we shall be better prepared to commence the investigation of some of the elementary bodies. The first group we shall consider is the *gazolytes*, consisting of oxygen, hydrogen, and nitrogen. In order to make experiments with gases, we must have a peculiar kind of apparatus, but it need not be expensive, and as we shall require it very frequently, it will be better to construct it at once. First of all we shall

Fig. 28.

want a spirit-lamp, and therefore you had better cut off two inches of brass tubing, and having fitted a small bottle (*Fig.* 28, *d*) with a cork, bore a hole in its centre with a red-hot wire, and insert the piece of tubing. Pass some cotton through the tube, (*a*) and fill the bottle up to the shoulder with spirit of wine. It is better to have a tin cover (*c*) fitted to the bottle, in order to prevent the evaporation of the spirit. Select a piece of glass tubing, about the size of a goose-quill, and long enough for your purpose (about eighteen inches); hold it over the flame of the spirit-lamp, and *heat it gradually*; it will soon begin to soften, and you should then bend it to the shape of the one in *Fig.* 29, and *let it cool gradually*. Fit a Florence flask with a sound cork, then make a hole in its centre to receive the bent tube, and place the flask upon the ring of a retort-stand (*a b*), as in *Fig.* 29. The *retort-stand* is only an iron rod, fitted to a heavy

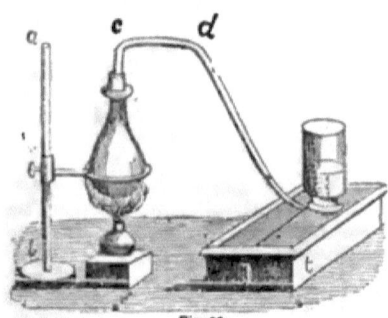
Fig. 29.

base, and furnished with movable rings, which can be fixed in any position by screws. The *pneumatic trough* (*t*) is generally made of tin, japanned, and has a movable shelf, to support the *receivers* of jars in which the gas is collected. It should be about 14 inches long, 9 wide, and 8 high, and when used is filled with cold water. When not able to procure a trough and convenient receivers, a common washing-basin will form a good substitute for the former, and a few pickle bottles for the latter.

When about to collect gases attend to the following rules:—1st. Fill the receivers by immersing them in the trough; then raise them carefully and place them mouth downwards on the shelf in your trough ready for use, taking care that the water is at least one inch above their mouths. 2nd. Before collecting the gas for experiment allow some to escape, because the first portions are always inferior. 3rd. Attend to the lutings and joints of the apparatus, to see that no gas escapes. 4th. When you apply heat to the apparatus be sure to remove the end of the gas-delivering tube (*c d*) from the water before you remove the heat, otherwise the flask may burst. 5. When gases are to be kept for any length of time grease the stoppers of the receivers. 6th. Do not collect gases *too long* before they are required for use, as they are apt to deteriorate. 7th. As some gases are soluble in water be careful in their preparation.

QUESTIONS.

104. *T.*—What is oxygen?

P.—One of the most widely diffused elementary bodies, and therefore placed first among the gaseous bodies.

105. *T.*—What is the name derived from, and by whom was it discovered?

P.—It is derived from two Greek words, *oxus* (ὀξύς), acid, and *gennao* (γεννάω), I give rise to; and therefore means the acid-maker. It was discovered in the year 1774, by Scheele in Sweden, and Dr. Priestley, in England; the former called it empyreal air, and the latter vital air; but Lavoisier named it oxygen. Its specific gravity is 1.1057.

106. *T.*—How **is** oxygen obtained?

P.—By mixing one-fifth of black oxide of manganese with four-fifths of dried chlorate of potash, and placing them in a flask, as in *Fig.* 29, then applying heat, **and** placing the end of the gas-delivering tube under the receiver. By this means the whole of the oxygen is given off from the chlorate of potash, with greater facility than when oxide of manganese is not used.

107. *T.*—Is this the **only** method of obtaining the gas?

P.—No. It may be obtained by using a short tube of hard glass, fitted with a perforated cork and bent tube, and sup-

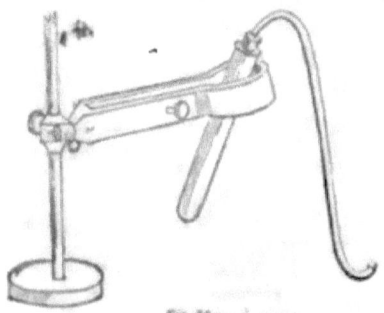

Fig. 30.

ported by means of Gay Lussac's Holder, (*Fig.* 30), **and** employing the red oxide of mercury (*red precipitate*) instead of chlorate of potash; but a better way is to use the same apparatus **as** before (*Fig.* 29), **and** place chlorate of potash in the flask **by** itself, and as soon as it boils the gas **will** be given off.

108. *T.*—Describe some of the properties of the **gas.**

P.—In **order to** do this I must make some experiments. I have a jar of the gas, and as I wish to plunge some substance into the jar, I must turn it up. Observe, I grease this square piece of glass well on one side, and place the greased side under water against **the** mouth of the jar, and now I can turn **it** up and place it on the table without any fear of the gas escaping [Experiment 14]. Here is a piece of copper wire, and you see that the end is turned up, thus. Now I will fix a small piece of wax candle to the part that is turned up, and pass the wire through a cork that fits the bottle exactly [Does so]. If *Fig.* 31 we light the candle and blow it out so as to leave a red-hot wick, and then plunge it into the jar, it will ignite and burn with a brilliant flame [Performs the Experiment]. Although oxygen burns so brilliantly now, yet it will not burn by itself, and is therefore called a non-combustible, but a supporter of combustion.

109. *T.*—Give me some **other illustrations** of its properties.

P.—[Experiment 15.] Here is another jar of the gas, and **you** see that instead of the candle, I have **a** piece of red-hot charcoal attached to the wire, and, when I plunge it into the gas it will burn most vividly. [Performs the Experiment.] Now, although this is very beautiful, it falls far short of another I will show you. [Experiment 16.] Here is a piece of thin iron wire coiled round to look like a corkscrew, and when it has been heated red-hot, by holding it over the spirit-lamp, I will plunge it into the jar of gas. [Performs the Experiment.] You see that the jar has broken; this was because I did not take the precaution to use a jar open at both ends, and the red-hot metal, which you saw fall in little globules, cracked the bottle. When this experiment is performed the jar should not be moved from the trough, and the greased glass placed at the upper part, by this means **the metal will** fall in the water.

110. *T.*—Is there **anything** peculiar about these globules?

P.—Yes; they are found to weigh more than the actual metal used, thus proving **that they** have combined with something **which has** weight; this is oxygen, and **the globules at** the bottom of the trough **are masses** of *black oxide* of *iron.*

111. *T.*—Can you give me any other experiments to illustrate its properties?

P.—Yes, but some of them are very dangerous; and we have performed enough to show that it supports combustion, and readily combines with many substances.

112. *T.*—Is oxygen necessary to our existence?

P.—Undoubtedly, but not in a pure state. You know that it is found in the air combined with nitrogen, in water combined with hydrogen, with metals forming oxides, in the tissues of vegetables and animals, and in our blood.

113. *T.*—What do you mean by oxygen forming oxides with metals?

P.—The gas combines and forms a compound which is called an *oxide.* These oxides are divided into three principal groups; 1. Those which resemble potash, soda, or the oxide of lead in their chemical relations, called *alkaline* or *basic oxides*, and sometimes *salifiable bases.* 2. Those which have properties directly opposed to the first group, called *acids*, which have a strong tendency to unite with the salifiable bases, such as sulphuric acid and potash to form the *salt*—sulphate of potash. 3. The *neutral* oxides, such as black oxide of manganese, which show little inclination to unite with other substances.

GENERAL QUESTIONS ON LESSON IX.
1. How are gases collected, and what apparatus **is** required?
3. **Describe the processes of** obtaining oxygen.
4. Give the properties of this gas.
5. Illustrate its properties by experiments.
6. Is oxygen essentially necessary?
7. Why does oxygen exist in **combination,** and not pure?

LESSON X.

WATER consists of the two elements—oxygen and hydrogen: we have examined the former, and it will now be our duty to consider the latter. When we procured oxygen **we** employed heat, but it is not required in the preparation of hydrogen, the apparatus **being** very simple, merely consisting of a common flask, or **bottle,** fitted with a good **cork** through which a tube-funnel (*b*) passes, to enable us to pour liquid into the bottle, and a gas-delivering tube (*a*) is also inserted into it, as in *Fig.* 32.

QUESTIONS.

114. *T.*—What is hydrogen?

P.—A **g**aseous body which we are unable to liquefy either by cold or pressure. It is inodorous, colourless, and tasteless when quite pure; **and** has **a** very low specific gravity compared with that of any other form of ponderable matter, being 0.069, while atmospheric **air is** estimated at 1,000.

115. *T.*—What do you mean by ponderable matter?

P.—Anything that has weight is said to be *ponderable*, such as oxygen and hydrogen gases; but certain things that cannot be weighed, like light, heat, and electricity, are called *imponderables.*

[See Q. 111, p. 22.]

116. *T.*—What is the name hydrogen derived from?

P.—Two Greek words, *udoor,* (ὕδωρ), water, and *gennao,* (γεννάω), I give rise to; it signifies a producer of water.

117. *T.*—How can we obtain hydrogen?

P.—By several methods. For example, if we wish to do so for experimental purposes, we usually place some granulated zinc, or zinc cuttings, in a wide-mouthed bottle (see *Fig.* 32) fitted with a glass tube to deliver the gas, and one to pour

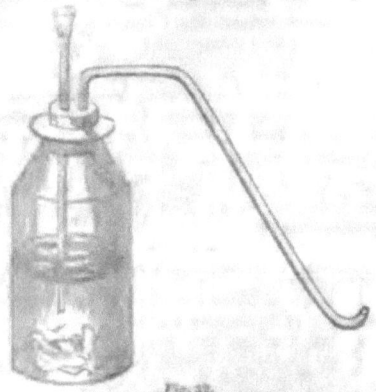

Fig. 32.

a fluid into the bottle; we then add dilute sulphuric acid (one part of acid to five parts of water) by means of the tube-funnel. You then see effervescence take place, and the gas rapidly issuing from the tube *a*. *Do not begin to collect any of the gas until all the atmospheric air has been expelled from the bottle*, or an explosion will take place. Some chemists collect two bottles, and afterwards reject the gas they contain, before obtaining any for experiments.

118. *T.* — Give some examples of the several methods of procuring this gas.

P.—Repeat the same process as that described just now [Q. 117], but substitute iron nails for the zinc, and the gas will be generated. Again, take a gun-barrel and place a quantity of iron turnings in it, fit one end with a long brass tube, and then heat the centre of the barrel red-hot, and pour water slowly into the other end; you will soon observe that gas escapes by the tube, and may be collected as usual, rejecting the first supply of course.

119. *T.*—What has become of the oxygen of the water?

P.—That combines with the red-hot iron turnings to form oxide of iron.

120. *T.*—I thought this gas was sometimes collected from water. How is it thus obtained?

P.—So it is; this is done by voltaic electricity, and when we consider electricity, I will describe the process.

121. *T.*—Give me some illustrations of its properties.

P.—In the first place it is the lightest of all ponderable substances, being nearly 14½ times lighter than atmospheric air, and 16 times lighter than oxygen. In order to prove this, I will perform an amusing **experiment**. [Experiment 17.] I have **removed** the gas-delivering tube from **the** bottle we had before, and inserted another of a different shape (A) to which a small balloon, made from the lining membrane of a turkey's crop, is attached. Of course, the dilute sulphuric acid has been added to the zinc in the bottle, and the gas generated

A

before the balloon was attached, so as to drive off the atmospheric air. [The balloon is seen filling as in *Fig.* 33]. Now that the balloon is full, I will tie a string round the neck of it, and set it free. [Does so]. You observe that it has ascended to the ceiling of the room, and if this was performed in the open air, the balloon would soon be out of sight. I have another pretty experiment for you. [Experiment 18]. You see that I have got a bladder filled with hydrogen, and fitted to a common tobacco-pipe, and you must also observe that I squeeze the neck of the bladder to prevent gas escaping. Now I will blow some soap-bubbles by dipping the bowl of the pipe into soap-suds, and then giving the bladder a squeeze under my arm you will see the soap balloons filled with hydrogen gas rapidly ascend.

Fig. 33.

122. *T.*—Is hydrogen an inflammable gas?

P.—Yes; but although it burns it does not support combustion.

123. *T.*—Prove that it is inflammable.

P.—[Experiment 19]. You see that I

have placed the end of the bent glass tube (*Fig.* 32, *a*,) under water, and that bubbles of hydrogen are escaping. I will apply a lighted taper to them, and we shall see that they will ignite and explode at the same time. [Applies the taper, and the bubbles explode]. Here is another experiment to prove it is inflammable. [Experiment 20]. You see that this bottle has some zinc cuttings and diluted sulphuric acid in it, and that instead of a glass tube, the cork (which fits tight) has a piece of tobacco-pipe adapted to it. I will allow some more of the gas to escape, so as to displace the air before I apply a light, and then you will see that it burns. [When the light is applied, the gas burns with a very faint light.]

124. *T.* What other peculiarities are there about hydrogen?

P.—[Experiment 21]. You observe that the hydrogen is still burning, [Uses the bottle with the tobacco-pipe, Experiment 20], and that the sides of the tumbler I now hold over it are covered with dew. This dew is water formed by the combustion of hydrogen, which unites with the oxygen of the air.

125. *T.*— As hydrogen burns without supporting combustion, and oxygen supports combustion without burning, it is probable that when combined a very rapid combustion will be the result. Is this the case?

P.—It is, and advantage has been taken of the fact, to produce the most violent degree of heat known, by means of an apparatus called the oxy-hydrogen blowpipe. In addition to this the oxy-hydrogen gas is thrown upon lime to produce a very brilliant light.

GENERAL QUESTIONS ON LESSON X.

1. What is there peculiar about the preparation of hydrogen gas?
2. Why is this gas named hydrogen?
3. Explain the difference between ponderable and imponderable bodies.
4. Give the various methods adopted to procure hydrogen.
5. Does hydrogen support combustion?
6. Give some illustrations of the properties of this gas.

LESSON XI.

THE next elementary substance we have to investigate is called Nitrogen, a gas that constitutes about four-fifths of the atmosphere, and is largely diffused in nature, especially in the organic kingdom. It was discovered in Scotland, in 1774, by Dr. D. Rutherford. Nitrogen means the generator of nitre, deriving its name from two Greek words, *nitron*, (νιτρον), nitre; and *gennaein*, (γενναειν) to produce; it is also, erroneously, called *azote*, from *a* (α) privative, and *zoe* (ζωη), life; meaning the life-destroyer, because an animal cannot breathe it without dying, whereas if they breathe oxygen it is so stimulating that they will go mad. Its specific gravity is 0·972, and the gas is devoid of taste, smell, and colour.

QUESTIONS.

126. *T.*—How is Nitrogen obtained?

P.—By burning phosphorus in air enclosed in a jar over water, as in *Fig.* 34. [Experiment 22]. Take a piece of phosphorus about the size of a large pea, place it in a small earthenware dish, and let it float on the surface of the pneumatic trough; then touch the phosphorus* with a piece of hot wire, and cover the jar over it. [Does so]. You observe, the jar is being filled with dense white fumes, produced by the combination of phosphorus with oxygen, to form phosphoric acid. The fumes have now disappeared, and you see that the water has risen about one-fifth of the height in the jar, and the phosphorus has

Fig. 34.

---

* Phosphorus is a dangerous thing to handle, as the warmth of the hand may cause it to ignite. When cut, it should be done under water, and always preserved in a bottle of water.

become extinguished because it has exhausted all the oxygen in the jar.

127. *T.*—Why did the water rise in the jar, and what became of the white fumes?

P.—The water rose in the jar because the air in the jar having lost about one-fifth of its volume, and the water occupies its place. The white fumes were dissolved by the water, and **pure** nitrogen **remains.**

128. *T.*—What has become of the one-fifth of the air in the jar?

P.—It is exhausted **by** the phosphorus in the process of combustion, being the oxygen of the air, for you know that 100 volumes of atmospheric air contains

  79 volumes of nitrogen
  21 ,, oxygen
  $\frac{1}{30} - \frac{1}{15}$ carbonic acid
and the vapour of water.

129. *T.*—As this method of preparing nitrogen is not altogether free from certain objections, prepare the gas by some other method.

P.—[Experiment 23.] Here is a porcelain tube filled with the turnings of copper, now when this tube is heated to redness and a stream of atmospheric air passed through the tube, the nitrogen will issue at the opposite end. [Does so.] You observe that the copper turnings, which have cooled, weigh more than they did before I put them into the tube; they have combined with the oxygen of the air, to form oxide of copper.

130. *T.*—Is there not another method of preparing the gas?

P.—Yes, by passing chlorine gas through a strong solution of ammonia; but as its preparation is attended with danger to inexperienced persons, I will not try it.

131. *T.*—Give me some illustrations of the properties of this gas.

P.—[Experiment 24.] Here **is a small** jar full of it; observe what takes **place** when I introduce a lighted taper. [**Does** so, and the taper is extinguished.] **The** reason the candle went out, is because nitrogen cannot support combustion, [Experiment 25]. This jar also contains nitrogen, and as I am going to add some lime-water to it, observe what takes place. [Does so, and no change is observed.] You seem surprised that there was not any change, but I never expected to see any; and only used these means to satisfy myself that the jar contained nitrogen and not carbonic acid, a gas that changes lime-**water** white by forming an insoluble salt **called** carbonate of lime.

GENERAL QUESTIONS **ON LESSON** XI.

1. What **is** nitrogen?
2. Give the derivation of **its** name and meaning.
3. Is nitrogen known by any other name?
4. How is this gas obtained, and is there any danger attending its preparation?
5. Give the composition of atmospheric air.
6. Illustrate the properties of this gas by experiments.

LESSON XII.

WE have **now to** examine the *halogens,* or *salt producers*:—Chlorine, discovered by Scheele, in Sweden, **in 1774;** Iodine, discovered by Courtois, in France, in 1811; Bromine, discovered by Balard, **in France, in** 1826; and Fluorine, first accurately examined **by** Scheele, in Sweden.

QUESTIONS.

132. *T.*—What is Chlorine?

P.—A greenish-yellow, pungent gas, **very** much resembling iodine, bromine, and fluorine. Its specific gravity is 2·5.

133. *T.*—What is the name derived from?

P.—A Greek word *chloros* (χλωρος), green, alluding to its colour.

134. *T.*—How is it prepared?

P.—By placing some finely powdered black oxide of manganese in **a** flask, and pouring some strong liquid hydrochloric acid upon it, and applying a gentle heat, as in *Fig.* 35. It may be prepared by mixing equal parts of the black oxide of manganese and salt together, and adding dilute sulphuric acid (equal parts of water and acid) to them when placed in the flask.

Instead of collecting the gas over water as usual, let the tube pass to the bottom of the receiver, which should be loosely covered with a piece of card; by this means, the chlorine will fill the bottle and displace the air; it may be collected over warm water, but then the gas expands from the heat.

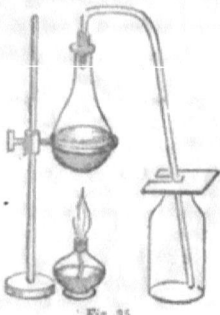
Fig. 35.

135. *T.*—Why is not **this gas** collected over water as usual?

P. Because cold water absorbs it. [Experiment 26.] You observe that a**bout** two-thirds of this bottle is occupied by chlorine, and the rest by water. I will shake it [does so, and the water **dissolves** the chlorine], and now you see that the yellow-green colour has disappeared, because we find that one part of water will **dissolve** two parts of chlorine, forming what is called *chlorine water*.

136. *T.*—**As you have** collected several **bottles of the** gas, **give some** experiments **to** illustrate its properties.

P.—Be careful not to **come too near,** because **this gas** is very irritating, and if inhaled, **is** injurious.* Now, you observe that I have several discs of millboard, well greased, to **go over the tops of the bottles,** and also that each disc has a piece of twisted **wire passing** through its centre. [Experiment 27.] I will plunge this wire, with the lighted **taper** attached to it, into **the** gas [does so]; **it** burns with a dull red light, and is now extinguished. [Experiment 28.] This wire has a piece of gold leaf attached; see how vividly it burns now that it is placed in the gas. [Experiment 29.] Here is some metallic antimony in fine powder [pours it into the jar of the gas]; now see what a beautiful shower of fire it produces. [Repeat Experiment 28, using copper leaf instead, and plunge phosphorus in the gas for another experiment.]

137. *T.*—What other properties does it possess?

P.—It **is a** powerful bleaching and disinfecting agent, which results from its strong affinity for hydrogen. [Experiment 30.] This wire holds a sprig of damp parsley; let us see what will be the effect of plunging it into the gas. [Places **it** in the jar]. It has lost its beautiful **green** colour, and is rapidly becoming **white.**

138. *T.*—What is IODINE?

P.—A solid body, which looks very like plumbago or black-lead, and smells like chlorine. Its name is derived from the Greek word *iodese,* (ιωδῆς), violet-coloured, and its specific gravity is 4·948.

139. *T.*—Give some illustrations of its properties.

P.—[Experiment 31.] I have placed a few grains of iodine into a flask; observe what a beautiful violet colour it gives out when heated over a spirit-lamp. [Experiment 32.] This tumbler contains a solution of starch, made with hot water, and allowed to cool; observe what takes place when I add this very small piece of iodine and stir the starch. [Does so, and the starch changes **to** a beautiful blue colour]. This **last** experiment **proves the** value of starch **as a** test for iodine.

140. *T.*—**How** is iodine procured?

P.—From *kelp,* or the half-vitrified ashes of sea-weeds; but the process is too long to enter into.

141. *T.*—What is BROMINE?

P.—It is a deep brownish-red liquid, with a very fœtid, disagreeable odour, as its name implies, being derived from the Greek word *bromos,* (βρῶμος), a noisome smell. Its specific gravity is 3.

142. *T.*—How is bromine obtained?

P.—From sea water; but the process is too long to describe; suffice it to say that chlorine is used to decompose the bromide of magnesium, in which form it is generally found, and that ether is then added, and

---

* When experimenting with chlorine, it is advisable to sprinkle a strong solution of ammonia about the table, and also to have a cloth moistened with it, near to the operator.

agitation employed, so as to dissolve the bromine; afterwards, caustic potash is added, and evaporation and other processes conducted.

143. *T.*—What are its properties?
P.—It is slightly soluble in water, more so in alcohol, and freely in ether. [Experiment 33.] Repeat Experiment 32, using bromine instead of iodine, and the colour is changed to orange-yellow instead of blue.

144. *T.*—What is FLUORINE?
P.—It is an element that has never been isolated, because as soon as it is separated from one compound, it unites with some other substance.

145. *T.*—How do we know that it does exist?
P.—Because it is found in the *fluoride of calcium* (fluor, or Derbyshire spar), fluoride of silver, &c. It is said to dissolve nearly everything it touches.

GENERAL QUESTIONS ON LESSON XII.

1. Name the discoverer of each of the halogens.
2. What is there peculiar about chlorine?
3. How is it obtained?
4. Illustrate the properties of chlorine by experiments.
5. What is iodine? How is it prepared? and what are its properties?
6. Illustrate the properties of iodine by experiments.
7. How is bromine obtained, and what are its properties?
8. How is fluorine obtained, and what is there peculiar about it?

LESSON XIII.

WHEN you have learned all about the elements of Chemistry, you should then study it more fully; because it is a science that requires **a life-time** devoted **to it,** and even then cannot be mastered, as fresh discoveries are made every **day.** It is on this account that I have not described the compounds of elements, such as oxides, hydrates, nitrates, chlorides, iodides, bromides, fluorides, &c. When you are better acquainted with the elements, you will learn that these substances form many compounds. For example—bromine vapour and hydrogen combine in equal volumes to form *hydrobromic acid*, and oxygen and carbon combine to form *carbonic oxide*.

QUESTIONS.

146. *T.*—What is Carbon?
P.—An elementary body, found in many different forms, constituting a large proportion of all organic structures, animal and vegetable, and found in a state of purity and crystallised, as graphite or plumbago, and as diamond. Thus, charcoal, black-lead, bone-black, lamp-black, and the diamond are, chemically speaking, **the** same substance.

147. *T.*—If the diamond, charcoal, and the **other** substances you have named are all **com**posed of the same substance, how is it that they differ in appearance?
P.—Because the arrangement of their atoms is different, as I explained to you before. [Q. 51.]

148. *T.*—Is graphite or plumbago pure carbon?
P.—Some specimens contain iron; but the finest specimens of Borrowdale plumbago consist of pure carbon.

149. *T.*—Is carbon combustible?
P.—Yes, we can burn the diamond as well as a piece of charcoal, or any other kind of carbon.

150. *T.*—What are its properties?
P.—It is a good conductor of electricity, and a bad conductor **of** heat. It is not acted upon by **air,** or water, at common temperatures, but readily burns in oxygen gas or common air when heated to redness, and leaves only **a** small quantity of ashes, but generates a **gas** called carbonic acid.

151. *T.*—What is carbonic acid gas?

P.—An extremely poisonous gas. It is incapable of supporting combustion, and therefore differing from *carbonic oxide*, which is a combustible that burns with a pale blue flame. The former contains its own volumes of oxygen, and the latter only half its volume of oxygen.

152. *T.*—How is carbonic acid gas obtained?

P.—By decomposing a carbonate with one of the strong acids, and collecting the same as chlorine, only with this difference, that we do not require heat, and that the gas should pass through a long tube filled with fragments of chloride of calcium. [Experiment 34.] Take a piece of marble, break it into small pieces the size of a pea, and put ten drachms of it into a bottle like that used for generating hydrogen (*Fig.* 33), then add six drachms of distilled hydrochloric acid (equal parts of water and acid) by means of the tube-funnel. [Experiment 35.] Repeat the above experiment, only substitute carbonate of ammonia instead of marble.

153. *T.*—Illustrate its properties by experiments.

P.—[Experiment 36.] Here is a jar of carbonic acid. I will plunge a lighted taper into it, holding the jar mouth upwards. [Does so.] You see that the flame is extinguished. [Experiment 37.] Here is a jar with some lime-water in it (A). You see that I pour the carbonic acid from the other jar (B) like you would water (see *Fig.* 36). [Does so.] Observe, the lime-water is milky, because an insoluble carbonate of lime has been formed. [Experiment 38.] I will now pour carbonic acid upon the flame of the spirit-lamp from the jar in my hand. [Does so.] You see it has extinguished it.

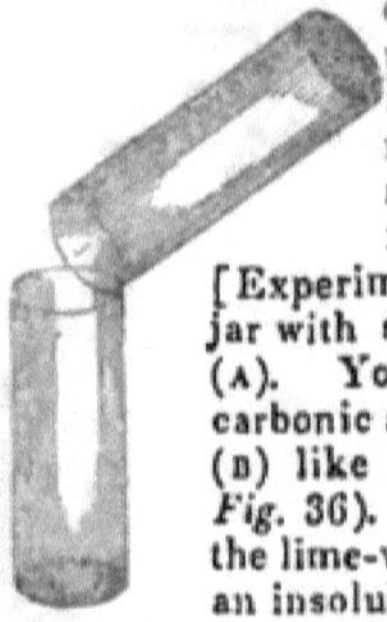

Fig. 36.

154. *T.*—What is SULPHUR?

P.—A simple elementary body, often found in a free state. It is too well known to require much description. In its chemical relations it bears great resemblance to oxygen. It is insoluble in water and alcohol, but soluble in bisulphuret of carbon, the fat oils, and oil of turpentine. It has no taste, nor smell, and is fusible.

155. *T.*—What is PHOSPHORUS?

P.—An elementary body, closely allied to sulphur, nearly colourless, and resembles partially bleached wax. It is insoluble in water, but dissolves in oils, alcohol, and sulphuret of carbon.

156. *T.*—How is it prepared?

P.—By decomposing the phosphate of lime in bones, by means of sulphuric acid, and then causing it to undergo a long process, which I will not describe, as it is not sufficiently useful.

157. *T.*—What is BORON?

P.—An elementary substance procured from borax, but as I have never seen it, (and I believe very few persons have,) it is as well to pass it over.

158. *T.*—What is ALUMINUM?

P.—A metal, and therefore I shall defer its description until another opportunity occurs of examining all the important metals.

[The pupil should consult Cat. XI.]

GENERAL QUESTIONS ON LESSON XIII.

1. What is the purest kind of carbon?
2. Describe and illustrate the properties of carbon.
3. What is carbonic acid gas? How is it obtained, and what are its properties?
4. What is sulphur, phosphorus, and boron?

V.—ELECTRICITY, OPTICS, AND ACOUSTICS.

INTRODUCTORY NARRATIVE.

LESSON I.

THE old **shire** town and royal burgh of Jedburgh, which is situated on the Jed water, in Roxburghshire, was formerly celebrated for its bold and strong castles, woodland fastnesses, **and** splendid ecclesiastical buildings, some of which were reckoned the finest in Scotland, as the ruins of Jedburgh Abbey now testify. To the lover of science, it possesses an additional interest, from being the birth-

place of the celebrated philosopher Sir David Brewster, who was born on the 11th of December, 1781.

His father, who was a worthy member of the church of Scotland, and rector of the grammar-school of Jedburgh, educated his son to follow in his footsteps, and therefore, after David had received a thorough preliminary education, he was sent to the university of Edinburgh, and having completed his studies, became a licentiate of the church of Scotland.

In the year 1800, when only nineteen years of age, the university conferred the honorary degree of M.A. on him; and he commenced the study of the science of optics by repeating Sir I. Newton's experiments on the inflection of light, from which he concluded that the phenomena of inflection are not dependent upon the nature of the body by which they are caused.

In a few years, ill health obliged him to give up the clerical profession, a circumstance that caused him much regret.

In 1807, the university of Aberdeen conferred the honorary degree of LL.D. upon him; and in 1808, the Royal Society of Edinburgh elected him Fellow of their body.

In 1808, he commenced editing the "Edinburgh Encyclopædia," a work that will ever be a memorial of his indefatigable labours in the cause of science. Besides contributing the articles on the sciences of electricity, optics, mechanics, hydrodynamics, astronomy, and expansion, he wrote upon the kaleidoscope, which he invented in 1816, microscope, anemometer, and other instruments, besides the biographies of many eminent scientific men. When engaged upon this work, he was one day much bothered by an abstruse calculation. Evening had arrived and it was not solved; he therefore ordered his carriage, and notwithstanding that it was late at night and he was much exhausted, yet he carried away his papers, and accompanied by his servant, to prevent him going to sleep, drove off to Minto, where he arrived early in the morning, and explained his difficulty to Lord Minto. The noble lord soon saw how it was to be solved, and while engaged in finishing the calculation, Brewster fell upon the floor quite exhausted, and was soon fast asleep. Few can imagine the mental and bodily exertion that he endured while editing this work, from the year 1808 to 1830, when it was completed.

In 1810, he married the eldest daughter of J. Macpherson, Esq., of Belleville, Inverness, by whom he has had several children.

In 1814, he visited France and Switzerland. In 1816, he received half of the physical prize of 3,000 francs of the Institute of France, the other half being adjudged to Dr. Seebeck, of Berlin, for the most important discoveries made in any branch of science in Europe during the two previous years. In 1819, he gained the Rumford gold and silver medals of the Royal Society of London, for his discoveries on the polarization of light.

In 1819, he was elected General Secretary of the Royal Society of Edinburgh, in consequence of the decease of Professor Playfair. In the same year he established the "Edinburgh Philosophical Journal," conjointly with Professor Jameson. Afterwards he conducted the "Edinburgh Journal of Science," and established the Society of Arts for Scotland.

In 1825, he was elected corresponding member of the Institute of France, and of the Royal Academies of Russia, Prussia, Sweden, and Denmark, and many other **scientific bodies.**

In 1826, he left Edinburgh to take up his residence on the banks of the Tweed, near to Melrose, where he had purchased a property, and where he still laboured at the "Edinburgh Encyclopædia," and other works. Beautiful as this part of the country naturally is, and interesting from many associations, yet it is rendered still more so by the beautiful ruin of Melrose Abbey, which was founded in 1136, by **King David I.**, or, as he is more commonly called, "St. David."

In 1828, he obtained the Keith medal of the Royal Society of Edinburgh, for the discovery of two new fluids contained in the cavities of the topaz.

In 1830, he published an admirable essay on polarization in the "Philosophical Transactions," for which the Royal Society of London awarded him one of their royal medals; and the following year he published the life of Sir I. Newton in the "Family Library."

He was elected Vice-President of the Royal Society of Edinburgh in the year 1831, and received the decoration of the Hanoverian Guelphic Order, with several other eminent and scientific men. In 1832, he was knighted by King William IV.

He now fills the Principal's chair in the united college of St. Salvador and St. Leonard, at the university of St. Andrew's, Fifeshire. And in the Great Exhibition of 1851, he was chairman and reporter of the jurors and associates in Class X. (Philosophical Instruments and their Dependent Processes.)*

Besides contributing various important papers and essays to the transactions of the several learned bodies with which he has been connected from time to time, and the journals he has conducted, he has also edited the works of others, translated Legendre's "Geometry and Trigonometry," and published several scientific works. Among the number, we must mention his "Letters on Natural Magic," which is one of the volumes of the Family Library; "The Martyrs of Science; or, the Heirs of Galileo, Tycho Brahe, and Kepler;" a treatise on "Optics," in "Lardner's Cyclopædia;" and the papers in the "Edinburgh Encyclopædia" which more materially interests us in the present instance.

ELECTRICITY.
QUESTIONS AND EXPLANATIONS.

1. *T.*—What is the term Electricity derived from?

P.—The Greek word *electron* ("Ηλεκτρον), amber.

2. *T.*—Why should amber give the name to electricity?

P.—Because Thales, one of the wise men of Greece, first discovered the electrical properties of amber, and all other bodies that possessed the same properties were said to be *electrical* or *amber-like*.

3. *T.*—What do you mean by the electrical properties of bodies?

P.—It has been observed by philosophers, that there are certain bodies or substances which acquire the property of attracting light bodies, when they are subjected to a peculiar kind of excitation by friction; and it has also been observed, that if the friction is carried on in a dark room, and the excitation be powerful, that faint flashes of light, or luminous sparks, are produced, and that there is a crackling noise attending the excitation, and also a peculiar odour.

4. *T.*—Give me some proof that friction

* Very recently he has been consulted respecting the famous diamond exhibited in the Great Exhibition, and known as the "Kooh-i-noor," or "Mountain of Light," and he has recommended that it be cut anew; he is also of opinion that it is not the true Kooh-i-noor, although a valuable diamond.

ELECTRICITY.

Lesson I.

does excite the properties you have mentioned?

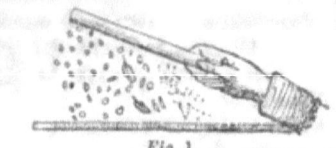

Fig. 1.

P.—[Experiment 1.] Here is a glass rod, and you see that when I touch the pieces of paper, elder-pith balls, feathers, and sawdust that are upon the table, that no change takes place. I will try this **rod** of brimstone. (Does so.) You see that there is no change; and if I were to try a piece of amber or sealing-wax it would be just the same. [Experiment 2.] I will now rub the glass rod with my silk handkerchief, which is quite dry. (Does so.) **You observe that** the pieces of paper, pith, balls, **feathers, &c.,** are attracted (see *Fig.* 1) towards the rod, and **if we** rubbed the amber, sulphur, or sealing-wax, the same effect would be produced. The cause of the phenomenon you have witnessed is called *Electricity*.

[The pupil should try Experiment 2, in the dark, and he will observe faint luminous flashes, and sparks, with a crackling noise, and peculiar odour. Let him repeat the experiment, and use oiled silk sprinkled **over** with Mosaic gold, or *aurum musivum*, or *mosaicum*.*]

5. *T.*—**How do you know** whether **a** body will **become electrical** by friction**?**
P.—By using the electrical pendulum. (See *Fig.* 2.) It consists of a piece of wire, bent as you see here, and inserted into a glass stand at one end, while the other end supports a pith-ball, which is suspended by a fine linen thread. If we place a body near the ball and it is not attracted, it is either non-electric or too slightly electric to produce any effect. If we rub resin, amber, sulphur, and

Fig. 2.

* For the method of preparing *aurum mosaicum*, see *Family Friend*, vol. ii. **p.** 56. (Old Series.)

glass, and apply them to the pith-ball, we shall observe that a sensible effect is produced upon it, for it is either attracted towards the substance presented, or it is repelled. Some bodies, such as wood, charcoal, and precious stones, scarcely produce any attraction and if we rub a metal we do not observe the least attraction.

6. *T.*—From what you have stated it would appear that some bodies become electrical by friction, **and** others do not acquire such a **property by that** means. Is it **so?**
P.—Yes; bodies are divided into conductors and non-conductors. The former called *anelectric bodies*, and the latter *idio-electric bodies*.

7. *T.*—Enumerate the non-conductors.
P.—Shell-lac, sulphur, amber, jet; all resinous bodies, pitch and wax; gums, including india-rubber and camphor; all vitreous and vitrified bodies; precious stones, gutta percha, bituminous substances, silk, dried furs, and skins, hair, wool, feathers, paper, porcelain, turpentine, various oils and fatty fluids, chocalate, all dry gases, the atmosphere, steam of high elasticity, ice at 0° Fahr.

8. *T.*—Enumerate the conductors.
P.—All metals, well-burned and dry charcoal, plumbago, concentrated and diluted acids, saline fluids, water, moist vegetable matter, living animal matter, flame, smoke, steam.

9. *T.*—Demonstrate **to me that some of** the substances you have enumerated possess the properties ascribed to them.
P.—If we use an electrifying machine and develop electricity, we render the conductor of the machine, which is a metallic body, electric. If we bring a metal cylinder, supported on a glass pedestal, in contact with the conductor, the metal will be electrified through its whole extent; if I lay hold of the cylinder, all its electricity will instantly disappear, because the human body is a good conductor.

10. *T.*—Your observations lead me to believe, that all *idio-electric* bodies or non-conductors are insulators. Am I correct?
P. Yes; and all *anelectric* bodies transmit or conduct electricity. A conductor of electricity can, therefore, only be electric while **it is** *insulated* or surrounded by

Lesson I.   ELECTRICITY.

perfect non-conductors. Water and steam are good conductors, and, therefore, we can understand how it is that electrical experiments will not answer in damp weather, because the atmosphere conducts it away.* But a dry atmosphere being a non-conductor, it insulates it.

11. *T.*—If you rub a metallic rod while it is held in your hand, why does it not become electric?

P.—Because the electricity which is developed by friction is transmitted to the ground by my body.

12. *T.*—Would it not be better to call bodies by **some** other names than conductors **and non**-conductors?

P.—**Yes**; **it** would be more correct to call them good and bad conductors.

13. *T.*—How many kinds of electricity are there **?**

P.—Six; viz., 1. Frictional electricity; 2. Galvanic or Voltaic electricity; 3. Thermo-electricity; 4. Magneto-electricity; 5. Magnetism; and 6. Electro-Magnetism.

14. *T.*—How many kinds of frictional electricity are there?

P.—Two; *vitreous* or *positive*, and *resinous* or *negative* electricity.

15. *T.*—Prove that such is the case.

P.—Here is **a** double electric pendulum,

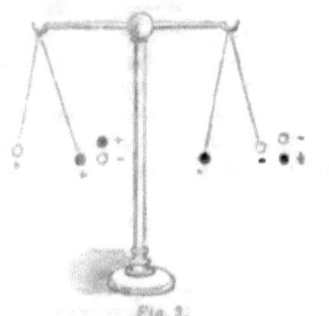

Fig. 3.

which consists of a glass pedestal (*a, b*) with two metallic arms, from each **of** which a pith ball is suspended by means of a fine silk thread. The one pendulum

* This is important, and should **be** remembered when performing electrical experiments, and care taken to have the glass feet, &c., well dried by warmth and friction.

has been made electric by contact with a glass rod rubbed with silk, and the other by a rod of shell-lac rubbed with fur. Now, observe what takes place. When I bring the shell-lac near to the ball that has been repelled by the glass rod, it will attract the ball. [Does so.] Now you will see that the reverse takes place on the other side. [Places the glass rod near **to** the ball.] You observe that the ball repelled by the shell-lac is attracted by the glass. We have thus proved that the electricity developed by glass is not identical with that evolved from resin, because the one attracts and the other repels.

16. *T.*—How are the terms positive and negative expressed?

P.—By the arithmetical signs of plus + and minus —, the former denoting the positive and the latter the negative electricity.

17. *T.*—From what you have **shown** me, it appears that certain phenomena occur when substances that possess electrical properties **come** in contact, or are presented **to each other.** Explain these phenomena.

P.—Bodies in dissimilar states of electricity attract each other; for example, + and — substances **in** similar states, repel each other; for example, when both are — or both +. When bodies are in an ordinary state, or unelectrified, they are said to be neutral. (See *Fig.* 3.)

18. *T.*—Does not electricity depend in a measure upon the nature of the surface?

P.—Yes; smooth glass rubbed with silk or wool becomes positive, but if it be ground or roughened by sand, it becomes negative under the same treatment.

GENERAL **QUESTIONS ON** LESSON **I.**

1. What **is meant by** bodies being electrical **?**
2. What is th**ere** peculiar about **electrical** excitation?
3. Prove that friction develops electricity.
4. How are bodies divided?
5. What do you mean by insulation?
6. Enumerate the various kinds of electricity.
7. How are **the** electrical conditions of bodies expressed?

LESSON II.

ELECTRICITY, according to Franklin, signifies a single imponderable fluid, which produces the phenomena of *positive and negative electricity*, by its relative excess or deficiency. Dufay and Symmer consider it to be two imponderable fluids, similar in their properties, but diametrically opposed in their mutual relations. The latter theory has been more generally adopted as a means of explaining electrical phenomena, and it has been considered that when these two fluids are united in one body, and they mutually neutralize each other in that body, it is in its natural condition; and when the two electricities are decomposed in a body, if the vitreous electricity predominates, it will become positively electric; but negatively, if the resinous electricity **predominates**. A difference has always been made between the electric and magnetic fluids. Very recently, however (Feb., 1852), Mr. Groves demonstrated before the members of the Royal Institution that electricity is not a fluid, but merely a quality of dynamic

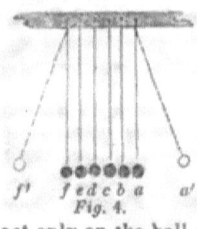
Fig. 4.

relations between molecules. We will perform his experiment for ourselves. [Experiment 3.] Here is a bar of wood supported at both ends, and having six small balls of ivory suspended from it ($a\ b\ c\ d\ e\ f$) by silk cords. Now let us imagine that the line of balls represents the particles of a bar or wire through which the electricity is to be transmitted. If we remove the ball a, and allow it to impinge or strike against the ball b, the whole line will not move forwards, but will appear to act only on the ball f at the other end of the row, causing it first to separate from the the rest and to be moved in the same direction as the ball which communicated the motion, viz., from the position of f to f'. The ball f' will, in turn, impinge on the ball e, and cause the ball a to be separated to the distance a', which is not quite so great as that of f' from its original position f. From this experiment, Mr. Groves concludes, that as the transmission of a force without motion, except at the extremities, is very evident, that electricity or the transmission of what is called the electric current, may be **referred to** a parallel agency. Mr. Groves cited as an example of the molecular disturbance of conductors **when** electricity is transmitted through them, **the** well-known expansion of a platinum **wire** when voltaic electricity is passed through it, and the appearance of little globules all along the wire when electric fusion was employed.

[The pupil should read Catechisms I. **and III.**, particularly pages 12, 14, and 70.]

QUESTIONS.

19. *T.*—**If +** electricity be given off by friction **in a** body, does it not follow that — electricity must be given off in an equal degree?

P.—Yes; and I will prove it to you by a simple experiment. [Experiment 4.] Here are two discs insulated by glass rods. The upper one, which I hold in my right hand, is made of glass, and the lower one of wood covered with leather, **which has** been rubbed over with amalgam. **Now,** when I rub these two **discs** together, you will not observe any traces of electricity as long as they are in contact; but immediately that I separate them, the one becomes positively electrified, and the other negatively. [Does so, and the result is as anticipated.]

20. *T.*—Do you imagine that bodies show a preference for either kind of electricity?

Fig. 5.

P.—No; the same body may

be rendered positively or negatively electric, according to the substance with which it is rubbed. Glass becomes positively electric when rubbed with wool or silk, and negatively when rubbed with fur.

21. *T.*—Are not bodies influenced by circumstances?

P.—Yes; colour, arrangement of the molecules, temperature, and the surface of the bodies produce different effects from those usually observed: for example, a black silk riband will be rendered negatively electric if rubbed with a white silk riband.

22. *T.*—How is electricity communicated?

P.—When free it may pass from one body to another, either by immediate contact, or by traversing a distance of more or less extent between the body communicating and the body conveying it. It may be communicated by passing from one body to another without actual contact, and then we observe what is called an electric spark. [Experiment 5.] I have a metal rod, and you will observe that when it is brought near to the conductor of the electrifying machine, that a vivid spark is produced, and also a snapping noise. [Does so, and the effect is observed.] If I placed my knuckles near a rubbed glass or shell-lac rod, the effect would be the same, only much milder.

23. *T.*—Is it possible to draw electric sparks from the human body?

P.—Yes; if you stand upon a stool with glass legs, and bring the body into contact with the conductor of an electrical machine; directly the machine is turned, you will feel a peculiar creeping sensation over the body. If I get upon another insulated stool, and place my knuckles near any part of your body, a spark will be emitted, and a shock given in proportion to the distance the electricity has traversed.

24. *T.*—How is electricity distributed?

P.—According to the amount of surfaces on passing from one insulated conductor to another. Suppose that a charged insulated conductor is brought in contact with the ground, it will lose all its electricity, because it is distributed over so large a surface. And further suppose two metallic balls, both the same size and insulated; the one on the right being electrified and the other not. When these two balls are brought in contact, the electrified one will lose exactly half its electricity.

25. *T.*—What are the best insulating substances?

P.—The vitreous and resinous non-conductors (see Q. 7), such as shell-lac, sulphur, dry glass, and also silk.

26. *T.*—We know that there are two kinds of electricity, because it has been demonstrated by experiment. I wish to know if one kind only can be developed at a time.

P.—Certainly not. One kind of electricity cannot be developed without the other, any more than one kind of magnetism. If a body is rubbed, the body and the rubber assume opposite states; the one is positively and the other negatively electrified. (See Q. 19.)

GENERAL QUESTIONS ON LESSON II.

1. Enumerate the theories respecting electricity.
2. Have you any reason to doubt the old theory that electricity is a fluid?
3. Can we excite equal degrees of positive and negative electricity at the same time by means of friction?
4. Can the same body have opposite states of electricity developed?
5. In what manner is electricity communicated and distributed?
6. Is it possible to excite positive electricity without developing negative electricity?

LESSON III.

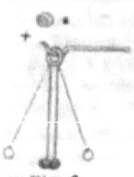

Fig. 6.

itself **when the two kinds of electricity are** uncombined, but also when they are combined; and therefore when an electric body is placed near to a body in a natural condition, disturbance takes place. This is easily demonstrated [Experiment 6]. Here is an insulated metal hook, with **a metallic ring** attached to it, **and two fine** metallic threads, having pith-balls **at their extremities.** Now when I bring this roll of resin (*a*), **which has been rendered −** electric by friction, near to the ring, the **two balls will be repelled, although the** resin **is at a** considerable distance from them; **and the** nearer **it is** brought **the more the** balls **diverge;** but immediately **the resin is removed the balls will fall together.** [Removes **the resin, and the balls are seen** as represented by the black balls in *Fig.* 6]. Now all this depends upon the separation of the electricities **which were combined** in the metallic ring and **pendulums** before the resin was placed **near to them;** and the reason is this, the − electricity is repelled towards the balls, whilst the + electricity **is attracted to** the ring.

When a body charged with one kind of electricity **is placed** near to other bodies, but not in contact, it communicates the opposite kind **of electricity** to them. Let us see that such **is the** case. Here is some **apparatus of a simple kind that you** may construct for yourselves.*

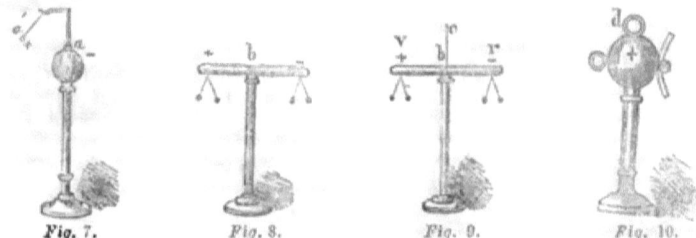

Fig. 7.   Fig. 8.   Fig. 9.   Fig. 10.

Fig. 10 represents the prime conductor of an electrifying machine; *Figs.* 8 and 9 are two **insulated metallic cylinders, placed end** to end, but not in contact with each other or **the conductor.** *Fig.* 7, **is an insulated** brass **ball, with a pith-ball** (*a′*) suspended to it, [Experiment 7]. **Now if I turn the** electrifying **machine,** the surface of *Fig.* 10 is positively **electrified, and acts upon** the insulated cylinder *Fig.* 9, so as to make the end *r* negatively electric, **and the end** *v* positively electric. This is by induction, **and** we observe that the central part *c* is neutral, and that the adjoining cylinder (*Fig.* 8) is also rendered negatively and positively electric at either end, as in the **other case;** and further, that the **brass ball** (*Fig.* 7) is rendered negatively electric on one side, and positively electric on **the opposite side, so as** to repel the pith-ball (*a′*).

QUESTIONS.

27. *T.*—What **is meant by** induction?
P.—It is the excitement exerted by a **body** already electrified **upon all** surrounding substances, **and is exerted at very sensible** and considerable **distances,** producing **a** state opposite to **its own in** the proximate parts, and a similar one in the remote parts. [See Experiment 7].

28. *T.*—Does the intensity of the electrical disturbance depend upon the proximity of the bodies?
P.—Yes, it diminishes with the distance

---

* For the method of constructing various kinds of Philosophical, Chemical, Electrical, and other apparatus, see the papers now publishing **in** the new series of the *Family Friend*, on " Practical Science."

Lesson III.   ELECTRICITY.   157

from the charged body (*d* Fig. 10); and if it is entirely removed, all the disturbance ceases, thus demonstrating that the excitement was only temporary or induced.

29. *T.*—Suppose that one end of an insulated cylinder (Fig. 9) is made to communicate with the ground by means of a conducting medium, what would be the effect?

P. While the electric body (*d* Fig. 10) still acted by induction, all the repelled electricity would be carried off by the earth, and the insulated conductor remain charged only with the electricity of the inducting body. If we remove the communicating medium with the earth and the inducting body, the insulated conductor will be charged throughout with the same electricity.

30. *T.*—What is an electroscope?

Fig. 11

P.—An instrument for showing the existence of electrical excitement. It may be constructed of two pith-balls (Fig. 6), or two strips of gold leaf, enclosed in a glass vessel, to prevent the action of currents of air, &c., upon them, (Fig. 11.) Sometimes the electroscope is furnished with a graduated arc, in which case it acts as an electrometer, or measurer of electricity.

31. *T.*—How is the electroscope used?

P.—If we wish to examine what is the nature of the electricity of a body, we charge the electroscope with a kind of electricity we know; for example, by holding a roll of shell-lac over the disc, and touching the plate with the finger, so as to carry off all the repelled electricity, and allow the other to be attracted and accumulated upon the plate. Now observe, [Experiment 8, holds a roll of shell-lac over the electroscope, which is touched with the finger, and no effect upon the gold leaves is observed], when I remove my finger from the disc, and also the roll of shell-lac, the gold leaves will diverge. [Does so and the leaves separate, as in Fig. 11]. Now it is evident that the instrument is charged with a kind of electricity contrary to that of the shell-lac.

To render this plainer, we have only to say that if we want a negative charge we must rub a glass rod with silk, and use that, because it is + electric.

32. *T.*—How do you account for the action of electric bodies upon the electroscope?

P.—By the laws of electrical induction.

33. *T.*—What apparatus do we require to develop frictional electricity?

P.—The apparatus is very extensive, because we also require some for collecting the electricity, as well as developing it. It will be better to describe each separately.

34. *T.*—How do you usually excite and collect electricity?

P.—By an electrical machine, which is generally a hollow cylinder, or a circular plate of glass. All frictional electrifying machines consist, 1st, of the electric body to be excited; 2ndly, of a rubber or exciter; and 3rdly, of an insulated conductor for collecting the electricity.

35. *T.*—Then it is not necessary to have a glass electrifying machine.

P.—Certainly not, any electric body will answer. In the Great Exhibition there was a gutta-percha machine. (C. 10, No. 444).

36. *T.*—Explain the construction of the cylindrical machine.

Fig. 12.

P.—It consists of a hollow cylinder of glass (c c), which is so fitted that it revolves upon pivots passing through upright pillars of glass (P P), the one end being furnished with a winch handle (H), by which it may be made to revolve. A cushion or rubber (R), which is covered with an amalgam,* is attached to a glass pillar fitted with a sliding base (b), so as to allow it to press with a greater or less force against the cylinder. A flap of oiled silk (S) is attached to the rubber and thrown loosely over the cylinder, and just where it terminates is a cross-piece of brass furnished with points, corresponding to one on the opposite side (A), this is connected with an insulated cylindrical conductor (N and P), and as the machine is placed between two of these conductors, one collects +, and the other − electricity.

37. *T.*—What is the use of the silk flap?

P.—To keep up the friction on the surface of the glass, so that the electricity excited by the rubber (R) may not be lost on its passage to the conductor (P).

38. *T.*—Can we produce positive and negative electricity at will?

P. Yes, if we wish to have a charge of vitreous or positive electricity, we put the conductor (N) in connection with the earth, so that electricity is continually supplied to the glass cylinder. If we wish for a supply of resinous or negative electricity we reverse the proceeding, and remove the + conductor (P), or connect it with the earth, so that the electricity thrown upon the glass is relieved, and a constant supply of the electricity we require afforded to the − conductor (N).

39. *T.*—Is it necessary to have the ends of the cylindrical machines permanently closed?

P.—No; it is better to have the ends sufficiently large to admit the hand, for the purpose of wiping out and drying the inside, because if they are closed, condensation takes place on the inside and prevents the proper action of the machine, and therefore the ends should be fitted with wooden caps which fit the openings exactly, and may be removed at any time.

40. *T.*—Describe the plate-glass electrical machine.

P.—It consists of a circular plate of

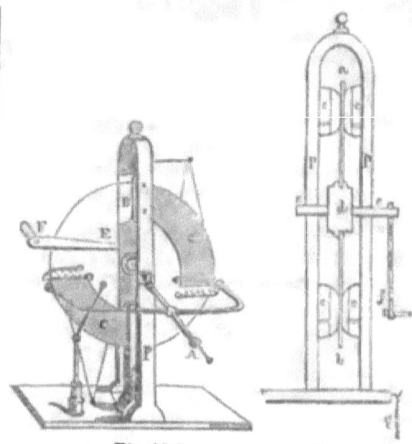

Fig. 13.   *Fig. 14.†*

glass, the diameter of which of course varies, some plates being only 9 inches, and others 80 inches in diameter. An axis passes through an opening in its centre, to one end of which is a winch-handle, and the whole is supported by the frame-work to which the rubbers are attached. This machine is furnished with a conductor, which, like that of the cylindrical one, is insulated, and has ends with points placed opposite to the termination of the silk flaps.

41. *T.*—What is an electrophorus?

P.—A simple electrical apparatus, depending upon the principle of induction. It consists of a cake of resin fused in a circular plate of metal which is larger than the resinous disc, and has a cover with an insulated handle, which is

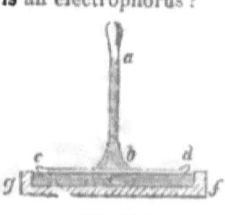

Fig. 15.‡

---

* *Fig.* 13. Plate-glass electrical machine. A, conductor. B, cushion or rubber, smeared with amalgam. c, c, silk flaps. F, glass plate. F, winch handle. P, frame-work or pillar.

† *Fig.* 14. End view of the machine, showing the arrangements of parts. a, b, plate of glass. c, c, c, c, cushions or rubbers. d, centre of glass with the axis. e, e, passing through it. f, winch handle. p, p, the frame-work or pillar. g, chain.

‡ *Fig.* 15. a, b, the insulated handle. c, d, the cover. e, disc of shell lac. f, g, conducting metal disc or sole.

---

* This is made by melting two ounces of zinc in an iron ladle and then adding one ounce of tin, after which four ounces of heated mercury should be gradually poured into the ladle and the whole well stirred, and when nearly solid the amalgam should be poured into some vessel and agitated so as to reduce it to powder placed upon the upper surface of the electrical plate.

42. *T.*—How is the electrophorus used?

P.—The cover is removed, and the surface of the shell-lac struck pretty smartly with a piece of dry silk, fur, or cat's-skin, so as to make it negatively electric; after which the cover is replaced. The electricity of the cake of resin acts inductively upon the two electricities hitherto combined in the cover; the + electricity is attracted, and will be found in the lower part of the cover, and the − electricity is repelled and accumulates in the upper part of the cover. [Exp. 9.] You observe that I have charged the electrophorus, and now I will bring my knuckle near the cover. [Does so, and a spark is elicited.] If I now touch the cover with my finger, all the − electricity will escape, and the + electricity remain in combination with the − electricity of the resin as long as the cover remains on. If the cover is removed the + electricity will be set free, and we can then get a spark of + electricity from the cover.

GENERAL QUESTIONS ON LESSON III.

1. What is the effect of an electric body being placed near to a body in a natural condition?
2. If we place any body charged with only one kind of electricity near to other bodies, what will be the effect, provided the electrical body does not touch the others?
3. Explain the meaning of induction.
4. What does the intensity of electrical disturbance depend upon?
5. Explain the use and **action** of the electroscope.
6. What are the usual means of developing frictional electricity?
7. Explain the various machines used for frictional electricity, and how they act.
8. What is the electrophorus, its use, and mode of action?

LESSON IV.

Our purpose is not to consider the difficult or abstruse matters relating to the laws of electricity, but rather to give a general outline of its leading features, which will bear the same resemblance to the subject that a skeleton map does to a complete one. A work, six times the size of our complete volume, would scarcely contain the index to electrical science; and, therefore, where our readers imagine they discover neglect, let them rather impute it to want of space than lack of knowledge.*

We know that as the distance increases between bodies, electrical attraction and repulsion diminish; this is proved by the oscillations of an electric pendulum.

As long as a body remains in a natural condition, that is, as long as the two kinds of electricity are uncombined, it is probable that they are uniformly distributed through the whole mass of the body. When the two kinds of electricity become separated, and a conductor is charged with free electricity, the individual elements of these freed electricities will repel each other, and continue separating until checked by some means. This is the reason that electricity is distributed over the surface of a conductor, because, as the body is a good conductor, it does not hinder the dispersion of the electricity.

QUESTIONS.

43. *T.*—Does the form of a body influence the distribution of electricity?

P.—Yes; the more round a body is the better, for as it departs from a round form,

---

* GRANDFATHER WHITEHEAD, feeling the want that existed of any *practical work* on science, has commenced a series of papers on "Practical Science," in the new series of the *Family Friend*, which is intended as an Appendix to the present catechisms, and an introduction to other scientific works.

the electricity is less equally distributed over its surface, and collects at points lying farthest from the middle.

44. *T.*—Do pointed bodies **affect the** accumulation of electricity?

P.—Yes. If a point is brought **near an** insulated conductor, the electricity will be more dense at that part, and therefore overcome the resistance of the air, which envelopes it, as if it were a non-conducting layer. Experiments prove that electricity flows readily from sharp-pointed bodies.

45. *T.*—Is the knowledge of the influence of pointed bodies practically applied?

P.—Yes, in the construction of lightning conductors.

46. *T.*—Suppose that we place two insulated electric conductors, similarly charged, near to each other, how will the electricity be distributed on their surfaces?

P.—The electric density will diminish between the conductors as they are placed near to each other, and increase at those points furthest from the point between the two, thus:

O O
a | *b* *c* | *d*
Fig. 16.

The sphere *a b*, and the sphere *c d*, when insulated, and placed near to each other, if charged with the same electricity, will cause a disturbance. The electricity of one sphere will repel that of the other, and therefore at *b* and *c* the density of the electricity decreases, while it increases at *a* and *d*. The nearer the spheres are brought together, the greater will be the increase of intensity at *a* and *d*, and the diminution at *b* and *c*.

47. *T.*—What would be the effect of bringing a non-electric conductor near to an electrified insulated conductor?

P.—It would become electric by induction, and act like a body charged with the opposite electricity.

48. *T.*—Suppose that the two spheres (*Fig.* 16) are placed in contact, what will be the effect?

P.—The density of the electricity will be *null* where they touch. If these spheres had been charged with opposite electricities, then the matter would be reversed, and on bringing the spheres together a spark would be produced, because the density of the electricity would be at *b* and *c* instead of *a* and *d*.

49. *T.*—The two spheres *a b* and *c d*, *Fig* 16, are charged with opposite electricities, the former with +, and the latter with − electricity. Now the electricity of the one sphere is attracted by that of the opposite sphere, and being prevented from escaping they combine. How must we manage to make the combination perfect?

P.—By separating the spheres with a Franklin plate.

50. *T.*—Explain what you mean by a Franklin plate, and its mode of action

Fig. 17.

P.—It is a plate of glass, partially coated on both sides with tin-foil (*a Fig.* 17), so as to leave the outer part free. If this plate is placed between the two spheres, the one part will be charged with + and the other with − electricity, so that the glass alone separates them; and as they are unable to penetrate the glass the combination is pretty perfect.

51. *T.*—Is it necessary to bring both sides of the Franklin plate into contact with the spheres to charge its sides with opposite electricity?

P.—No, because by charging the front side with + electricity it will act by induction upon the combined electricities of the other side; and as soon as we place that side in connection with the earth, the + electricity will pass into the earth, and the − electricity will be induced to the back surface As the − electricity of the back surface repels the + electricity of the front surface, it enables electricity to pass again from the conductor to the front surface, which again repels it, and thus increases the − electricity of the back surface. By acting in this manner, we may charge one surface with +, and the other with − electricity.

52. *T.*—How can we make this plate discharge its electricity at once?

P.—By means of the discharging-rod (*Fig.* 18), which, as it touches both surfaces at once, puts them into connection with each other,

Fig. 18.

so that the accumulated opposite electricities of the two surfaces pass from one to the other. To use this rod apply one ball to one surface, and then apply the other, when a vivid spark and explosion will be produced.

53. *T.*—What is the Leyden jar?

Fig. 19

P.—A glass jar or bottle coated with tin-foil **inside** and **outside, as high as** (*a Fig.* 19) in the one on the table, and therefore leaving a rim of naked glass above the tin-foil. The mouth of it is fitted with a wooden cap, which has a brass rod passing through its centre, to the upper end of which a brass ball is attached, and a brass chain to the lower part.

54. *T.*—What is the principle of the Leyden jar?

P.—A modification of Franklin's plate.

55. *T.*—Are not several of these jars sometimes united?

P.—Yes; this is done in order to obtain a very strong charge; and in this case **we** are obliged to employ larger jars, and then the brass ball of each jar is connected with its fellow, and all the external coatings of the jars are in connection with each other, as well as the inner coatings. When this combination takes place the apparatus is called an *electric battery*.

GENERAL QUESTIONS ON LESSON IV.

1. What is the effect of the distance being increased between bodies?
2. Is there any objection to our using angular and sharp edges to conducting bodies?
3. Explain the distribution of electricity on the surfaces of conducting bodies.
4. How does a Franklin's plate act?
5. How can we discharge a Franklin's plate?
6. Explain what is meant **by a Leyden** jar and **an** electric battery.

LESSON V.

WE know that when electricity has accumulated in a body and is discharged, that a light is produced, but that the body will not afford the least appearance of light as long as a state of electric equilibrium subsists, and the two electricities are undisturbed. The distance at which a spark can be drawn from an electric body depends upon the conductability of the substance, the power of the electric discharge, and the size of the surface. A powerful charge is required to make round bodies emit sparks spontaneously, but angular or pointed bodies will emit sparks with a very weak charge. Sparks are multiplied by interrupting the conductor by which the electricity passes to the earth. This may easily be proved by experiment. [Experiment 9.]

Fig. 20.

Take a plate of glass of the same shape as *Fig.* 20, and fasten a brass ball to **the** top of it, and connect this brass ball with another at the bottom, by means of rhomboidal or diamond-shaped plates of tin-foil pasted on the glass, but so arranged that they do not touch each other. Connect the lower ball with the outer coating of a Leyden jar, and the upper ball with the knob of the jar, you will then see sparks between each piece **of** tin-foil. [Does so, and the effect produced in the dark is beautiful]. [Experiment 10.] I have here a glass plate (*Fig.* 20) which is painted with different colours, red, blue, and yellow, and covered with pieces of tin-foil, the same that some of the liberated electricity be abstracted from the zinc, so as to cause its density to be less than 1, **we should** then find **that the loss of the + electricity from the zinc** plate would be immediately compensated for by **the electro-motor force, while** an equal **amount of −** electricity **to that of** the newly-formed **+** electricity **passing to the zinc plate, would pass to** the **copper plate, and thence to the ground.**

73. *T.* − Is your voltaic pile now formed?

P.—No; I have only **a pair of plates, and voltaic piles may consist of any number of plates from 4 to 500 or more, and** I have not yet used the moist cloth, which must now be placed upon the zinc, when it will be found that the liberated + electricity will pass from the zinc to the moist cloth; now the effect of this action is **a loss of electricity in the zinc,** which is therefore immediately supplied, so that the **density of the + electricity of** the **zinc and cloth will be equal or 1. We will now place a copper plate upon the moist cloth, and we shall find that + electricity is distributed over it, and has a density of 1, so that we now say that the under copper plate in connection with the ground, has a density of 0, while + electricity of a density = 1 is on the zinc plate, the moist cloth, and the upper copper plate.**

74. *T.*—Then it appears, **that a voltaic pile consists merely of a series of plates of copper and zinc, with an intermediate substance, moist cloth, and that they are arranged in the following order,—copper, zinc, cloth, copper, zinc, cloth, copper, &c.**

P.—Exactly so, and **the density of the** electricity is proportioned to **the number** of pairs **of plates used.** For example, if we pile the elements in the order you have mentioned **to the** number of 100, it will be found that **the freed + electricity upon the 100th zinc plate will have a density of 100.** One end **of this pile is called the zinc end, or positive pole, and the other the copper end, or negative pole.**

75. *T.*—What would be the effect of insulating the negative pole, and connecting **the positive one with the ground?**

P.—The density of the freed electricity of the zinc end would be 0, and the − electricity would be distributed over the whole pile, its density increasing towards the copper end.

76. *T.*—If these two poles are connected, what would be the effect?

P.—A constant reunion of the electricities developed **in the pile, but if** they are separated a little, we shall observe an uninterrupted current of sparks pass from one to the other.

77. *T.*—What **do you mean by a galvanic circuit?**

P.—All apparatus serving to produce a continual electric current are called galvanic circuits, and are generally constructed **of two** metals and one fluid, similar **to the voltaic pile, which is not** so useful **as the trough apparatus.**

78. *T.*—What do you mean by the trough apparatus?

P.—It consists of several square plates of copper and zinc soldered together, and placed perpendicularly in a wooden trough lined with a coating of resin. The plates are so arranged that there is an interval between each pair, and this is filled with acidulated water, which acts like the moist cloth of Volta's pile.

79. *T.*—Am I correct in supposing that there are different forms of the galvanic circuit?

P.—Yes; there are many. When there is only a pair of conductors immersed in a fluid, it is called a single circuit; when two or more pairs are immersed, it is called a compound circuit; and they are also called voltaic batteries.

80. *T.*—Is it possible to have a **powerful battery in a small compass?**

P.—Yes; I have one here (*Fig.* 22). It is called a Smee's battery, and consists of two plates of amalgamated zinc (z z), with a plate of platinized silver (s) between **them;** these plates, you observe, are confined to a piece of wood (w) by a binding screw (d), and the whole immersed in a vessel containing dilute sulphuric acid (A).* By means of this battery we obtain immense power without much trouble, and ensure a pretty steady action. Here is another battery (*Fig.* 23) which is called Daniell's constant battery

Fig. 22.

---

* One part of acid to seven of water

Lesson VII.   ELECTRICITY.   145

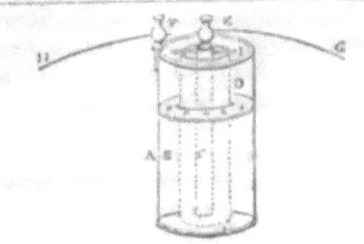

Fig. 23.

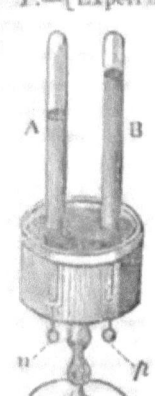

Fig. 24.

because it produces a long-continued and uniform current. The outside vessel (A), you observe, is made of copper, and is filled with a strong solution of *sulphate of copper*, or "blue vitriol" (B). You see that there is another cylinder placed within this, but separated from the copper vessel by a shelf (D), which is full of holes. Upon the shelf are some blue lumps; these are crystals of sulphate of copper, placed there to maintain the strength of the solution. Within this second cylinder, which is a porous earthen tube, is a rod of zinc (C), supported by a cross piece (I), and surmounted by a cap and screw (E), which confines a wire (G); a similar cap and screw (F) is affixed to the outside vessel, and confines a wire (H). Both these wires transmit the electric current from the battery.

81. *T.*—How can we determine the direction of the current of voltaic electricity?

P. By remembering that the polarity or disturbance commences at the surface of the metal attacked, and starts from that point; it then passes through the liquid to the second metal or conducting body, and returns by the wire.

82. *T.*—You said (Q. 120, p. 123,) that you would describe the process of obtaining oxygen from water by voltaic electricity; please to do so now.

P.—[Experiment 12.] Here is a shallow cylindrical glass vessel (*Fig.* 24), furnished with two glass tubes (A and B), which are filled with water acidulated with sulphuric acid, and **placed over two small plates of platinum connected with two platinum wires passing through the bottom of the vessel (*n* and *p*)** We will now connect these wires with the two poles of a Smee's battery. [Does so.] You see that bubbles of gas are rising in each tube from the platinum plates. You see that the gas in the tube over the negative pole or zinc end, occupies twice the space of the gas in the other tube; the former is hydrogen, and the latter oxygen.

[See Lessons IX. and X., Catechism IV., for the characteristic properties of each.]

GENERAL QUESTIONS ON LESSON VI.

1. How may the electric equilibrium of two solid bodies be disturbed?
2. What do you mean by an electro-motor power? and give the scale of tension?
3. Explain what is meant by a voltaic pile, and how it is constructed.
4. Explain the theory of the action of the voltaic pile.
5. What do you mean by the poles of a voltaic battery?
6. Explain the difference between a trough apparatus, a Smee's, and a Daniell's battery.
7. How is water decomposed by voltaic electricity?

LESSON VII.

WE have seen that the galvanic current will produce heat and light, and that it will decompose water. If space permitted, we might enter into the consideration of its action upon salts, particularly the alkalis; however, we may notice that it decomposes many salts, and that we are indebted for many of the elegant articles that adorn our mansions to its agency, whether they be the pictures delivered by the Art Union of London, or the services of electro-plate that are ranged upon our tables.

ELECTRICITY.

Lesson VII.

There is a law which is called the electrolytic law, that no electric current, or comparatively only a very weak one, can pass through a fluid without its passage being attended by chemical decomposition. This occurs in every cell of every galvanic apparatus as long as the circuit is complete, and the quantity of the electric current is proportionate to the amount of decomposition in each cell.

We have now to consider other actions of the galvanic current—its magnetic actions. For a considerable period it had been known that powerful electric charges, under certain circumstances, affected the magnetic needle. Experiments were made, but in the year 1820, Oersted discovered a means of causing electricity to act certainly and constantly upon a magnet.

QUESTIONS.

83. *T.*—How can we magnetize soft iron so as to form magnets?

P.—By passing a current of electricity at right angles to it, in which case the iron will acquire magnetic polarity, either temporary or permanently, as the case may be, the direction of the current determining the position of the poles. [Experiment 13.] I have a bar of soft iron in my hand, and you observe that it is bent into the form of a horse-shoe; here is some copper wire which is covered with silk for the purpose of insulation, and you observe that I have now wound it firmly over the bar of iron, so that the windings are all close together; we will suspend the horse-shoe bar to a hook in the beam by means of the ring at the top of it. [Does so.] Now let us try if it will support the keeper, or even an iron nail. [Tries them, and they fall to the ground.] Let us place the ends of the wire into communication with a small voltaic battery, and try the keeper again. [Does so, and the keeper adheres firmly, so as to be able to bear a very heavy weight as in *Fig.* 25.] If we disconnect the wires, the weight and keeper will fall to the ground. [Does so, and they instantly fall.]

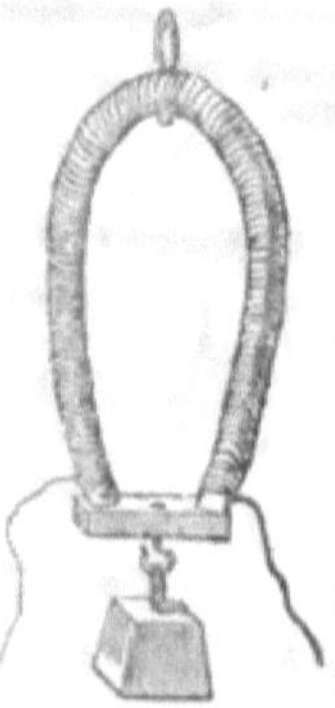

Fig. 25.

84. *T.*—Which is the north, and which the south pole of this magnet?

P.—Where the + current enters, a north pole is formed, and a south pole where the — current enters.

85. *T.*—Then it would appear that the wire of an electric current is a magnet. Is this the case?

P.—Certainly; and it shows attractions and repulsions for other electric wires. For example, if the wires of two circuits are placed side by side, and are free, they will be mutually repelled if the direction of the current is the same in both, and attracted if the currents are contrary.

86. *T.*—Can motion be produced by the galvanic current?

P.—Yes; a continuous motion may be produced by the magnetizing action of the galvanic current; but the apparatus is too extensive for me to demonstrate it to you. Attempts have been made by Jacobi, of St. Petersburgh, and Wagner, of Frankfort, to apply the galvanic current practically as a moving power; but the expense is a serious objection to its use.

87. *T.*—Has any practical application been made of the magnetization of soft iron by galvanic currents?

P.—Yes, in the construction of the electric telegraph, the arrangements of which admits of a perfect correspondence being carried on, resulting from attraction and repulsion.

88. *T.*—What do you mean by thermo-electricity?

P.—It is simply electricity, developed by heat.

89. *T.*—How is this produced?

P.—We know that an electric current develops heat on passing through an inferior conducting substance, or if its passage is interrupted. This is by no means anything new; but within the last twenty years, Professor Seebeck, of Berlin, has discovered that heat may be made to produce a current of electricity. This is managed as follows: two metals are soldered together, whose susceptibility to heat is unequal, and as often as heat is applied to the two places of junction, an electric current is produced and maintained as long as the difference of temperature continues. Bismuth and copper answer very well for this purpose.

90. *T.*—Is it necessary to employ metals?

P.—No; it is found that if hot water and cold water are mixed together, that electricity is produced, and that the hot water becomes negative, and the cold water positive; but the reverse takes place with acids; for if a hot acid is mixed with a cold one, the former becomes positive, and the latter negative.

91. *T.*—You said that bismuth and copper answered very well; can you inform me of any other metals that are used?

P.—Certainly. This table will **exhibit** the order of the principal metals in regard to thermo-electric combinations; and the farthest asunder any two metals are placed in this Table, the more powerful is the union formed by them.

Antimony.	Brass.	Cobalt.
Arsenic.	Rhodium.	Palladium.
Iron.	Lead.	Platinum.
Zinc.	Tin.	Nickel.
Gold.	Silver.	Mercury.
Copper.	Manganese.	Bismuth.

Each metal causes a positive current to pass upon any metal above it, and a negative upon any metal below it; therefore, if bismuth and antimony were soldered together, a negative current would pass from the antimony to the bismuth, and a positive one from the bismuth to the antimony; negative electricity radiates from the junction through the bismuth, and positive electricity through the antimony.

92. *T.*—Is it possible to form a compound thermo-electric circuit?

P.—Yes; by joining several bars of metals together; but then the heat requires to be applied to each joining: thermo-electric piles may be constructed as well as voltaic piles.

GENERAL QUESTIONS ON LESSON VII.

1. How can we form temporary magnets?
2. How do you know the north from the south pole of a magnet?
3. Is it possible to cause motion by the galvanic current?
4. Upon what principle is thermo-electricity produced?
5. Describe the method of obtaining an electric current by heat, and name the metals generally employed.

LESSON VIII.

For many obvious reasons we have placed magnetism, the subject of the present lesson, last on our list.

We have already seen that the property of attracting iron may be imparted temporarily **to iron**, and permanently to steel; but certain iron ores which have this property are found in the earth, and are termed *natural* **magnets**. *Artificial magnets* are generally made in the form of rods, needles, and horse-shoes.

QUESTIONS.

93. *T.*—Suppose that you throw a magnetic-rod into iron filings, what will be the condition of it when removed?

P.—The iron filings will be collected at both ends, but not in the centre, because it is found that the magnetic influence is greater at the extremities or *poles* than in the centre.

94. *T.*—Suppose that I broke the magnetic-rod in the centre, and plunged the two pieces into the iron filings, what would be the effect?

P.—Exactly the same, because each portion would become a perfect magnet, having its neutral line and two poles.

95. *T.*—If you suspend a magnet by a silk cord (as in *Fig.* 26), what will be the effect? or bringing one pole of a magnet near either of the two poles of the one that is suspended?

ELECTRICITY.   Lesson VIII.

P.—If we present one pole of a bar-magnet held in the hand to the pole *a* (*Fig* 26,) it will be repelled, while *b* will be attracted. If we reverse the magnet, and present the other pole to *a*, it will be attracted and *b* repelled.

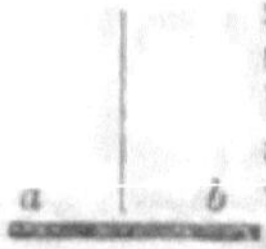

Fig. 26.

96. *T.*—What is the reason of the phenomenon you have described?

P.—Because it is a **law in magnetism** that *similar poles* **repel each other,** *and contrary poles* **attract each other.** The two poles of the magnet in the hand are opposite poles, because they **are** of a different nature.

97. *T.*—Is it possible to impart temporary magnetic influence to iron?

P.—Yes. [Exp. 14]. Here is a bar magnet (*a b*), and a small bar of iron (*c*). You observe when I dip the bar of iron into some iron filings that no magnetic effect takes place; but when the bar of iron is presented to the magnet, then it is attracted and supported by it. I will now dip the **bar** of iron into the iron filings, and observe what takes place. [Does so, and the **iron** filings are attracted in **a tuft, as** in *Fig.* 27.] This clearly demonstrates that *under the influence of* **a** *magnet, iron itself becomes magnetic.* I will remove the iron bar, and you will then see the iron filings **fall off,** because no further attractive force remains. [Does so, and the iron filings drop off.] [Experiment 15.] Instead of using iron filings I will employ small cylinders, attaching four of them to the first (as *d Fig.* 27), and you will then find that a chain is formed, of which the magnet is the first link, but that as soon as the magnet is removed, the chain will fall apart, because there is no magnetic power to hold the links together. [Performs the **Experiment**].

Fig. 27.

98. *T.*—If the pole of a bar magnet supports a piece of iron which is in danger of falling from its weight, **what will be** the effect of bringing the contrary **pole** of another magnet immediately over it?

P.—The iron would fall off, because, the second magnet disturbs the actions of the first, and decomposes the magnetic influence **in** the iron. [Experiment 16.] Here is a bar-magnet (*a b*, *Fig.* 28), with a piece of iron (*c*) attached; if I bring another bar-**magnet near to** it, **so that the opposite** pole *b'* **is placed over the** pole *a*, the piece of iron (*e*) **will** fall off. [Does so, and it falls as represented in *Fig.* 28.]

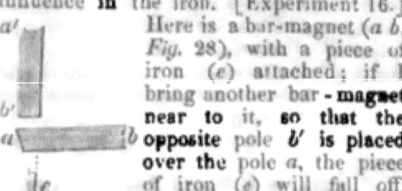
Fig. 28.

99. *T.*—Can you render any other metal magnetic besides iron?

P.—Yes, nickel and cobalt may also become magnetic.

100. *T.*—What do you mean by the armature of a magnet?

P.—It is generally **a piece of soft iron** brought into contact with the magnet, in order to preserve its power by means of the magnetic decomposition **going** on in the soft iron.

101. *T.*—What is meant by the direction of magnets?

P.—It has been observed, that when **magnets** are suspended horizontally, or **magnetic** needles revolve upon a fixed **point in an** horizontal plane, that they **always point** one particular end to a particular spot or point in the horizon. If you turn this point away from this point, back it comes again; consequently there must be a magnetic force which acts at all points of the earth's surface; and we find that this force distinguishes between the two poles, attracting one and repelling the other like a magnet. From observing this, we have been enabled to name the two poles of the magnet; thus one is called the north pole, and the other the **south** pole.

102. *T.*—Then the north pole of the magnet points to the north, and the south pole to the **south**?

P.—Certainly not. The north pole of the magnet points to the terrestial magnetic south pole, and the south pole to the magnetic north pole.

103. *T.*—What do you mean by the declination of a magnetic needle?

P. It is the deviation of the needle from the astronomical meridian. Thus it may declinate east or west, which is the same as saying that it turns towards one or **the** other side of the astronomical meridian.

Lesson IX. OPTICS.

104. *T.*—What do you mean by the inclination of the needle?

P. Its deviation from the horizontal position; thus one point of the needle approaches the earth, or what is technically called *dips*, and this we find increases or decreases according to our position near or from the equator and the poles.

GENERAL QUESTIONS ON LESSON VIII.

1. Is the magnetic influence uniform in a magnetic bar?
2. What is the difference between the ends and the centre of a magnet?
3. What are the ends of a magnet called?
4. Is there anything peculiar about the attractive force of magnets?
5. Is the magnetic force increased by using two magnets instead of one?
6. Explain the meaning of the terms direction, declination, and inclination of a magnetic needle.

[GRANDFATHER WHITEHEAD refrains from entering into the discussion of animal electricity, because the subject is too abstruse for the greater part of his pupils, and not so practically useful as the subjects already considered].

OPTICS.

INTRODUCTION.—The science of Optics reveals to us the intimate nature and affections of light; and as we judge of the various objects around us, chiefly by our sense of sight or vision, the science of optics becomes interesting to us all, and enables us to comprehend many of the highly interesting, curious, and important phenomena connected with vision; and hence its name, which is derived from the Greek word *optomai* (οπτομαι), to see; therefore the science of optics signifies the theory of light and vision.

In investigating this science, we have to consider the following points. 1. The general properties of light, and its effect on the organ of vision. 2. The reflection of light from the surfaces of bodies. 3. The refraction of light, or the change it undergoes in passing through transparent bodies. 4. The phenomena of colours. 5. **Peculiar** modifications of reflected and refracted light.

LESSON IX.

SOME bodies admit of the passage of light, and of other bodies being seen through them; they are therefore called transparent.* Some are exactly the reverse of this, and are called opaque; others only admit of bodies being imperfectly seen through them, and are called semi-transparent, or half-transparent; others are visible by their own light, and are called luminous; and some can only be seen by means of the light obtained from the luminous bodies.

We have now to treat of the theory of direct light, or *optics proper.*

* **The** word *transparent* is derived from the Latin words *trans*, through or beyond, and *parens*, apparent. This word is frequently used instead of *diaphanous*, which signifies the same, and is derived from the Greek word *diaphanees* (Διαφανης), shining through.

QUESTIONS.

105. *T.*—What is light?

P.—Rapid undulations or vibrations produced by very minute particles or luminous bodies in a thin and elastic medium, called the luminous ether, which is interposed between them and the seat of our vision.

106. *T.*—How do these undulations produce light?

P.—By stimulating the optic nerve by means of vibrations, and producing an effect which we call light.

107. *T.*—How does light proceed?

Fig. 29.

P.—In a straight direction from the luminous body which produces it, towards the part upon which it acts. Thus from every luminous point rays of light proceed in all directions, as seen in this diagram (*Fig.* 29).

108. *T.*—What do you mean by a ray of light?

P.—It is the smallest portion of light which can emanate from a luminous body, and is generally represented as a mathematical line, although it is really an infinitesimal pyramid.

109. *T.*—What do you mean by a medium?

P.—It is any transparent space through which light passes, such as air, water, and glass. Even empty space is a medium.

110. *T.*—What is a luminous body?

P.—It consists essentially of ponderable matter, and the ultimate physically perceptible atoms are called *luminous points*; therefore as every body is made up of molecules or atoms, so is a luminous body made up of an assemblage of luminous points.

[The pupil should read Lesson III., p. 11.]

111. *T.*—Are all bodies luminous?

P.—No, some are *opaque*, as stones, metals, wood and clay, and do not suffer light to pass through them. This property however depends upon their thickness, for all bodies will admit of the passage of some degree of light if we make them sufficiently thin. For example, if we affix a thin gold leaf to a glass plate, and hold it to a strong light, we shall perceive a blueish-green light through it. Others are *transparent*,—as water, air, and glass. These bodies yield a passage to light, so as to allow us to observe the form of objects beyond them. *Translucent* bodies (such as thin paper and ground glass), admit of the transmission of some portion of light, without however allowing the form or colour of objects being recognised if they are far distant. I cannot give you a more familiar illustration of the *comparative*, but not the actual degrees of distinction between opacity, transparency, and translucency, than the common fowls' egg-shell. If you hold it when boiled, and full against the light, you will have a good definition of opacity. Now empty it, and on holding it against the light, you will observe that some parts of the shell are darker than others, which are spotted as it were with light, and that there is also a thin membrane lining the shell. Now the shell itself will represent opacity, the light spots on it translucency, and the membrane transparency. Be sure to remember, however, that this is only the comparative degrees of distinction, because the whole of them are translucent.

112. *T.*—You mentioned before (Question 105) that a ray of light proceeded in a straight line towards the part upon which it acts, now when it reaches that part what takes place?

P.—As long as the ray remains in the same medium it advances in a straight line, but as soon as it comes in contact with another body it is partly thrown back, or *reflected* from its surface: if the body is transparent, the light partly enters the body in an altered direction, and is then *refracted*.

113. *T.*—Does light travel fast?

P.—Yes, its velocity is so great, that it traverses all distances upon earth in an imperceptibly small space of time. It travels over 195,000 English miles in one second, and therefore would require eight minutes and thirteen seconds to traverse the space between the sun and the earth; while a cannon-ball, going at the rate of 1,200 feet in a second, would require fourteen years to pass through the same space.

114. *T.*—How do you account for shadows?

Lesson X.

OPTICS.

P.—Light being transmitted in straight lines, it follows that a dark body exposed to rays of light must throw a shadow, because the light does not pass through it. I will illustrate this in a familiar

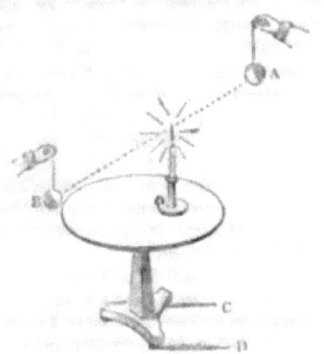

Fig. 30.

way. [Experiment 17.] Place a lighted candle in the centre of a small table (as in *Fig.* 30), then tie a thread to the stalk of an apple, and hold it high above the light (as A *Fig.* 30); tie another thread to another apple, and I will hold it nearly on a level with the table (as B *Fig* 30); now you observe that the half of each apple is light, and the other part dark, the lighted part being nearer to the candle, and the dark part farther from it. Now there is no actual shadow cast from the apples held in the hands; but if you look at the stand of the table you will observe that there are shadows (C & D) thrown from it; this is because the natural light strikes the other side, and therefore the part beyond it forms the limits of the shadow. In this manner we can understand how the shadow of a body exposed to the sun's light is sharply defined close behind it, while at a greater distance it becomes undefined.

GENERAL QUESTIONS ON LESSON IX.

1. Describe light.
2. How is light produced?
3. How is light transmitted? and what is meant by a medium?
4. Describe the difference between opacity, transparency, and translucency, and also what is meant by diaphonous.
5. What takes place when a ray of light is interrupted in its course?
6. How fast does light travel?
7. Explain how shadows are formed.

LESSON X.

THE intensity of light diminishes in proportion as the squares of the distances increase. This is a known fact of much importance in optics, and should therefore be remembered.

Before entering more fully into the science, it will be well to explain some of the terms in common use. Thus a *pencil* is a slender portion of rays, or a small bundle of them; a *beam* is a large bundle of pencils. Rays are said to *diverge* when they separate from each other as they depart from the luminous point; and *converge* when they approach closer to each other, until they meet in a point. All rays are originally divergent, but they are made to converge by the aid of some substance having a reflective or refractive power. The *focus* is the point from which rays diverge, or to which they converge. The *principal focus* is the point to which parallel rays are made to converge by reflection or refraction. *Parallel rays* are those which continue a direct course side by side, at the same distance from each other, thus _____, but no such rays really exist. The *focal distance* or length _____ is the distance between the focus and the reflecting or refracting _____ body. *Reflected rays* are thrown back from the surface upon which they fall, but *refracted rays* are not thrown back, but pass through the medium in an altered direction. [See Question 110.]

QUESTIONS.

105. *T.*—What is light?

P.—Rapid undulations or vibrations produced by very minute particles or luminous bodies in a thin and elastic medium, called the luminous ether, which is interposed between them and the seat of our vision.

106. *T.*—How do these undulations produce light?

P.—By stimulating the optic nerve by means of vibrations, and producing an effect which we call light.

107. *T.*—How does light proceed?

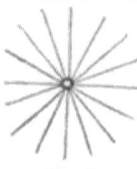

Fig. 29.

P.—In a straight direction from the luminous body which produces it, towards the part upon which it acts. Thus from every luminous point rays of light proceed in all directions, as seen in this diagram (*Fig.* 29).

108. *T.*—What do you mean by a ray of light?

P.—It is the smallest portion of light which can emanate from a luminous body, and is generally represented as a mathematical line, although it is really an infinitesimal pyramid.

109. *T.*—What **do you mean** by a **medium**?

P.—It is any transparent space through which light passes, such as air, water, and glass. Even empty space is a medium.

110. *T.*—What is a luminous body?

P.—It consists essentially of ponderable **matter,** and the ultimate physically perceptible atoms are called *luminous points*; therefore as every **body is** made up of molecules or atoms, so **is a** luminous body made up **of an assemblage** of luminous points.

[The pupil should read Lesson III., p. 11.]

111. *T.*—Are all bodies luminous?

P.—No, some are *opaque,* as stones, metals, wood and clay, and do not suffer light to pass through them. This property however depends upon their thickness, **for** all bodies will admit of the passage **of** some degree of light if we make them sufficiently thin. For example, if we affix a thin gold leaf to a glass plate, and hold it to a strong light, we shall perceive **a** blueish-green light through it.

Others are *transparent,*—as water, air, and glass. These bodies yield a passage to light, so as to allow us to observe the form of objects beyond them. *Translucent* bodies (such as thin paper and ground glass), admit of the transmission of some portion of light, without however allowing the form or colour of objects being recognised if they are far distant. I cannot give you a more familiar illustration of the *comparative,* but not the actual degrees of distinction between opacity, transparency, and translucency, than the common fowls' egg-shell. If you hold it when boiled, and full **against** the light, you will have a good **definition** of opacity. Now empty it, **and on holding** it against the light, **you will observe that some parts** of the **shell are darker than others,** which are spotted **as it were with** light, and that there is also **a thin membrane** lining the shell. Now the shell itself will represent opacity, the light spots on it translucency, and the membrane transparency. Be sure to remember, however, that this is only the comparative degrees of distinction, because the whole of them are translucent.

112. *T.*—You mentioned before (Question 105) that a ray of light proceeded in a straight line towards the part upon which it acts, now when it reaches that part what takes place?

P.—As long as the ray remains in the same medium it advances in a straight line, but as soon as it comes in contact with another body it is partly thrown back, or *reflected* from its surface: if the body **is transparent,** the light partly enters **the** body **in an** altered direction, and **is** then *refracted*.

113. *T.*—Does light travel fast?

P.—Yes, its velocity is so great, that it traverses all distances upon earth in an imperceptibly small space of time. It travels over 195,000 English miles in one second, and therefore would require eight minutes and thirteen seconds to traverse the space between the sun and the earth; while a cannon-ball, going at the rate of 1,200 feet in a second, would require fourteen years to pass through the same space.

114. *T.*—How do you account for shadows?

Lesson X. OPTICS.

P.—Light being transmitted in straight lines, it follows that a dark body exposed to rays of light must throw a shadow, because the light does not pass through it. I will illustrate this in a familiar

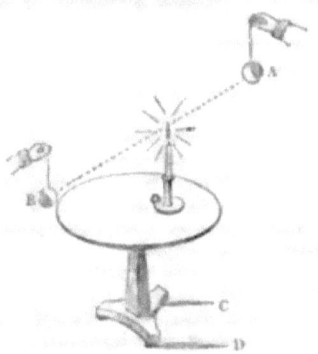

Fig. 30.

way. [Experiment 17.] Place a lighted candle in the centre of a small table (as in *Fig.* 30), then tie a thread to the stalk of an apple, and hold it high above the light (as A *Fig.* 30); tie another thread to another apple, and I will hold it nearly on a level with the table (as B *Fig* 30); now you observe that the half of each apple is light, and the other part dark, the lighted part being nearer to the candle, and the dark part farther from it. Now there is no actual shadow cast from the apples held in the hands; but if you look at the stand of the table you will observe that there are shadows (c & d) thrown from it; this **is** because the natural light strikes the other side, and therefore the part beyond it forms the limits of the shadow. In this manner we can understand how the shadow **of a** body exposed to the sun's light is **sharply** defined close behind it, while at a **greater** distance it becomes undefined.

GENERAL QUESTIONS ON LESSON IX.

1. Describe light.
2. How is light produced?
3. How is light transmitted? and what is meant by a medium?
4. Describe the difference between opacity, transparency, and translucency, and also what is meant by diaphonous.
5. What takes place when a ray of light is interrupted in its course?
6. How fast does light travel?
7. Explain how shadows are formed.

LESSON X.

The intensity of **light diminishes in** proportion as the squares of the distances increase. This is a known fact of much importance in optics, and should therefore be remembered.

Before entering more fully into the science, it will be well to explain some of the terms in common use. Thus a *pencil* is a slender portion of rays, or a small bundle of them; a *beam* is a large bundle of pencils. Rays are said to *diverge* when they separate from each other as they depart from the luminous point; and *converge* when they approach closer to each other, until they meet in a point. All rays are originally divergent, but they are made to converge by the aid of some substance having a reflective or refractive power. The *focus* is the point from which rays diverge, or to which they converge. The *principal focus* is the point to which parallel rays are made to converge by reflection or refraction. *Parallel rays* are those which continue a direct course side by side, at the same distance from each other, **thus** ———, but no such rays really exist. The *focal distance* or length ◁——— is the distance between the focus and the reflecting or refracting ——— body. *Reflected rays* are thrown back from the surface upon which they fall, but *refracted rays* are not thrown back, but pass through the medium in an altered direction. [See Question 110.]

QUESTIONS.

115. *T.*—What is meant by catoptrics?

P.—It is that part of the science of optics which treats of the laws of reflected light, and the phenomena of vision produced by reflection. The term is derived from the Greek word *katoptron* (κάτοπτρον), a *mirror.*

116. *T.*—If a ray of light be admitted into a darkened room, and allowed to fall upon a polished metallic surface, what will be the effect?

P.—It will be returned or reflected in such a manner that the angle of incidence shall be exactly equal to the angle of reflection. For example, if *n i* (*Fig.* 31) be the direction of the incident ray, and *i p* a perpendicular drawn from the surface of the mirror *m m,* the ray will be reflected in such a direction *i d,* that the angle of reflection *d i p* is equal to the angle of incidence *n i p.* Hence it is clear that the ray makes the same angle with the perpendicular, both before and after its reflection.

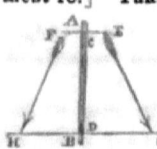

Fig. 31.

117. *T.*—What is the relative position of the image of an object when seen in a reflecting plane?

P.—It is such that every part of the image will appear as far behind the plane as the object itself is before it. [Experiment 18.] **Take a mirror (A B** *Fig.* 32), and hold any object (such as a knife, pen, or arrow), in the position shown in **F H** in this figure, and you will see the image of the object reflected, as E G in the annexed figure. Now if we examine the diagram, we shall find that the lines F C and H D are equal to the lines C E and D G, and therefore the image appears as far behind the plane of the mirror as the object before it.

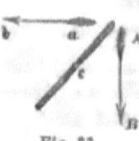

Fig. 32.

118. *T.*—Does the position of the mirror alter the position of the image of the object reflected in it?

P.—Yes. [Experiment 19.] You observe that I have a pencil here (A B, *Fig.* 33,) which is placed perpendicularly, and I now place a mirror (c) at an angle of about forty-five degrees, with its reflecting surface towards the pencil; now if you look in the mirror you will observe that the image of the pencil is horizontal instead of being perpendicular. [Looks in the mirror, and observes the image to be in the same position as the arrow *a b, Fig.* 33.] Now I will reverse the position of the pencil and place it horizontally, and you will then observe that the image appears to be perpendicular. [Does so.]

119. *T.*—Why do we observe the reflection of our figure in a mirror recede when we recede, and approach as we approach the mirror?

P.—Because the lines and angles of incidence are always equal to the lines and angles of reflection. [See Q. 114.]

120. *T.*—How can you observe the profile of your face?

P.—By standing between two mirrors placed thus and looking at A, so that a three-quarter view of the face is observed, then turning the eyes towards B you will observe your profile distinctly reflected in the mirror. By altering the position of the mirrors the reverse effect is obtained.

Fig. 34.

121. *T.*—How do you account for the profile of your face being observed?

P.—Because the image which is delineated behind one mirror serves as an object to be reflected from the surface of the other.

122. *T.*—Upon what principle is the kaleidoscope constructed?

P.—The multiplication of the reflection of an object caused by placing it between two mirrors inclined towards each other at any angle. For example, here is a diagram showing two mirrors inclined to-

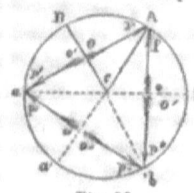

Fig. 35.

wards each other at an angle A C B, and having an object O P placed between them. The consequence of this arrangement is, that several images will be observed, all situated in the circumference of a circle. This may be understood better by drawing the image in its place behind each mirror, with the image formed in turn by each object. Thus we observe that the image, O P, in the mirror, A C, is $p\,o$, while its image in B C is $o'\,p'$, and therefore the reflection of $p\,o$ in $b\,c$ will be $o''\,p''$, while the image of $o'\,p'$ in A C will be $p'\,o'$. Therefore it appears that $p''\,o''$ is the image of both $p''\,o'$ in the mirror $b\,c$, and of $o'\,p'$ in the mirror $a\,c$, one of the images covering the other, if the angle n c A be 60°, as in the diagram; that is to say, the sixth part of a circle. If the angle be greater or less, the image $p''\,o''$ will be twofold.

123. *T.*—Does the angle formed by the mirrors materially affect the number of the images?

P.—Yes; if the mirrors had inclined at an angle of 45°, or 36°, or one-eighth or one-tenth of the whole circumference, we should have, inclusive of the object itself, eight or ten images. The number of images increases as the angle diminishes, their number becoming infinitely great if the angle of the mirrors be null; that is, if the mirrors be **parallel** to each other.

124. *T.*—We have hitherto been considering the reflection of objects from plain surfaces; but suppose that the mirror in which the object was reflected was convex, what would be the effect?

P.—The image would be reduced, or present a miniature picture of the object placed opposite it. The image must always be smaller than the object, because the rays which form them become convergent in their passage to the eye of the spectator. Another peculiar effect observed in the image reflected in a convex mirror is its defective outline; and this is caused by the imaginary or virtual focus of reflection varying for different parts of the same figure, so that the central part alone is correct.

125. *T.*—Do concave mirrors **exhibit** any remarkable phenomena?

P.—Yes; and some of them are very curious and interesting, depending upon the situation of the object with respect to the mirror and the observer.

126. *T.*—Is there not something very remarkable in the image of an object reflected in a concave mirror?

P.—Yes; the image is inverted, or turned upside down. Some curious optical deceptions are produced by means of concave mirrors, which almost appear supernatural; and a singular natural phenomenon, known as the "Spectre of the Brocken," is caused by the reflection from a concave surface. This is observed at a distance from the highest peak of the Hartz Mountains, in Hanover.

GENERAL QUESTIONS ON LESSON X.

1. Explain the meaning of the terms pencil, and beam of light; divergent, convergent, reflected, refracted, and parallel rays; focus, principal focus, and focal distance.
2. What is that part of optics, which treats of reflected light, named?
3. What takes place when a ray of light falls upon a plain mirror?
4. Does the position of a mirror influence the reflection of an object?
5. Can the image of an object be reflected from another mirror? and what is the effect produced?
6. Explain the principle upon **which** the kaleidoscope is constructed.
7. State the peculiarities of convex and concave mirrors, and explain the reasons for their existence.

LESSON XI.

HITHERTO we have considered the laws relating to the reflection of light, but we have now to investigate the phenomena of the refraction **of** light, or the science of dioptrics.* By refraction we mean the deviation or change of direction suffered by a ray of light in passing from one medium to another, and before proceeding further,

* From the Greek dioptomai (Διόπτομαι), to see through.

we will try two simple experiments. [Experiment 20.] I have placed a shilling at the bottom of this teacup, and if you walk back, so that you can merely see the edge of it, I shall be ready to perform the experiment. [The pupil does so.] I will pour some water into the teacup, and the shilling will then appear to rise more and more, as the level of the water rises in the vessel, until at last the whole piece of money will become visible, because the refracting power of the water is greater than that of the air. [Performs the experiment.] The next experiment is still more simple. [Experiment 21.] Here is a tumbler of water and a spoon; now you will observe, when I place the spoon in the water, that it will appear as if it was bent. [Does so, and the spoon appears bent.] This is because the light reflected from the spoon is refracted as it issues from the water. An oar, a stick, or any straight object, will produce the same effect. I will illustrate the atmospheric refraction of light by a simple diagram (*Fig.* 36). Here we have four lines, A A, B B, C C, and D D, parallel to one another; let these represent the strata of the atmosphere, which become denser as they approach the surface of the earth; s represents a star, from which a ray of light proceeds in a straight line s *a*, until it enters the atmosphere at *a*, its direction is then changed into the line *a b*, then when it reaches the line

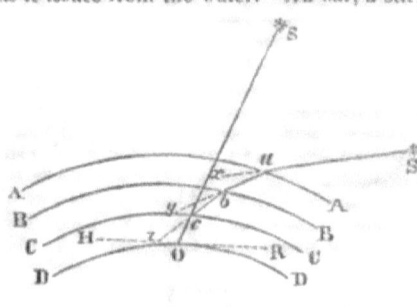

Fig. 36.

B B into *b c*, and again when it reaches the line C C into *c*, finally reaching the eye at o. The effect of this would be to make the star appear at s', which therefore raises it from its true position by refraction, the same as the shilling in the teacup.

QUESTIONS.

127. *T.*—Are rays of light always changed in their direction when passing from a rarer into a denser medium?

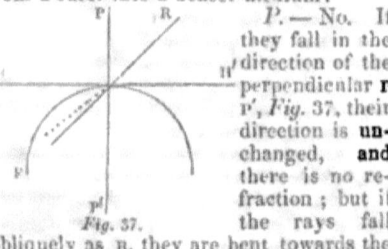

Fig. 37.

P.—No. If they fall in the direction of the perpendicular **P** P', *Fig.* 37, their direction is **unchanged, and there is no refraction**; but if the rays fall obliquely as R, they are bent towards the perpendicular. The opposite of this takes place in every respect where the rays pass from a denser to a rarer medium.

128. *T.*—If what you have stated about the medium be correct, different substances must possess different powers of refraction. Is this the case?

P.—Partially so. A solution of salt is a more powerful refractor than pure water, oil of turpentine more refractive than salt and water, and oil of aniseed even still more powerful than the turpentine.

129. *T.*—How is this? You have said before that the denser a body is, the greater is its refractive power.

P.—It has been found that combustible bodies have greater refractive power than incombustible substances of equal or greater density. It was the knowledge of this that led Sir Isaac Newton to believe that the *diamond* was an inflammable substance.

130. *T.*—What substances are generally employed by opticians for exhibiting the phenomena depending upon the refraction of light?

P.—Glass and transparent crystals, but chiefly the former.

131. *T.*—Does the form of the refractive body exercise any influence upon the relation of the refracted rays?

P.—Yes. By varying the obliquity of

the surfaces of the refractive body, we may vary the degree and direction of the refraction of the rays. We may bring the rays of light to a focus by means of a refractive body, the surface of which presents parts with different degrees of obliquity.

132. *T.*—What are **the usual forms** given to lenses?

P.—There are **seven kinds: 1st, the**

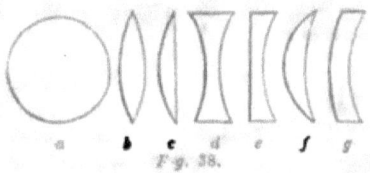

Fig. 38.

spherical kind, made of a globe of glass (*a*) filled with water, or solid; 2nd, the *bi-convex*, or one that has both external surfaces convex (*b*); 3rd, the *plano-convex* (*c*), which has one plain and one convex surface; 4th, the *bi-concave* (*d*), or one that has both surfaces concave externally; 5th, the *plano-concave* (*e*), or one that has one surface plain and the other concave; 6th, the *concavo-convex*, having one surface concave and the other convex, this kind is called a *meniscus* (*f*), because it is like a little moon; 7th, another form of *concavo-convex* (*g*), which is also considered to be a *meniscus*. The 2nd (*b*), 3rd (*c*), and 6th (*f*), are thicker at the centre than the edges, and are called convergent lenses. The divergent lenses are thinner in the middle than at the edges, such as the 4th (*d*), 5th (*e*), and 7th (*g*).

133. *T.*—Are there any other kinds of glasses used in optics?

P.—Yes, several; but with the exception of prisms or triangular glasses, and plain tablets, the others are not so generally used, such as for polarisation of light.

134. *T.*—What do you mean by **the polarisation of light**?

P.—The separation of a ray of light into two rays, each differing from the other in its properties; the most curious of these is that of producing colour in several ways from a ray which appears to be colourless.

135. *T.*—Do you mean to say, then, that a ray of light has any colour?

P.—Decidedly; and the most curious and important of the properties of light is that of imparting colour to bodies; and it will, perhaps, appear rather absurd to some persons to hear that a green leaf is not green. It may be absurd, but to a certain extent it is true. The colours of all the objects that surround us are due to the effect of light, the colour of a substance resulting from its surface being adapted to reflect its peculiar colour.

136. *T.* How is the influence of light in the production of colour modified?

P. By refraction; and this is readily demonstrated by means of a prism of glass, or by the following simple experiment. [Experiment 22.] Place a piece of paper upon the table, and then place a wine glass, with a stem cut (as in the accompanying figure) into nine or more planes, upon the edge of the paper, taking care to arrange them on the table so that a ray of light from the sun shall pass through the stem, just as I do now. [Does so, and the paper is found to be coloured.] You see that there are several colours upon the paper. First you see there is violet, which is a compound colour; then indigo, another compound; then blue, an original colour; then green, a compound; yellow, an original; orange, a compound; and red, an original. You see that these colours are in bands of unequal extent, and so blended, that it is impossible to say where one begins and the other ends. If the refraction of a ray of light is performed in a darkened room with a prism and a mirror, an oblong image is formed on the wall, which is called the *spectrum*, and which exhibits **the** prismatic colours we have seen.

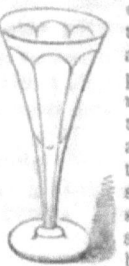

Fig. 39.

137. *T.*—What **do you mean by prismatic** colours?

P.—They are the simple colours of the rainbow, and are so called because they are produced by decomposing a ray of light by means of a *prism*.

138. *T.*—Has this knowledge been practically applied to any useful purpose?

P.—Yes, to several; and the improvements in achromatic lenses is chiefly owing to it.

139. *T.*—What do you mean by achromatic?

P.—A substance without colour, the term being derived from two Greek words, a (*a*) *privative*, and *Kroma* (Χρῶμα), colour. The term is applied to these lenses because the coloured fringes and other defects observed in images formed by a single lens are removed.

GENERAL QUESTIONS ON LESSON XI.

1. What do you mean by refraction?
2. Explain how refraction takes place, and illustrate it by simple experiments.
3. Does refraction always take place when a ray of light passes from a rarer to a denser medium?
4. Do all substances possess the same power of refraction?
5. Describe the various kinds of lenses.
6. What is meant by polarisation of light?
7. What are the colours of the solar spectrum?

LESSON XII.

THE organs of vision are usually described under the head of optics, but I think it better that they should be described when treating of anatomy, and we will now enter upon the consideration of some Optical Instruments.

Optical instruments are so various, that it would be impossible to describe one-fourth of them in our volume, we shall therefore only consider the most common, commencing with the Telescope.

QUESTIONS.

140. *T.*—What is the most simple kind of refracting telescope?

P.—The astronomical, which consists of two convex lenses, an object-glass, and an eye-glass, the foci of which are in the same place. Here is a diagram (*Fig.* 40) that will explain it. Let A B represent the rays from the moon falling upon the object glass C D, then the image formed upon this glass being seen through the eye-glass E F, will have its apparent diameter magnified accordingly. The image will be inverted with respect to the object, but this is not of any consequence for the purposes to which it is applied. Its power may be calculated thus,—if the object-glass have a power = 20, and that of the eye-glass = 8, the object will be magnified to 20 × 8 = 160 times.

Fig. 40.

141. *T.*—Describe the camera obscura?

P.—It consists of a rectangular box, A B C D, with a circular aperture in front, fitted with a moveable tube T, having a convex lens at its extremity. In the body of the box is a mirror, E I H D, placed at an angle of 45°, and at the upper and back part a plate of ground glass, E F G D. The rays of light proceeding from the object Q P, pass through the lens, form an inverted image in its posterior focus, which is received upon the mirror, and is reflected upon the ground glass.

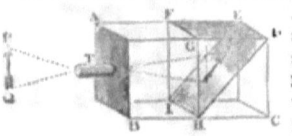

Fig. 41.

142. *T.*—What is the camera lucida?

P.—It is an instrument similar to the camera obscura in its effects, but smaller, and therefore used chiefly for drawing distant objects. It consists of a quadrangular glass prism, by which the rays from an object are twice reflected, and thus form an image on a sheet of paper placed underneath it. As the prism revolves upon an axis, it can be turned to the proper position.

[Grandfather Whitehead does not consider it necessary to describe the microscopes, magic-lanterns, &c., as they are only modifications of the same principles as those already laid down.]

Lesson XIII. ACOUSTICS.

GENERAL QUESTIONS ON LESSON XII.

1. Describe the principle of the dioptrical telescope.
2. How is the power of this telescope calculated?
3. Describe the camera obscura.
4. What is the camera lucida?

ACOUSTICS.

INTRODUCTION.—The science of Acoustics forms a very considerable branch of physics, being that part which treats of the nature of sound, and the laws which govern the origin, propagation, and perception of sound. The term acoustics is of Greek origin, being derived from the word *akouo* ('Ακούω), to hear, and sometimes the science is termed Phonics, which is also a word derived from the Greek word *phone* (Φωνη), **a voice, or** sound.

LESSON XIII.

WHEN atmospheric vibration takes place, we experience the sensation of sound. If a bell rings, or a bird sings, the knowledge that such is taking place is conveyed to our brain by means of the vibrations produced in the atmosphere, which cause wave-like motions in the air. These waves of sound are collected by the *concha*, or external ear, from which they are conveyed along the auditory canal or external auditory passage, and impressed upon a fine nervous membrane, called the drum of the ear or tympanum, which is situated at the bottom of the auditory canal. The tympanum augments the vibrations by its extreme elasticity, and transmits them to the internal ear partly by means of a chain of little bones, which are placed behind it, and partly by means of the air striking another membrane, and causing vibra-

Fig. 42.*

tions there. The vibrations are then admitted into the labyrinth, which is a bony maze, consisting of three portions, viz., the vestibule, the semicircular canals, and the cochlea, being, in fact, the true auditory organ. The auditory nerve having received the necessary impressions, conveys them to the brain. I have thought it necessary to inform you thus much of the structure of the ear, before entering upon the science of acoustics; but when we consider the anatomy of our bodies, we shall learn more about the internal arrangements of this curious structure.

QUESTIONS.

143. *T.*—Is air necessary to the formation or propagation of sonorous vibrations?

P.—No. It is the usual medium; but a solid, liquid, or aërial body will answer, provided it forms a continuous connection between the sounding body and the ear.

144. *T.*—Why is it necessary to have a continuous connection?

P.—Because sound cannot be conveyed through a vacuum.

145. *T.*—How do you know that sound cannot be conveyed in a vacuum?

P.—Because if a small bell be sus-

---

* Fig. 42. *a*, the *tympanum* or drum; *b*, the *malleus*, or little hammer; *c*, the semicircular canals, containing the auditory nerves; *e e e*, the *concha*, or external ear; *d d*, the auditory canal, or external auditory passage.

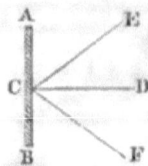

Fig. 45.

same manner as a ray of light, because the vibration of sound is propagated in right lines, and therefore the angle of reflection must always be equal to the angle of incidence. Here is a diagram to explain what I mean. Let A B be a wall or any dense surface, and suppose that a sound is propagated from F and travels in an oblique line, it will impinge upon the wall A B, in the direction F C, and be reflected from C in the line C E, forming an oblique angle with the wall A B. If the sound was emitted from D, and proceeded in the straight line D C, it would return again in the same line, and be heard again at D, producing what is called an echo.

161. *T.*—What is an echo?

P.—It is a reflected sound, and may be double, triple, or even quadruple, according to the number of surfaces from and to which the sound may be reflected.

162. *T.*—Does the reflection of sound always produce an echo?

P.—No; because instead of producing an echo, it may concentrate the vibrations so as to make the sounds heard very distinctly at a great distance. For example, if the sound is repeatedly reflected from a curved surface; so that if the sound is propagated or emitted in the focus of one reflecting surface, it will be conveyed to the ear placed in the focus of the other reflecting surface.

Fig. 46.

Here is a diagram (fig. 46) that will explain my meaning. Suppose that a sound like the tick of a watch could not be heard in the line A B, it may be so increased by reflection as to be distinctly heard. Thus it may go from A to C, and from C to B, by a motion of lesser reflections from *d e c b a*, alternately terminating at B. This is the principle of the Whispering Gallery at St. Paul's Cathedral, London; and the speaking-trumpet is also constructed upon the principle of the reflection of sound.

163. *T.*—How do you account for discordant sounds like cracked bells?

P.—There is a double vibration, and the sound waves interfere with one another; consequently, we have discord.

164.—*T.* Why is sound conveyed better by night than by day?

P.—Because the air is less disturbed by accidental vibrations or currents, and is of a more uniform density.

165.—*T.* Why do windows rattle when a salute is fired?

P.—Because the vibrations of the air are communicated to the glass by impinging upon the panes, the same as upon a wall.

[See Q. 160.]

GENERAL QUESTIONS ON LESSON XIV.

1. How are musical sounds produced?
2. How many notes are there in music?
3. Can you account for the musical notes?
4. How does sound travel?
5. Explain how echoes are produced.
6. Why do we hear discordant sounds?

Explanation of Answer No. 157.

London: Printed by William Tyler, Bolt-court.

www.ingramcontent.com/pod-product-compliance
Lightning Source LLC
Chambersburg PA
CBHW030308170426
43202CB00009B/916